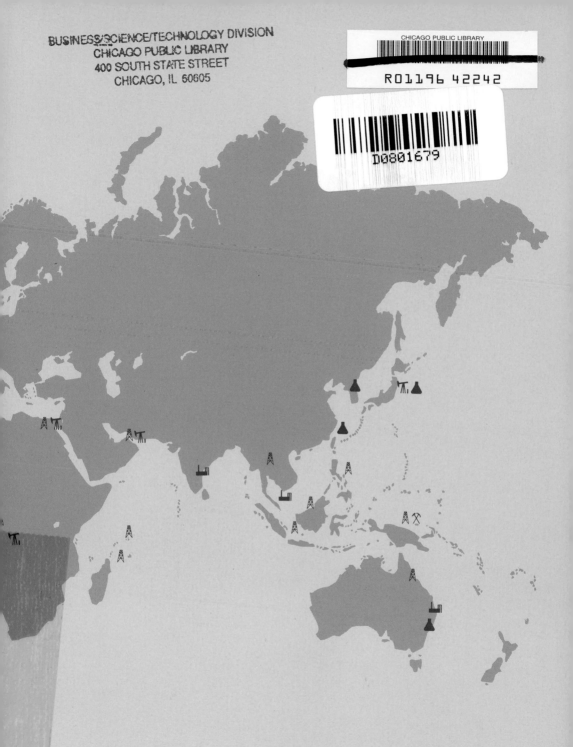

Chemical Operations   Mining Operations

Challenge and Response

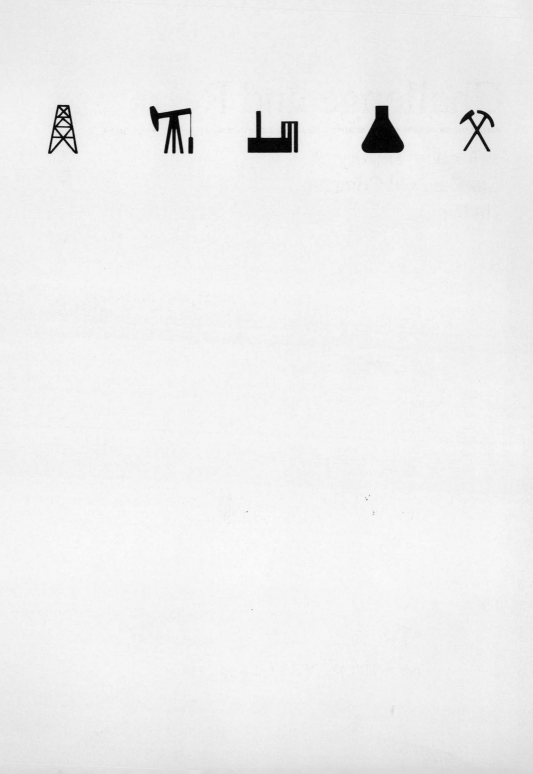

Challenge and Response

A Modern History of
Standard Oil Company
(Indiana)

Emmett Dedmon

JAN 2 9 1985

THE MOBIUM PRESS / Chicago 1984

Library of Congress Catalog Card Number: 84-60010

ISBN: 0-916371-00-X

Designed by Mobium Corporation for Design and Communication,
    Chicago, Illinois

Printed and bound at R. R. Donnelley & Sons Company,
    Crawfordsville, Indiana

Contents

v

Illustrations

Charts

Acknowledgments

Because Standard has had a sense of history, the company archives are rich in the recollections, experiences, and first-hand descriptions of those who served the corporation as long as half a century ago. This has made it possible to describe events not from second-hand sources but in the original words of those who actually took part in the decisions and actions.

An earlier history of Standard, written by Paul H. Giddens, was published in 1955 and brought the history of the company up to 1951. Following publication of his book, which provided much valuable source material for this modern history, Dr. Giddens interviewed a series of executives who played vital roles in the postwar evolution of the company. Of course, not all of those interviewed saw events from the same perspective, but their various viewpoints made it possible to add additional human dimension to the development of Standard in these years.

The author is deeply indebted to John E. Swearingen, whose name might well be on the cover of the book as co-author. Standard's chairman was endlessly patient not only in recalling the major elements of this history and in editing the several editions of the manuscript, but also in taking the time to add to the author's understanding of the oil business.

I am indebted also to Joe P. Hammond, who added perspective to the total project, and to his associate, Albert G. Fiedler, Jr., who eased my way through the many interviews necessary to compile this history and also served as my technical expert as well as editor. Finally, the project could not have been completed in its present form without the expert editing, checking, and additional research of George R. Ewing. He proved not only an excellent editor, but a compatible collaborator in the final stages of the manuscript.

Finally, it is the author's hope that somehow he has been able to capture the pride in Standard which seems to permeate the entire organization from trainee to annuitant. To the men and women of Standard, I am also grateful for their interest and cooperation.

Emmett Dedmon

Chicago, Illinois
August 15, 1983

About the Author

Emmett Dedmon began his career as a writer and editor with the Chicago Times upon his graduation in 1939 from the University of Chicago. Within months he enlisted in the U. S. Army Air Corps as a cadet, taking leave from his position as assistant foreign editor of the Chicago Times.

He parachuted from a burning bomber over Bremen in 1943 and wrote his first book, "Duty to Live," on scraps of paper while he was a prisoner of war in Germany. After the war, Dedmon advanced from reporter-rewrite and various editor assignments at the Chicago Times and at the Chicago Sun, and served as news editor and feature editor after the two newspapers became the Chicago Sun-Times. He rose to vice president and editorial director of the Chicago Sun-Times and the Chicago Daily News, both publications of Field Enterprises, resigning when the Daily News ceased publication in 1978.

The list of seven books authored by Dedmon includes China Journal, an account of Dedmon's three-week visit to China as a member of a delegation of newspaper editors, and Fabulous Chicago, a history of the city, which stood on the New York Times non-fiction best seller list for almost four months when it was published in 1953. The history was reissued with new material in 1982.

Dedmon's broad familiarity with leaders of Chicago and the nation and his knowledge of modern and historical events are illustrated in part by honorary degrees bestowed upon him and by the organizations with which he was associated in executive positions. Among his honors are the Notable Nebraskan Award from his native state, an honorary LL.D. degree from Nebraska Wesleyan, and the Doctor of Humane Letters from both George

Williams University and Roosevelt University. He was a member of the Chicago Club and served on executive committees of both the Commercial Club of Chicago and the Economic Club of Chicago.

A trustee of the University of Chicago, Dedmon had been chairman of the Visiting Committee on The College, and of The Center for Far Eastern Studies. He was a trustee of the Newberry Library and of the Chicago Historical Society, a member of the Society of American Historians, and was past president of the Society of Midland Authors. He had been a director of the American Society of Newspaper Editors and of the Associated Press Managing Editors Association. In 1982, he was elected to the Chicago Journalism Hall of Fame.

Shortly after he approved the final transcript of his Modern History of Standard Oil Company (Indiana), Dedmon yielded to a lingering illness and passed away on September 18, 1983.

Accounts of developments that became effective in September, 1983, were updated in the manuscript by Standard Oil staff.

George R. Ewing

Albert G. Fiedler, Jr.

Preface

Incorporated in 1889 as one of the companies in John D. Rocke-feller's Standard Oil Trust, Standard Oil Company (Indiana) began its existence as an independent enterprise in 1911 with assets torn away by court order from the holding company organization that succeeded the Trust.

These assets were a substantial inheritance, but for large periods of its first 50 years, the company seemed intent on hoarding that inheritance rather than allowing it full play in the mainstream of the world economy where it might flourish.

A striking exception was a period in the 1920s under Colonel Robert W. Stewart, who led the company on a vigorous search for its own crude oil supply and expanded it by acquisition into an international enterprise. But after Stewart was forced from office in 1929, the company reverted to such cautious ways that it soon became known in the industry as "the sleeping giant."

Asleep or not, it had the inherited strength of the giant from which it had emerged. This history concerns itself with the awakening of that giant and the multiplication of those innate strengths which had lain dormant for so many years.

The assets of a company such as Standard (Indiana) are of a special kind; they exist in nature's most complex and versatile minerals, which, being in the ground, have no value in them-selves. Only as dedicated men and women search for, find and produce them, and make them available in the marketplace, are they valuable in the scheme of industrial civilization. This book is meant to chronicle the achievements of some of the people who, in finding ways to develop these natural assets, ultimately created a business institution which reflects and contributes to the health of the American economy.

Because Standard (Indiana) is prominent among many companies that are custodians, in a sense, of natural mineral resources, its history—its successes and failures—reveals much about the nation whose laws and regulations govern the use of those resources. In telling the story of Standard Oil Company (Indiana) and its principal developments, particularly those over the past quarter of a century, it is a necessary and welcome concomitant that such a history tells much about America and its history during this same period.

Standard Oil Company (Indiana) is a holding company whose subsidiaries and affiliates, directed by their own managements, conduct a substantial part of its worldwide business activities. The term "Standard" is sometimes used informally in this book to refer to the parent company and its subsidiaries and affiliates or to one or more of them.

John E. Swearingen, chief executive officer, 1960–1983.

The Fundamental Challenge

Outsiders may look at a corporation and see it as a kind of monolith, represented by a stack of stock certificates, an annual report, and a listing on a stock exchange. The fact is that a corporation, even the largest, is created by people and is as dependent upon people as is the smallest business enterprise. The success or failure of the corporation depends both on the degree of its acceptance by the people it serves and on the nature and the quality of the people whose daily labor represents the totality of the company.

In the middle and late 1950s, two successive presidents of Standard Oil Company (Indiana)—Alonzo W. Peake and Frank O. Prior—sought to bring these two factors into a more favorable conjunction through a series of moves to introduce more modern management principles into the company and to awaken Standard from the comatose state in which it had drifted for almost two decades.

Large institutions are not changed easily, however. Despite the moves by Peake and Prior, the condition of the company when John E. Swearingen convened a senior management conference in 1964 remained much as it had been when he became chief executive officer upon Frank Prior's retirement in 1960.

Swearingen's remarks at that conference provide a contemporary profile of the company that is remarkable for its candor.

"Our problems have been a very long time in the making," he told the conference. "The erosion of our position in the oil business goes back at least 20 years, and it may take another 20 years before we realize all of the ambitious goals we have set for ourselves . . .

"Our difficulty is not survival; it is mediocrity. If we could be content with a large, respectable, stable enterprise that poorly repays its investors' confidence, this could be a company that would certainly last out our time. If some of you are satisfied to be part of such an enterprise, I suggest you submit your resignations; they will be accepted in the order in which they are presented. I won't be satisfied until we stand in the front rank of companies in the oil business—and I know you won't either."

Earlier in the day, Swearingen had spoken on "The Fundamental Challenge." In his talk, he not only detailed the problems facing the company, but the methods he felt should be used in dealing with them. The plans outlined in this talk were to set the course and tone of the corporation for the next two decades.

"Our company has long been run on the basis that no one ever makes a mistake," he told the assembled executives. "This has led to a situation in which subordinates feel obliged to check with their superiors on every decision before it is made and where everyone is afraid to take responsibility for a new or unorthodox approach. Because we are afraid of making mistakes, we are more concerned with not doing the wrong thing than with doing the right thing. This means a built-in barrier against progress and change—when in doubt, we don't."

This same thinking was reflected in a practice endemic in the company "for people to let their thinking be controlled by what they imagine the boss wants rather than by what seems to them to be correct," he said. "A promising idea is not pursued because it is believed a superior would not approve of it. Or where changing circumstances have markedly affected the desirability of a program but it is carried through on the original basis because a senior executive has shown a personal interest."

Effective decentralization obviously was called for, Swearingen said, adding that decentralization is a term which can mean different things to different people. "In my view, decentralization means delegation of authority to take action within prescribed policy limits, combined with a realistic, timely, and concise system of reporting the action taken. This means authority must be placed in individuals—not diffused—and accountability must be fixed and reckoned. We cannot tell a man how to do his job in detail or expect him to check in advance every major decision. To make decentralization work, your subordinates must have a clear cut understanding of what you expect of them. Sure, we have job descriptions, but these for the most part are generalized statements of what a man is doing, not what he should be doing."

Swearingen also noted that the company had paid little attention to such things as communication and motivation. Major parts of operations were separate and independent subsidiaries, with people working in their own specialized areas to achieve poorly defined and limited objectives. As Swearingen said, the company seemed to think of people "as cogs in a complex piece of machinery, and obviously a cog needs little real communication or motivation about what the machine is trying to do. But the concept of people as units to be systematized and directed is both wrong and ineffective—and leaves untapped the great potential of creativity and performance that we desperately need if Standard is to meet its challenge."

It was an historical fact; the company was severely compartmentalized—sales were sales, refining was refining, production was production. There was an obvious need to break down barriers born of compartmentalized specialties, and to secure cross-pollination of ideas among the company's more than 40,000 employees.

In 1961, Swearingen had taken the first step toward breaking down these barriers by appointing task forces to study the operations of the company and its major subsidiaries. Each panel contained representatives from more than one subsidiary—one way of forcing managers to learn about the other fellow's problems whether they wanted to or not.

The task force reports and projections for the next 10 years were not too encouraging. But the company forged ahead to develop its first Ten-Year Plan. It was this plan which provided the basis for the presentations to the 1964 Senior Management Conference.

"The Plan" as it was referred to, had emerged in 1963 at the end of the second of four phases of effort which Swearingen spelled out as necessary to the future growth and profitability of the company. They were:

1. Reduce operating costs.
2. Improve investment efficiency.
3. Improve organization and management.
4. Develop a positive thrust forward.

After reviewing the performance of the company with respect to the objectives of the first and second phases and the effect on profit potential, Swearingen made this bleak summary:

"To put it crudely, then, in the planned projections of our three largest subsidiaries (names of these subsidiaries current at

3

the time Swearingen made these remarks in 1964 were American International Oil Company, Pan American Petroleum Corporation, and American Oil Company), International has growth but inadequate profit; Pan American has profit but limited growth; and American's current plan shows little of either."

Swearingen then went on to state in his most forceful manner what he felt the proper balance between growth and profits should be:

"With an apparent conflict between growth and profitability, it is very tempting to ask for a decision in favor of one or the other. I sometimes feel that this is what some of our people are asking for. 'Make up your mind,' they seem to say. 'Do you want profit or do you want growth?' If only the parent company would make a decision one way or the other, everybody would know what to do and life would be much simpler.

"The answer to this apparent dilemma should actually be clear and self-evident . . . In the first place, the dilemma is not a real one; in any company worth its salt, there should be no contradiction between profit and growth. We want both; the investing public wants both; and you and I, as employees, want both.

"Growth in volume of business without a realistic growth in profits we must completely reject as an objective for the company as a whole or for any of its subsidiaries," he said. "This company has followed the growth-without-profit route for too long a time, and we are not going to do it any longer."

Swearingen was equally adamant in rejecting profits without growth. Standard at the time was a company which was over-invested in all parts of its business; it would have been easy to emphasize cutting costs and payrolls to produce an increased profit level. There were a number of reasons why this was not a good idea.

First, there is always a ceiling on growth in profits without an expansion of the base on which these profits have to be earned. Second, the investing public determines the price-earnings ratio of a stock by comparing the way one company does business with that of its competitors in the industry, including an anticipation of future earnings and dividends. If the investing public were to see a company abandon the growth potential of the industry to more aggressive competitors, the public would reduce the amount it was willing to pay for the stock accordingly. Third, if short-term profit had been the only objective, there were many things

Standard could have done. The company could have eliminated all research, given up all advertising, and stopped all exploration and exploratory drilling; these actions would have resulted in a dramatic and immediate increase in earnings, but the success would have been short-lived.

"As a matter of principle, profitability and growth do not really conflict; they reinforce each other," Swearingen said. "A profitable company has the funds to grow; and starting as it does with an efficient operation, it can develop further efficient operations. A growth company creates not only a favorable image on the outside among investors, but an essential vitality and enthusiasm within the company itself. I want to work for a growth company; so do you; and so do people everywhere, because we all know that in such a company we will have greater opportunity for our own growth—in earnings, in opportunities for advancement, and in job satisfaction."

But if the emphasis of the objectives was on growth and profits, the emphasis on the means to reach these goals was on people. As a vital part of the program, Swearingen told his associates that "we must all of us become completely preoccupied with people—their development, their motivation, their freedom to think and to act and even to make mistakes." More wildcat drilling in the realm of ideas was needed, he said.

Although the principal business of the day was an analysis of the problems the company faced, Swearingen ended his remarks on an optimistic note:

"This is a great company—but its greatness lies in its past and in its potential for the future rather than in its present performance. Most of us who are here today, myself included, are new to our present responsibilities and can take no credit for past greatness. Yet the responsibility for the present is largely ours, and the responsibility for the future is entirely ours.

"We have a cautious, slow-moving, over-systematized, over-controlled company—but a company which has in it able though often frustrated people. Over the years we have set our sights too low, and been too tolerant of mediocre results. We must break this pattern. Our company has aptly been described as a sleeping giant. It has been great in the past; it has the capability to be great again if we can stir it awake. This is our fundamental challenge."

Independence from the Trust

Standard Oil Company (Indiana) had its origins in the need of John D. Rockefeller and his associates in the Standard Oil Trust for a refinery which would be close to the thriving and expanding midwestern marketing area to process crude oil coming from a newly discovered oil field near Lima, Ohio. The site they chose for the refinery was a barren patch of Indiana land near the sand dunes on the southern shore of Lake Michigan at a rail siding named after "Pap" Whiting, a colorful railroad character. To build and operate the refinery and market its products, the Trust incorporated a Standard Oil Company in the state of Indiana on June 18, 1889.

The great commercial potentialities of oil were just beginning to be realized. It had been only 30 years since America's first commercial oil well was drilled at Titusville, Pennsylvania, by a one-time railroad conductor named Edwin L. Drake. Drake's discovery soon brought other speculators and adventurers to the area. In two decades, oil production had grown to the point where, by the 1880s, more than 80 per cent of the world's petroleum consumption was supplied by Pennsylvania oil fields.

Ironically, from the very beginning there were those who were convinced the world would soon run out of oil. In an address before the American Institute of Mining Engineers in 1886, the state geologist of Pennsylvania predicted direly that " ... the amazing exhibition (discovery) of oil which has characterized the last 20, and will probably characterize the next 10 or 20 years, is ... a temporary and vanishing phenomenon."

One of John D. Rockefeller's associates, John D. Archbold, testified in court that he would be willing to "undertake to drink all of the oil" to be found west of the Mississippi. Fortunately, he was not around when the great oil fields of Texas, Oklahoma, and California were discovered.

Because of the fears of a diminishing supply, the opening of a new oil field near Lima, Ohio, in 1885 was considered an important development. Unfortunately, oil from the field was known as "sour crude," meaning that it was highly laced with sulfur; its odor was described at the time as something akin to a rotten egg, and it earned the sobriquet of "polecat oil."

Despite the odor, Rockefeller bought up millions of barrels of the stuff and organized an "Oil Fuel Brigade" to popularize the use of oil for heating and as a fuel for manufacturing plants, an effort that was successful. Unfortunately, the odor of the kerosene produced at the Lima refineries caused much of it to be returned —charges collect.

Determined to find a way to remove the rotten-egg-like sulfur scent from Lima crude, Rockefeller turned to a one-time German pharmacist named Herman Frasch, who was then establishing a national reputation in the United States as an industrial chemist and had sold one of his processes to The Standard Oil Company (Ohio), a Rockefeller company. Later, Frasch developed a process to remove sulfur from crude oil by treating it with copper oxide. At the end of the refining process, the objectionable odor had been removed and the sulfur had been converted to copper sulfide. It was the Frasch process—still unproved commercially—on which Rockefeller was betting when the Whiting refinery was established to refine crude oil by using this new technique.

To assist Frasch at Cleveland and Lima, John D.'s brother, Frank Rockefeller, in June, 1889, hired William M. Burton, a young Ph.D. in chemistry, who had just completed his work at Johns Hopkins University. As construction of the Whiting refinery proceeded, Burton was transferred in 1890 to the new plant as a chemist to do routine work—testing paint samples, analyzing samples of copper compounds, and making sulfur determinations. He was later to remember arriving "on a very hot day in June. The general appearance of the situation was anything but attractive. Sand burrs, sand fleas, scrub oaks predominated."

In this setting, and amidst the noise and bustle of construction on the refinery, Burton converted the second floor of the one-time Wuestenfeldt farmhouse and an old cowshed in the rear into a laboratory. That laboratory was an important beginning; it was to become Standard's first research department.

In the fast-growing midwest, demand was increasing for

7

kerosene, which as it turned out, would be the refinery's principal salable product for a number of years. Lubricating oils and greases also were in demand, and a market for fuel oil was developing. Ohio refiners and their counterparts elsewhere sold gasoline to varnish makers, paint dealers, cleaners, to homes and hotels using machines to make gas from gasoline, and to municipalities using gasoline lamps. As kerosene production increased, surplus gasoline became a problem although not as severe as it had been for the nation's first refiners who sometimes dumped gasoline into creeks or rivers.

The dominance that Standard (Indiana) achieved in the midwest may be measured by the fact that between 1900 and 1911, it sold 88 per cent of all kerosene and gasoline purchased in its territory. It maintained this position not only through aggressive marketing practices such as its rural tank-wagon deliveries, but by undercutting the price when independents, peddling products refined from newly discovered Kansas and Oklahoma oil, attempted to invade its territory.

The practice of lowering prices in one locality but not in another in order to eliminate a competitor gave rise to a demand by smaller oil companies and jobbers for passage of what were known in those early days of the century as "anti-discrimination" laws. In the early 1900s, Iowa passed the first such law, requiring oil companies to maintain uniform prices throughout the state; by the end of the decade similar laws were on the books in 13 states in Standard's market area.

These were but skirmishes on the fringe of a far more serious public opinion and legal battle engaging the Trust and its adversaries. Even as the Standard Oil Trust was forming new companies and expanding into new markets, its size and business practices were being attacked in the courts, by the press, and by two presidents of the United States. "Trust-busting" was a popular phrase of the day and had been exploited skillfully by Presidents Grover Cleveland and Theodore Roosevelt. The passage of the Sherman Anti-trust Act in 1890 spurred public demands for the federal government to intervene and break up large industrial combinations which had proliferated during the expansionist era just prior to 1900.

The principal target of public ire, probably because it could be identified with the personality of a single man—John D. Rockefeller—was the Standard Oil Trust, created in 1879 and refined by an agreement signed on January 2, 1882. An innovative step toward more efficient administration of an integrated enterprise, the Trust embodied a new legal form that made it easier to keep information about operations from the public. Although secrecy was deemed essential in the business world of that day, this may have been a fatal flaw.

The Standard Oil Trust became a favorite target of the "muckrakers," as investigative reporters of that day came to be known. Henry Demarest Lloyd began his attack on the Trust with "The Story of a Great Monopoly," published in *The Atlantic Monthly* in 1881. To keep up with public demand for the article, the magazine went through an unprecedented seven printings. But perhaps the most influential of all the muckraking attacks on the Standard Oil Trust was that of Ida M. Tarbell, who wrote a series of articles on the Trust which were published over a period of two years in the monthly magazine, *McClure's*, and were then published in book form in 1904.

The government, sensing a public issue of great popular appeal, filed a series of suits in both state and federal courts against the Standard Oil companies. An Ohio Supreme Court decision on March 2, 1892, prohibited continuation of the trust agreement, and Rockefeller and his associates liquidated the Trust.

To manage the assets and business affairs of the liquidated Trust, the Rockefeller organization in June, 1899, amended the charter of one of the Trust companies, Standard Oil Company (New Jersey), to make it a holding company. The holding company drew fire on November 15, 1906, when the government brought suit in United States District Court at St. Louis charging that Standard Oil Company (New Jersey) and 70 affiliated corporations and partnerships had engaged in a continuing combination and conspiracy in restraint of trade in violation of the Sherman Anti-trust Act of 1890. The government asked the court to order the combination dissolved.

The court assigned a former judge, Franklin Ferris, to act as hearing officer and to gather testimony. The hearings, which extended over almost three years, resulted in testimony by more than 400 witnesses and the introduction of 1,371 exhibits. Altogether the completed transcript ran to 21 printed volumes totalling 14,495 pages.

The hearings were concluded in January of 1909 and in November of that year, after hearing arguments and studying the evidence, the United States District Court at St. Louis ruled that

38 Standard companies, including Standard (Indiana), were guilty of conspiring to restrain trade in violation of the Sherman Act. As a result of its finding, the court entered a decree prohibiting Standard (New Jersey), as the holding company, from voting the stock or exercising any control, supervision, or influence over the acts of the 37 other companies also found guilty. (Complaints against 33 of the companies and partnerships were dismissed as without merit.)

It was inevitable that an appeal in the case would be taken all the way to the United States Supreme Court. The implications of the case went far beyond a single industry. Many business and corporate leaders feared that the Sherman Act might be construed as making the sheer size of a corporation possible grounds for government legal action—a cause of action which was to reappear in Justice Department claims more than 70 years later. Others feared that all future consolidations and mergers might be outlawed. The stock market lingered in the doldrums while the justices pondered the appeal in Washington.

On Monday, May 15, 1911, Chief Justice Edward D. White announced late in the afternoon that the Court was ready to give its decision. The courtroom quickly filled as senators, congressmen, and newsmen rushed in to hear an opinion, which, whatever its view, was bound to be regarded as of historic importance.

Before dealing with the Standard (New Jersey) case specifically, Justice White outlined the court's view of the intent of the Sherman Act. The Sherman Act, the court held in an opinion applied many times since, should be interpreted "by the light of reason, guided by principles of law." This view, in effect, said that bigness, combinations, or mergers were not in themselves illegal unless there was clear evidence of restraint of trade.

Then, in ruling on the case against Standard (New Jersey), the court held there had indeed been a restraint of trade and that the structure of the company was therefore unlawful. It upheld the lower court's order, thus bringing to an end the life of probably the most noted and efficient holding company in the history of American business. The court made only two modifications in the lower court's decree, one extending the time for compliance from thirty days to six months and the other permitting the companies to continue in business pending compliance with the decree.

Though the effect of the decision was traumatic, a new surge of business confidence spread throughout the country. The stock market rose six per cent in the three days following the decision.

Nor did investors lose confidence, because of the decision, in the discredited holding company and in companies formerly under its umbrella. Trading in Standard (New Jersey) stock zoomed when it was learned shareholders would be given proportional stock in the former subsidiary companies at the dissolution.

The fractional amounts of proportional shares of stock were eye-boggling. Because of the relatively few shares of Standard (Indiana) stock held by the Jersey company, for example, the holder of one share of Jersey stock was to receive in stock of the newly independent Standard Oil Company (Indiana), 9,990/983,383 of one share. On December 1, 1911, more than 200,000 stock certificates for such fractional shares were sent out by registered mail to 6,078 stockholders. And, thus, for Standard (Indiana), a new era as an independent midwest industrial enterprise began.

Standard (Indiana) not only acquired a substantial financial base, it also acquired a name that was famous in its own right. While this was in one sense an advantage, it was to cause great confusion in the public mind through the years, and would result in a series of lawsuits as the company sought to protect the integrity of its name in its basic marketing area.

One of the first problems facing the newly independent company arose before the 1911 dissolution in the form of gasoline demand which first increased moderately with the birth of the automobile age, then snowballed. In two years, the number of motor cars and trucks in the United States doubled from 312,000 in 1909 to 639,500 in 1911.

The increase in automobiles and trucks alone meant that the nation would require 80 per cent more gasoline in 1912 than it had consumed in 1911. This estimate did not include the output of 1,350 manufacturers who were producing farm tractor gasoline engines and stationary engines fueled by gasoline. Neither did the estimates take into account the gasoline needed by the infant dry-cleaning industry and increasing use of gasoline for lighting and cooking.

The rapidity with which the gasoline crunch developed made it imperative for the oil industry not only to increase the volume of crude oil processed—and crude oil production wasn't keeping up with demand—but to squeeze as much gasoline out of a barrel of crude oil as was technically possible. It was the same challenge Standard and the rest of the industry were to face many years later during the gasoline shortages of 1979.

11

The possibility of squeezing the barrel intrigued the scientific minds of a few chemists during the first decade of the 1900s. But not more than 20 well-trained chemists were working in the entire petroleum industry and not all of them were experimenting with new processes to increase gasoline yield. Applications for patents were filed on just three new gasoline yield processes during the first few years of the century, one in each of the years 1907, 1908, and 1909.

For Standard (Indiana) the field of opportunity was limited by the chartered purpose the founding Standard Oil Trust assigned to it: refining and marketing. As he pondered his company's charter boundaries, the refinery gasoline yield of 15 to 18 per cent, and the implications of the gasoline shortage, Burton, who had advanced to assistant general superintendent of the Whiting refinery in 1893 and to general manager of manufacturing for Standard (Indiana) in Chicago in 1903, made a move in 1909 that put Standard to work on the yield problem.

Without enlightening the parent company, Standard Oil Company (New Jersey) in New York, and Standard (Indiana)'s directors in Chicago on what he was about, Burton discussed his proposal with the chief chemist at the Whiting laboratory, Robert E. Humphreys, like Burton a Johns Hopkins Ph.D. in chemistry. No basic research on the chemistry of petroleum had been done at Whiting and Humphreys was enthusiastic about the opportunity. He had come to Whiting in 1900 and since 1907 had been in charge of the laboratory. But the routine analyzing of samples, making sulfur determinations and the like viewed by management as the work to be expected, was boring to an inquiring mind. With Humphreys were F. M. Rogers and, a year later, O. E. Bransky, both also Johns Hopkins Ph.D.s.

At first, the scientists tried to achieve the cracking or breaking down of the several crude oil components by simply increasing the amount of heat applied and attempting to raise the temperature of the oil. When this approach did not work, they decided to apply heat under pressure on the premise that this would raise the reaction temperature and accelerate the cracking process. It was a risky course; at the time fires were commonplace at the refinery, and applying heat under pressure would add the additional risk of an explosion.

Little was then known about the performance of steel under high temperatures and pressures. The experimental horizontal, cylindrical container vessel fired from beneath, which was to replace pot stills, was a dangerous question mark. At the time, no reliable information existed on the tensile strength of steel above 750° Fahrenheit, and Burton and Humphreys estimated a temperature of 850° Fahrenheit might be required. Welding had not yet come into use; boilers were held together by rivets, also with unknown performance characteristics under elevated temperatures and pressures.

After two years of experimentation, Humphreys and Burton were able to demonstrate toward the end of 1910 that it was both safe and practical to produce gasoline—then called "synthetic" gasoline—by cracking high boiling-point oil under high temperature and high pressure. However, Burton had hard going when he presented his request to the parent company in New York for permission to build 100 of his proposed 8,000-gallon stills. Board members feared explosions such as had occurred in early steam boilers for trains and ships. Then too, there very likely was an underlying reluctance within the dissolution-threatened parent company to risk the estimated $1 million cost on an as yet commercially untried process. The proposal was vetoed.

However, one of the first major decisions made by the board of directors of the newly independent Standard (Indiana) was to appropriate capital funds for this same Burton expansion project. That they approved the necessary expenditure—for 120 stills instead of 100, as a matter of fact—was to prove a great boon to the fledgling company. On January 7, 1913, Standard (Indiana) was granted a patent under Burton's name on the new process.

Even as the first of the Burton-Humphreys stills were being built, a few inventive minds began developing improvements to that pioneering process and other inventors began seeking competitive processes.

Of the former, perhaps the most important among early advancements was the tube still originated by Edgar M. Clark and patented on December 1, 1914. Clark's academic training, unlike that of Burton and Humphreys, ended with elementary school. But Clark possessed mechanical aptitude, inventive genius, and energy. He went to work for Standard in 1890 as a common laborer, became assistant superintendent of the Whiting refinery working for Burton, and in 1907 manager of the Wood River, Illinois, refinery (near St. Louis), then under construction.

The tube principle was suggested in part by Clark's observation of horizontal steam boilers then in use and by his effort to create a still that would not be subject to hot spots that slowed

13

operation of the Burton-Humphreys stills. The tube principle was incorporated into the Burton-Humphreys design and the first tube cracking still called the Burton-Clark was installed at Wood River refinery in 1914.

A number of competitive processes were later successful, 10 in 1920 and 1921 alone: Coast, Fleming, Emerson, and Dubbs in 1920; and Jenkins, Greenstreet, Cross, Holmes-Manley, Tube and Tank, and Isom in 1921.

Other companies began clamoring to be licensed to use the Burton-Humphreys process soon after a patent was granted. The economic stakes were gigantic. The process doubled the amount of gasoline produced from a single barrel of oil. The price of gasoline was soaring throughout the world—from 9½ cents a gallon in 1911 to 17 cents in 1913 in the U.S.; in Europe motorists were paying 50 cents a gallon in London and Paris and as much as $1 a gallon in some other locations, a price Americans were not to pay until 66 years later.

Overcoming the fears of some directors that licensing might result in the competition's gaining a share of Standard (Indiana)'s own market, the company licensed 14 refiners to use the process, at first limiting the contracts to an experimental two years. The results were spectacular. Between 1914 and 1919, the company received more than $11 million in royalties, "all velvet" as one director described it at the time.

The most difficult of the licensing negotiations proved to be with Standard (New Jersey), which took umbrage at the royalty demands and sat out negotiations for a year. Finally, after another year had passed, the former parent company reluctantly signed the licensing agreement requiring it to send monthly royalty checks to its former subsidiary. It had been Burton's proposal to forge ahead with 100 stills even before building the large experimental cylindrical still that had been vetoed at headquarters when Standard (Indiana) was still controlled by the eastern company.

In recognition of Burton's work, the company gave him $100,000 in early 1916. John D. Rockefeller, Jr., impressed by Burton's achievement in developing the new process, suggested, as a large stockholder in Standard (Indiana), that the company give Burton $400,000 more. After a strong personal protest from Humphreys—who had done much of the detailed research—the award was adjusted so that both men shared in payments over a period of years. By 1927, Burton had received more than $400,000 and Humphreys almost $200,000.

Although the pioneering work of Burton and Humphreys was generally recognized, Standard (Indiana) soon found itself involved in a series of claims from other patentees that the Burton-Humphreys process used procedures which infringed on others' patent rights. One of these involved a dispute with The Texas Company (Texaco Inc. after May 1, 1959) over the Holmes-Manley process to which The Texas Company had rights. Although Standard disputed The Texas Company claims, it wanted the rights to install the Holmes-Manley process, which provided for a continuous flow of crude oil into stills and made it possible to handle seven times as much crude oil per day in a unit as the Burton-Humphreys "batch" cracking method. This dispute ended in 1921, when for reasons of mutual interest, Standard and The Texas Company signed an agreement in which each agreed to license the other to use its process without royalty payments. Standard (Indiana) began installing the Holmes-Manley continuous process in 1925. It was the first time the company had used anything but the Burton-Humphreys cracking process.

As similar agreements came into being among Standard (Indiana) and other oil companies, the parties to the agreements were popularly described as members of the "Patent Club," a descriptive term originated by the Standard-Texas Company agreement.

This association, in turn, drew the attention of the United States Justice Department, which filed an anti-trust civil suit on June 25, 1924, in the Federal District Court for the Northern District of Illinois against the members of the "Patent Club"— Standard (Indiana), Standard (New Jersey), The Texas Company, Gasoline Products Company, and 46 other oil companies.

The government's anti-trust prosecution worked its way from a master's hearings up to the United States Supreme Court. Decisions were made, overturned, and made again at the various appellate levels. Finally, the United States Supreme Court, in a unanimous decision delivered by Associate Justice Louis D. Brandeis on April 13, 1931, ruled in favor of the oil companies, holding that there had been no actions taken which tended to create a monopoly.

One of the more serious civil suits filed against Standard had been that of Universal Oil Products Company. In a petition filed in 1916, Universal claimed that the Burton-Humphreys process infringed on patents granted to Jesse A. Dubbs to which Universal had the rights. This suit was not settled until January 6, 1931, when, in a complex series of agreements between claimants and counterclaimants among various oil companies, the so-called "Peace of 1931" was signed. During the 15 years of litigation, Standard (Indiana) alone had spent more than $1 million in defense of its patents. The settlement and the U.S. Supreme Court decision removed the uncertainty that had hung over the whole art of cracking and the way was cleared to use existing processes without litigation.

The unique role of the Burton-Humphreys experimental still had been to open the way for doubling the amount of gasoline which could be obtained from a barrel of crude oil. Another impact of Burton's own achievement as a chemist and subsequently as a company executive, was as a forerunner to the increasing role of scientists in the company's management. Many technical men were to be transferred from the laboratory to management positions, establishing a company tradition.

"The system of this company," declared Russell Wiles, one of its early patent attorneys, "is founded on the premise that a scientifically trained man is a good man for any job; the scientific staff does not cooperate with the manufacturing staff—it has become the manufacturing staff." Wiles made the statement in 1922 in his remarks at a New York ceremony when Burton was awarded the Perkin Medal, the highest chemistry honor in the United States.

The original charter of Standard (Indiana) provided that it engage in crude oil refining, and transportation and marketing of oil products. In 1911, when Standard (Indiana) and other Standard Oil companies were separated from each other, Standard (Indiana) consisted of a marketing organization with operations in nine states of the upper Mississippi Valley, and three refineries situated at Whiting, Indiana (near Chicago); Wood River, Illinois (near St. Louis); and Sugar Creek, Missouri (near Kansas City). The Whiting refinery at the time was the third largest in the country and the largest west of the Atlantic seaboard. Much of the company's activities centered around it.

The advent of World War I diverted some of the refinery's productive capacity to defense purposes. The first medicinal white oil to be produced from U.S. crude oil was refined at Whiting by a process developed by Standard scientist O. E. Bransky. Toluene, produced from coking operations at the refinery, went into the manufacture of trinitrotoluene (TNT), and 285 million candle tapers from the refinery's candle factory were used

16

as army trench candles. Whiting's new mechanical shop was put at the disposal of the Emergency Fleet Corporation to make ship parts.

Punctuated by the World War I period, the first decade of its independence saw Standard (Indiana) move aggressively to expand its market territory and to multiply the number of its sales outlets. Between 1911 and 1918, the company doubled the number of bulk plants and extended its deliveries—predominantly by horse-drawn tank wagon. Standard (Indiana)'s territory by the end of the decade contained more than one-third of the population of the United States, more than 50 per cent of the motor vehicles registered in the country, and more than 50 per cent of the tractors.

The company also acted to motorize its delivery system. Strange as it may seem, since the automobile had been around for some years, the company's first motor tank truck on the streets of Chicago did not appear until 1911. It was a huge and cumbersome vehicle, known as a Biddle-Murray truck—the only one of its kind ever constructed. It did, however, establish the feasibility of using motor vehicles to deliver gasoline and fuel oil. Salesmen also were motorized. Beginning in 1913, they were equipped with Ford roadsters; by 1915, Standard was the country's largest purchaser of Ford motor cars.

Many things taken for granted today had to be developed as the company adjusted to the age of the automobile; precedence in the marketplace had to be given to gasoline rather than to kerosene, which had been the company's primary product a scant 20 years earlier. One of the resulting industry innovations was the service station—later an American landmark in every village and city and on every highway.

Allan Jackson, then manager of Standard (Indiana)'s Joliet division, is usually given credit for developing a standardized type company station about 1917. It consisted of a small brick building with a flat roof and a canopy extending over one of two driveways in front of the building. The canopy was supported by brick posts at either end, which also served the practical function of preventing careless or inept drivers from crashing into the pumps standing between the posts. A few of these stations were still to be seen in some of the rural byways of the midwest at the beginning of the 1980s.

Before service stations were built, many dealers served their customers from pumps at the curb (and before that from large barrels or cans). These curbstone dealers often fought to prevent service stations from being built. Other opposition came from garage owners, who saw the stations as a threat to their business.

In 1915, the garage association in Chicago ordered its members to buy gasoline and oil only from companies not associated with service stations. As a result of this fight, Standard lost 200 garage accounts to the company that later was to be named Texaco, which at the time had no service stations of its own in the area.

As aggressive and subsequently productive as Standard's marketing moves were, the management saw that the company could not really continue to grow until it developed its own crude oil supply. Therefore, the decision was made to broaden the articles of incorporation and as amended on March 23, 1917, the articles gave the company authority to engage in other branches of the oil business.

The following year marked the end of an era for the company. W. P. Cowan, who had been president during the formative years following the 1911 dissolution of the Standard (New Jersey) holding company organization, died on August 14, 1918. L. J. Drake, the man chosen to succeed him, also died after only two months in office. They and their associates left a solid financial legacy. With relatively few shares of stock outstanding and a policy of retaining a high percentage of net earnings in the business, earnings reached a high of $146.03 a share in 1917 and the stock market price had zoomed to $945 a share—six times earnings.

Up to this time the chief executive officer had held the title of president. Two men had served alternate terms as president of Standard Oil Company (Indiana) while it was a member company in the Standard Oil Trust and later a subsidiary of Standard Oil Company (New Jersey), the holding company that supplanted the trust. W. H. Tilford was the first to be elected. He served from 1889 to 1890, and was succeeded by James A. Moffett. Moffett was president from 1890 to 1892, Tilford, again, from 1892 to 1904, then Moffett served from 1904 to 1911, the year of the dissolution of the holding company organization.

At the suggestion of John D. Rockefeller, Jr., as a major stockholder, Standard (Indiana) decided to elect a chairman as chief executive officer after L. J. Drake died, and to give Burton— who had already been voted a director—the title of president. The feeling seemed to be that despite Burton's great talents, he lacked

18

the administrative strengths to guide the total operation of the company.

The man chosen as chairman on October 14, 1918, was the first executive not to have been associated with the operating side of the business. He was Colonel Robert W. Stewart, a lawyer from South Dakota who had come to Chicago in 1907 and since that time, as a general attorney in the Alfred D. Eddy law firm, which handled Standard (Indiana)'s legal business, had been active in most of the company's legal cases. Since 1915, when Eddy retired, Stewart had been Standard's general counsel and a member of its board of directors. It was Stewart who was to dominate the company and put the imprint of his personal style on it over the next ten years.

Colonel Stewart and the Search for Oil

3

Colonel Robert W. Stewart was an impressive man in size as well as in demeanor. More than six feet tall and weighing about 250 pounds, his title, as well as his military bearing, came from service with Theodore Roosevelt's "Rough Riders" during the Spanish-American War. Having grown up on a farm, Stewart regarded a long, hard day's work as the natural state of things and demanded equal commitment from his associates. He worked hard, but he also played hard, at fishing, cards, golf, and hunting; in sports or at work he had a driving desire to be a winner. For Standard, this translated into a determination to make the company supreme in its field.

In pursuit of that goal, Stewart chose as one of his principal tasks the development of crude oil supplies that would be owned or controlled by the company. But he also moved dramatically to change the company's relationships with its employees and the public. Company officers soon were travelling around the country and explaining company policy to employees at various company installations. Stewart had a strong belief that the company should tell its story and hold nothing back.

"A permanent attitude of secrecy is a confession of weakness," Stewart declared, "for it implies that the management has policies of such a character as to make secrecy necessary. A well-managed company has no such policies, and secrecy is unnecessary except relating to plans still in the stage of development. Secrecy encourages suspicion, and suspicion among either customers or employees hinders a business; it never aids it."

That this was a radical change for the company may best be illustrated by an episode which occurred during construction of the Whiting refinery—carried out, as were most projects at the time, with all precautions being taken to assure secrecy. A reporter from *The Chicago Tribune* heard about the construction under way at the Indiana dunes and attempted to find out what was going on. After having found one employee named Marshall who at least was willing to speak with him, he filed this report on September 22, 1889:

". . . The one lone fact in the situation which Mr. Marshall had grasped was that he was in the office of the Standard Oil Company of Indiana. As to what was being done at Whiting he was entirely ignorant. They might be erecting a $5 million oil refinery or they might be putting up a pork packing establishment. He didn't think it was a pork packing establishment, but he wasn't sure. . . . In fact, his understanding of what the company was doing was extremely foggy. He could not even offer an opinion whether or not the Standard Oil Company was the same as the popularly known Standard Oil Trust. He didn't know whether Lima oil could be refined . . . and he had forgotten where he was on the night of May 4."

Stewart's view was different. "It is my firm conviction," he wrote in an employee publication, "that every business has, or should have, more to sell than the commodities which are its ostensible reason for being. This may be something more than mere service as that overworked word is generally understood. It is the assurance of reliability and responsibility, the certainty of fair play, honesty, and ability in management. These are all things of real, tangible value, and the public has an abiding interest in all of them.

"I am firm in my conviction that the personnel of a business organization, as well as its policy, its purposes, its current activities, its volume of business, and its products all are matters of public interest, and that these matters should be given as wide publicity as possible. . . .

"I believe that the public at large has still to learn the basic fact that when an honest business, which is rendering a real service, is made to suffer loss, the public suffers too."

To put his case before the public, Stewart not only made many personal appearances before employees and citizens groups, but initiated a massive campaign of institutional advertising. In 1919, and continuing for 10 years, he used the pages of newspapers in Standard's marketing area to tell the company's story. The headlines of the advertisements reflect the nature of Stewart's business philosophy. Under such headlines as "Who Owns the Standard Oil Company (Indiana)?" "Democracy in

Industry," and "The Standard Oil Company (Indiana) and Its Competitors," the principles, practices, and profits of the company were candidly disclosed and explained.

Product advertising was also used to promote and protect Standard (Indiana)'s market share in the midwest. Annual expenditures for all advertising increased from about $1 million in 1919 to more than $4 million in 1926—the largest sum spent on advertising up to that time and a sum not to be matched for another 20 years. The company was also an early user of radio advertising, its first sponsored program being a concert by the Standard Oil Band of Whiting, in 1922.

As important as these efforts to build business confidence in the company were, however, they were secondary to Stewart's principal task of developing owned or controlled crude oil supplies. A sense of urgency was fired by periodic prophecies of doom about the adequacy of world oil supplies highlighted in 1922 by a United States Geological Survey forecast that U.S. oil reserves would be depleted by the early 1940s, using the exploration and production techniques known at that time. A factor also was competition with certain companies which, like Standard (Indiana), had been assigned specialty roles when they were part of the former Rockefeller organization, e.g., Standard (Indiana), refining and marketing; National Transit Company, transportation; Standard (Kansas), Prairie Oil and Gas Company and some others, exploration and production.

Crude oil supply was a serious matter. After the dissolution of the holding company organization in 1911, Standard (Indiana) was dependent upon Prairie Oil and Gas for most of its supply of crude oil. During World War I, however, Prairie was required to supply refineries along the Eastern seaboard to keep them operating at capacity for military reasons; thus, it couldn't provide sufficient supplies for the inland refineries it served.

The general shortage in the midwest continued after the end of the war. The oil industry's costs of drilling and production skyrocketed while crude oil prices remained relatively constant. As a result, drilling was unable to keep up with the increased demand for crude oil to be converted into gasoline. With a huge investment in refineries, an extensive marketing system, and no crude supply of its own, Standard faced a critical situation. The company's refineries were operating sometimes at 50 per cent of capacity or less because of insufficient crude oil supplies.

22 In 1919 Stewart arranged for Standard to acquire Dixie Oil

Company, which had been incorporated in 1917 by a Chicago lawyer to operate an oil lease near Shreveport, Louisiana, and a few months later achieved another major step toward establishing a crude oil supply. But the story of that step began years before with roots in the success of the revolutionary high-temperature, high-pressure oil cracking method—the Burton-Humphreys cracking process.

While Standard was building cracking stills at Whiting, Wood River, and Sugar Creek in 1913, an apparent no-solution problem developed for two companies in Wyoming, where the great Salt Creek oil field had been found in 1908 and oil production and refining were on the rise. They were Midwest Oil Company and Franco Petroleum Company—the largest oil producers and refiners in Wyoming. A ready market flourished for all of the gasoline their refineries could produce. But comparatively large volumes of crude oil had to be processed for a minimum amount of gasoline; the highest yield of gasoline from a barrel of crude oil processed in their refineries was only 18 per cent.

Their major problem was what to do with the fuel oil—57 per cent of the barrel—after kerosene (25 per cent) and gasoline had been taken off. The market in Wyoming was too limited to absorb large volumes of fuel oil, and rail transportation costs to distant midwest markets made that avenue uneconomic.

The solution came when Standard accepted a Midwest Oil-Franco Petroleum proposal for Standard to build Burton-Humphreys cracking stills at Casper, Wyoming, to produce gasoline from the unwanted fuel oil.

The ink was still fresh on the contract the three companies signed on July 1, 1913, when a new company—Midwest Refining Company—was organized to take over assets of Franco Petroleum as well as contracts for purchase of crude oil, pipelines, refineries, and marketing facilities of Midwest Oil, and the fuel oil processing contract with Standard.

Approximately six years later, as Stewart scoured the country looking for crude oil to buy or deals to acquire companies with crude oil production, Standard decided to acquire Midwest Refining—Stewart's first major step toward an owned or controlled crude oil supply after the Dixie Oil acquisition. Stewart initiated the purchase of Midwest Refining shares in early 1920. Standard had 33 per cent stock interest by the end of that year, and 99.93 per cent by 1928 when Midwest Refining was formally absorbed into the Standard organization.

Midwest Refining obviously was a good buy. It controlled about 65 per cent of Wyoming's 16.8 million barrels annually of crude oil production, including production from the Salt Creek field north of Casper through 20-year contracts with the principal producing companies. It also owned or controlled about 46 per cent of the pipeline mileage serving Wyoming fields and refiners, and processed about 86 per cent of all the crude oil refined in Wyoming.

While these and other acquisitions progressed or were sought, Stewart acted to improve the means of getting crude oil to Standard's refineries. As the 1920s began, Standard (Indiana) had no pipelines—the most efficient transportation method—serving its refineries at Whiting, Wood River, and Sugar Creek.

Crude oil Standard purchased in Kansas and Oklahoma was pumped by Prairie Pipe Line Company, a subsidiary of Prairie Oil and Gas Company, to the refinery at Whiting through a trunk line completed in 1905; to Sugar Creek through a line from Humboldt, Kansas, built about 1905; and to Wood River via a spur from the trunk line at Carrollton, Missouri, begun in late 1913 as diminished Illinois production fell short of Wood River refinery needs. Additional supplies for Whiting had become available after 1917 when Sinclair Pipe Line Company completed a trunk line from Drumright, Oklahoma, to East Chicago, near Whiting. The line route essentially paralleled the Prairie Pipe Line Company system. Large volumes of Standard's Kansas and Oklahoma crude oil purchases consigned to Whiting were transported through the Sinclair system until about 1920 when Standard quit using it because Sinclair increased its tariff rate.

On February 9, 1921, in an agreement with Harry F. Sinclair, head of the Sinclair Consolidated Oil Company, Stewart acquired for Standard a half-interest in the Sinclair Pipe Line Company for $16,390,000 in cash. This acquisition scuttled Standard's preliminary plans to build a parallel pipeline between Drumright, Oklahoma, and Chicago, and was the opening move in Standard's plan to establish its own transportation system.

Sinclair's commitment to increase the capacity of the 20,000 barrels per day Sinclair pipeline was part of the deal. And, although Standard was able thereby to increase its crude oil input to refineries by about 10,000 barrels daily, total supplies fell short of meeting Standard's needs. A step to help meet these needs was taken on the same day in 1921 when Standard and Sinclair Consolidated, each with 50 per cent interest, organized the Sinclair Crude Oil Purchasing Company.

1. The Salt Creek oil field in Wyoming as it appeared in November, 1922. A 1983 view is shown on page 84.

One of Stewart's more ambitious projects failed to materialize. During the summer of 1921, he initiated negotiations for a merger of Standard (Indiana) and Gulf Oil Corporation, controlled by the family of Andrew W. Mellon. Gulf was one of the most successful petroleum companies outside the group of original Standard Oil companies. An integrated company, it was particularly strong in production and oil reserves, which Standard badly needed. Neither company competed with the other in marketing to any great extent, and in a merger they would complement one another. The negotiations extended into 1922, but collapsed over the issue of whether Stewart was giving sufficient value to Gulf's properties.

In 1925, Stewart was to be more successful. That was the year Standard acquired controlling interest in Pan American Petroleum and Transport Company, one of the largest crude oil producers in the world, from Edward L. Doheny and his family. The acquisition amounted to a merger of the two companies, except for California properties which Doheny retained.

Through Pan American Petroleum and Transport, Standard secured an interest in some of the finest oil fields in the world, including about 1.5 million acres in Mexico and a 3 million acre concession in and around Lake Maracaibo in Venezuela; refineries in Mexico, Venezuela, Germany, and at Baltimore, Maryland, Destrehan, Louisiana, and Savannah, Georgia, in the

25

United States; one of the largest tanker fleets in the world; and marketing operations (principally for gasoline, kerosene, and bunker fuel) in South America, Europe, and North America including East Coast outlets of its 50 per cent owned The American Oil Company and American Oil's subsidiary Lord Baltimore Service Stations, Inc.

The assets of the two companies totaled nearly $584 million, and their securities were valued at nearly $800 million on the open market. Most importantly from Standard's viewpoint, Pan American Petroleum and Transport properties greatly strengthened the company's crude position. In 1919, Standard produced just over 96,600 barrels of oil (about 265 barrels daily); in 1929, with the Pan American Petroleum and Transport acquisition the major contributor, the company's production was more than seven million barrels (about 20,000 barrels daily), a gain of more than 75 times.

Standard's acquisition of control of Pan American Petroleum and Transport was considered the most significant event in the oil industry since the dissolution of the Standard (New Jersey) holding company organization in 1911. The *National Petroleum News* commented: "Those who know the intense ambitions of Colonel R. W. Stewart, to make his company a vital factor in the petroleum world and the extent to which he controls the board of directors of his company, can well appreciate this latest move in the working out of plans he has carried on his mind for a long time." The *New York Times* commented: " . . . if petroleum is to have another Rockefeller or, more modestly, another Harriman or Jim Hill, Stewart may play the role."

This prophecy was not to be fulfilled. The course of events that were to deflect Stewart's broadening career began in 1920 when a colorful wildcatter named Colonel Albert E. Humphreys discovered the Mexia oil field in Texas. The following year, two sensational wells started a scramble among oil companies to buy production from Mexia, soon labeled the "World's Wonder Field."

Aware that Stewart had set a course to improve Standard's crude oil supply situation, Henry M. Blackmer, president of Midwest Refining Company, initiated a deal for the Humphreys interests to sell Mexia oil to Prairie Oil and Gas Company and to Sinclair Crude Oil Purchasing Company in which Standard owned 50 per cent interest.

While Blackmer negotiated and Stewart resisted Humphreys'

offers to trade Mexia oil for Standard stock, Humphreys, thinking Blackmer was dealing for Prairie Oil and Gas and Sinclair Crude Oil Purchasing, agreed to Blackmer's offer to buy more than 30 million barrels of Mexia oil at $1.50 per barrel, 50 cents under the $2.00 posted price.

In the meantime, Standard's board of directors learned that Pure Oil Company, seeking to buy all of the Mexia production during delays in the Blackmer negotiations, had settled for ownership interests in Humphreys' companies and 50 per cent of the oil to be produced up to 40,000 barrels a day.

Dispatched by Standard's board of directors to try to buy the remainder, Stewart found that Blackmer now said he was in a position to sell more than 30 million barrels of oil to any buyer. Stewart also heard for the first time what Harry F. Sinclair had found out only the day before: Blackmer had arranged for Continental Trading Company of Canada—actually a paper corporation—to buy the oil and resell it at $1.75 a barrel, 25 cents over Humphreys' price.

A premium of 25 to 50 cents per barrel was common among crude oil buyers and sellers at the time, and a handshake deal was closed between Continental Trading as seller and Prairie Oil and Gas and Sinclair Crude Oil Purchasing as buyers. Standard would acquire rights to buy Mexia oil production through its ownership interest in Sinclair Crude Oil Purchasing Company.

When it came time to sign contracts, questions arose about the qualifications of the unknown Continental Trading Company of Canada. That matter was resolved by a performance guarantee contract to be signed by James E. O'Neil, president of Prairie Oil and Gas, and Stewart and Sinclair for Sinclair Crude Oil Purchasing Company.

Prior to the time set for the signing ceremony, Sinclair complained privately to Blackmer saying the 25-cent-per-barrel fee was exhorbitant and that he expected his company to share in it. Blackmer agreed that this would take place, and the signing of the contracts, still subject to approvals by directors of each of the purchasing companies, proceeded.

When the contracts were presented to Standard's directors on November 19, 1921, for board approval, Stewart told them, "Somebody is making 25 cents a barrel out of this thing. If that is material, don't take these contracts. Give them up. If you want this oil at this price, that is the price I am told you have got to pay for it and I believe that is what you will have to pay for it."

Because of the board's confidence in Colonel Stewart, the contracts were approved; but when Stewart and the others affixed their signatures to the contracts, a chain of events began that led to Stewart's downfall.

The first development in the chain was to lead to the disgrace and conviction of a member of the cabinet of the President of the United States. In 1921-1922, Albert B. Fall, Secretary of the Interior (March, 1921-March, 1923), leased certain U.S. Naval Oil Reserves to Edward L. Doheny, president of Pan American Petroleum and Transport Company (prior to Standard's acquisition of that company in 1925), and to Mammoth Oil Company, one of the companies in the Harry F. Sinclair organization. The lease to Doheny was for Naval Oil Reserves Numbers 1 and 2 in California, known as Elk Hills, and the lease to Mammoth Oil was for Naval Oil Reserve Number 3 in Wyoming, known as Teapot Dome.

Seven days after the Mammoth Oil lease was signed on April 7, 1922, U.S. Senator John B. Kendrick of Wyoming received a telegram from the Rocky Mountain Oil and Gas Producers Association of Casper, Wyoming, protesting the alleged letting of a contract to Mammoth Oil without competitive bidding.

A growing outcry about alleged irregularities in connection with the leasing of both Elk Hills and Teapot Dome naval oil reserves led to hearings beginning in 1922 before the Senate Committee on Public Lands and Surveys.

At the hearings, Doheny testified that he had loaned Fall $100,000 on November 30, 1921. Other witnesses brought out that Fall, until recently in strained financial circumstances, had quite suddenly expended large sums of money on his New Mexico ranch. Colonel J. W. Zevely, an attorney for Sinclair, testified Sinclair had loaned Fall $25,000 in the summer of 1923 on which no interest had been paid. On the basis of such testimony and subsequent court action, Fall was convicted in the Supreme Court of the District of Columbia on charges of receiving a bribe from Doheny in connection with the lease of Elk Hills.

This event and other disclosures prompted Congress to direct President Calvin Coolidge to institute and prosecute suits to cancel Mammoth Oil's Teapot Dome lease. Coolidge appointed Atlee Pomerene, a former U.S. senator from Ohio then in the practice of law, and Owen J. Roberts, an attorney who in 1930 became an associate justice of the U.S. Supreme Court, as special counsel.

On March 12, 1924, Pomerene and Roberts for the United States filed suit in the U.S. District Court at Cheyenne, Wyoming, against Mammoth Oil Company to cancel the lease for Teapot Dome on grounds Fall and Sinclair had defrauded the United States. The two prosecutors also named Sinclair Crude Oil Purchasing Company, as buyer of Teapot Dome oil production, and Sinclair Pipe Line, as a transporter, as co-defendants.

In preparing for the trial, Pomerene and Roberts examined records of banks in which Fall had accounts and found reference to 3½ per cent U.S. Liberty Bonds. The Treasury Department traced these bonds by their numbers to Continental Trading Company. The two prosecutors at this point weren't able to find out much about that company, only that it had been organized in Canada by H. S. Osler, president, in 1921, had purchased Liberty Bonds in the total amount of $3,080,000, and was dissolved in 1923.

Their next attempt to learn more about Continental Trading resulted in a dead end also. Whether they turned in the direction they chose because of knowledge they had of Osler's and Continental Trading's role in the Mexia oil deal, or whether for some other reason, is unclear. But they found that the president of Prairie Oil and Gas Company, James E. O'Neil, had resigned in September, 1923, and was in Europe; the president of Midwest Refining, Henry M. Blackmer, had left for Europe in February, 1924; and the chairman of Standard (Indiana), Robert W. Stewart, had shed no light on Continental Trading when he testified in September, 1924, before a grand jury which was considering evidence toward filing criminal charges against Sinclair, Fall, and Doheny. They were frustrated also when Osler pleaded privilege of counsel and refused to answer questions after Pomerene and Roberts sought through Canadian courts to force his appearance to testify at the Cheyenne trial.

Osler did submit a deposition dated November 24, 1924, however, in which he said the business of Continental Trading consisted primarily of keeping accounts. The New York branch of the Dominion Bank of Canada received payments from Prairie Oil and Gas and Sinclair Crude Oil Purchasing for Mexia oil, made remittances to the Humphreys companies, and followed instructions to invest the balance, resulting from the 25-cent difference between the $1.50 per barrel Humphreys selling price and the $1.75 per barrel price paid to Continental Trading by Prairie Oil and Gas and Sinclair Crude Oil Purchasing. The deposition said Osler would take 2 per cent for his commission and divide the balance among his clients in Continental Trading.

Apparently to explain the short life of Continental Trading, Osler deposed that by the spring of 1923 a shortage of crude oil and an anticipated price rise had not occurred. Further, Mexia field production had dropped, and it appeared likely that the contracted amount of oil would never be delivered. Therefore, the deposition said, Osler advised his clients to sell the contract to Prairie Oil and Gas and Sinclair Crude Oil Purchasing. When this was done (for $200,000 each to Prairie and Sinclair), Continental was dissolved in 1923. While this information was interesting, it didn't include names of Osler's clients—the owners of Continental—and they were what Pomerene and Roberts wanted.

Hoping that eventually Osler would be forced to testify, Pomerene and Roberts got the trial postponed to March 9, 1925. Three days after the trial opened on that date in Cheyenne, the Appellate Division of the Supreme Court of Ontario ruled that Osler must testify. However, Osler then was en route to Egypt on a hunting trip.

Sinclair, now under indictment on criminal charges stemming from the grand jury investigation, also was out of the prosecutors' reach, leaving Stewart as the potential star witness. But in spite of a diligent search, Stewart couldn't be found. When the trial opened, John D. Clark, vice president of Standard and assistant to Stewart, stated that Stewart was out of the country on business, a trip soon to be revealed as related to Standard's purchase of controlling interest in Pan American Petroleum and Transport Company.

Adverse public opinion about business ethics fomented by reports on these developments and by reports on the trial itself, including attacks on John D. Rockefeller, Jr. and leaders of companies involved directly or indirectly in the scandals, spurred Rockefeller, as a concerned major stockholder in Standard (Indiana), to urge Stewart's immediate return. Stewart did return on March 27 to testify, but the trial had ended on the day before.

The trial failed to prove that the Liberty Bonds purchased by Continental Trading and referenced in Fall's bank accounts had come to Fall from Sinclair. Presiding Judge T. Blake Kennedy's decision upheld the validity of the Mammoth Oil-Teapot Dome lease, finding no fraud. Appealed, the matter proceeded through the courts and on October 10, 1927, the Supreme Court sustained the decision of the U.S. Circuit Court of Appeals, Eighth District, holding that the Teapot Dome leases were procured through fraud and corruption and should be cancelled, and they were.

Stewart's next involvement began a week after the Supreme Court decision on Teapot Dome as a subpoenaed witness in the trial of Harry F. Sinclair in which Sinclair faced criminal charges of defrauding the government in leasing Teapot Dome. But the trial ended on November 2, 1927, in a mistrial after Sinclair was accused of shadowing the jury.

Again having business out of the country (in Venezuela) and not knowing when the second Sinclair trial would begin, Stewart contacted Pomerene and Roberts who told him he wouldn't be needed until April 2, 1928. Stewart left on his trip on December 28, 1927. During his absence, the Senate on January 4, 1928, adopted a resolution by Senator George W. Norris of Nebraska calling for the Senate Committee on Public Lands and Surveys to continue its investigations and trace the Liberty Bonds of Continental Trading that had not been linked to Fall.

Pressured by the Senate committee and newspapers, Rockefeller urged Stewart to abandon his business trip as being less important than his testimony, even though Stewart had frequently repeated that he was involved in no wrongdoing. Committee hearings began on January 24, and Stewart, failing to benefit by the understanding with Pomerene and Roberts that he wouldn't be needed in the second Sinclair trial until April 2, appeared before the committee on February 2.

Stewart held his own during the first hours of questioning by Senator Thomas J. Walsh. But he refused to answer two key questions: his knowledge of the distribution of the Continental Trading bonds, and whether he had discussed the bonds with Sinclair, on grounds that he was under subpoena to testify on these subjects at the second Sinclair trial. The questions drew the same response from Stewart on the second day of the hearings. After noon, Stewart was excused and, in executive session, the committee directed Walsh to prepare a report and a resolution calling for Stewart's arrest for contempt of the Senate. The Senate adopted the resolution shortly after 5 p.m., and the Sergeant at Arms and his deputy arrested Stewart at the Willard Hotel.

It was a momentous event. L. L. Stephens, the Standard (Indiana) attorney, secured the assistance of two local attorneys and worked through the night in preparing a petition for a writ of habeas corpus which, if granted in time, would at least postpone Stewart's being brought before the bar of the Senate. Just before

Stewart was to appear as the Senate convened at noon on the next day (February 4), the Supreme Court of the District of Columbia issued the writ and freed Stewart on $1,000 bond. The Senate then directed the matter to the district attorney for grand jury action.

During the habeas corpus proceedings over the next few days, the Senate committee found more of the Continental Trading bonds when the then chairman of Prairie Oil and Gas Company, W. S. Fitzpatrick, revealed on February 4, 1928, that O'Neil had received some of them. Told that he was near death, O'Neil had gone to Canada from France and arranged for the bonds to be turned over to Prairie in May, 1925.

On February 23, Justice Jennings Bailey discharged the writ and Stewart again stood under arrest. It was for only a few minutes, however. An appeal was filed in the Court of Appeals of the District of Columbia, and Stewart, freed on bond, again escaped appearing before the bar of the Senate.

On that same day, Henry M. Blackmer's attorney told the committee about Continental Trading bonds Blackmer had received in connection with the Mexia oil deal, and on March 1 and March 13, the former chairman of the Republican National Committee testified that in 1923 Harry F. Sinclair had made a donation and made loans to that committee in Liberty Bonds.

On March 1, 1928, at Standard (Indiana)'s annual meeting, Stewart was reelected to the board although Rockefeller declined to vote his proxies either for or against him, and the board reelected Stewart chairman. Before the month was half over, a grand jury in Washington indicted Stewart for contempt of the Senate. Stewart pleaded not guilty on March 15 before the Supreme Court of the District of Columbia and was released on $5,000 bond.

Stewart was held under subpoena during the second trial of Harry F. Sinclair on criminal charges which began on April 19, 1928, but was never called to testify. When the trial ended, Stewart no longer had grounds for refusing to answer the two key Senate committee questions. Further, a Senate subcommittee, in examining bank deposits Stewart had made in 1922 and 1923, found that Stewart had deposited interest from coupons of 3½ per cent Liberty Bonds in his personal account. Stewart and Standard's tax commissioner, Roy J. Barnett, were subpoenaed to appear before the Senate committee on April 24, 1928.

Their testimony told the story of Stewart's motives in the Mexia oil deal and his handling of Liberty Bonds that came to him from Continental Trading. Serial numbers of these bonds matched numbers of bonds purchased by Continental Trading except for some bonds Stewart owned personally that he had traded for coupons from the Continental bonds. Stewart deposited some of the coupons in his personal bank account and converted some to cash.

The bonds had remained in Standard's vault until April 21, 1928. On that day, Stewart called a meeting of the board of directors to apprise them of the facts. The directors were stunned. They were a subdued group as Stewart led them to the vault to show them the bonds. The directors wanted no part of the bonds and voted to turn them over immediately to the Sinclair Crude Oil Purchasing Company which had been the direct party to the Mexia contract. The total amounted to $759,500 in bonds and $38,000 in interest coupons.

Sinclair was acquitted of the criminal charge on April 21, 1928, and appeared before the Senate Committee on Public Lands and Surveys on May 1, 1928. He testified that he had given some of the Continental Trading Liberty Bonds he received to Fall and some to the Republican National Committee, and delayed turning over the remaining bonds to Sinclair Crude Oil Purchasing as profit deriving from the Mexia oil deal until the criminal suit against himself had been concluded, and the attention in the Congress turned to other matters.

All of the 3½ per cent U.S. Liberty Bonds purchased by Continental Trading Company had now been traced. The investigation was finished.

The investigation by the Senate Committee into the Teapot Dome and Elk Hills leasing scandal involving Fall, Sinclair, and Doheny had taken an unanticipated turn which led to the unrelated Mexia oil deal with serious consequences for Stewart.

Stewart was acquitted of contempt and perjury charges stemming from the conflicts between his testimony on February 2-3 and that on April 24, 1928. The Mexia oil deal and the Teapot Dome-Elk Hills deals were separate and unrelated. Standard and Stewart weren't involved at all in the lease scandal. They had no connection with the Teapot Dome field except as a buyer of production through Standard's ownership interests in Midwest Refining Company and Sinclair Crude Oil Purchasing Company, and none at all with Elk Hills. But there was to be a dramatic epilogue.

John D. Rockefeller, Jr. and his associates, who had refrained from voting their stock for Stewart at the annual meeting earlier in 1928 to show their displeasure at the emerging revelations of the investigation, now asked for his resignation. Stewart demurred, asking instead that he be allowed to take a leave of absence for a year, with the understanding that he would not stand for re-election. Rockefeller, who still was under great public pressure, insisted on a resignation.

When Stewart refused, saying it would amount to an admission of guilt, Rockefeller took up the challenge. He announced that he and a group of his associates headed by Winthrop Aldrich would solicit proxies for the election at the 1929 annual meeting of a slate of directors which would not include Stewart. The proxy fight which followed was the most spectacular in the history of American business up to that time.

"A generation can bring about astonishing changes," *The Chicago Tribune* commented. "No one would have believed 25 or 30 years ago that a Rockefeller would ever have to appeal for public support to gain control of an oil company bearing the name 'Standard' or, indeed, of any oil company, whatever its name. No one would have believed that a Rockefeller would be engaged in such a struggle and fighting on the side of a more scrupulous business morality. That is what has happened; no one has said that Mr. Rockefeller is anything but sincere, and no one is likely to say it. Time and their own acts have softened public opinion toward the Rockefellers, father and son."

During the proxy fight, Stewart made much of his record with the company, which was truly impressive. In 1918, Standard (Indiana) had net assets of $117 million; in 1928, company assets had grown to $460 million. In 1918, the company owed banks $35 million; in 1928, it had no outstanding liabilities and cash amounting to $112 million.

Stewart waged a vigorous campaign for proxies among the smaller stockholders, including the many employees who had stock made available to them under Standard's stock purchase plan installed by Stewart. However, the management slate could not compete with the large blocks of stock controlled by Rockefeller and the additional proxies which came to him from other large, individual stockholders and bankers who felt that Stewart's actions had reflected badly on all business.

When the annual meeting was held at Whiting on March 7, 1929, Rockefeller's slate, which included all the current directors except Stewart and one other, L. L. Stephens, polled about 60 per cent of the shares voted and Stewart only 32 per cent. Among the directors retained was Edward G. Seubert, then president of the company.

Seubert and the other directors, who were also operating department heads, had sided with Stewart in the fight, but Rockefeller believed they had no other course. The exception was Stephens, who the Rockefeller committee had decided was "unwarrantedly partisan" in supporting Colonel Stewart's campaign for proxies.

Because Rockefeller had wisely limited the objective of his proxy battle to ousting Stewart and had not allowed his relations with other members of management to deteriorate, the struggle with Stewart caused very little disruption to company operations. Seubert, who had been serving as president under Stewart since 1927 when Burton retired, was re-elected president and named chief executive officer. Stewart, who presided at the meeting, accepted his defeat with dignity and no public expressions of illwill.

Also reassuring to Standard's management was the decision of Rockefeller to slate Melvin A. Traylor, president of the First National Bank of Chicago, as the first non-employee director in Standard (Indiana)'s history. The addition of an outstanding Chicago businessman to the board was a signal to stockholders that the proxy fight would not result in a shift of power to eastern interests, as had been feared, and that Standard (Indiana) would remain a midwest-based and operated institution.

Seubert—"Keep Your Eyes on the Cash Box"

4

Edward G. Seubert, the man chosen to succeed Stewart, was of a far different mold. He had begun his career as a 15-year-old mechanic's helper at the Whiting refinery where his father was head of the pipe department. Within a year, he was working as a clerk in the office; because of an aptitude for figures, he moved from one promotion to another until he had arrived in the general office in Chicago as assistant to the treasurer. As an accountant and one who understood figures, Seubert was brilliant. He was elected a director in 1919 and vice president in 1920.

John E. Rouse, a vice president of Standard's oil and gas production subsidiary, once quoted a bit of wisdom from an unknown philosopher who said, "Pity the company which falls into the hands of its accountants." But that is exactly what happened to Standard (Indiana). Seubert's emphasis on capital conservation caused the company to be described later as the "Montgomery Ward of the 1930s," a reference to the business philosophy of Sewell Avery who kept Ward sitting on a pile of cash during and after World War II while Sears was expanding into a dominant position in the marketplace.

Seubert was not only cautious by nature, but he made frequent trips to New York to consult the Rockefeller interests and banks before making any major decision. It is difficult to determine whether they asked him to do this or whether his cautious character merely made him a "leaner" rather than a leader. Seubert's self-appraisal tells much about the man. "There haven't been any big moments in my life," he once said. "My life has been a steady experience of prosaic hard work." His chief philosophy, expressed even in a speech to employees, was: "Keep your eyes on the cash box, boys."

Seubert's personal life reflected penurious habits. He lived with two sisters on the south side of Chicago, and according to company legend, whenever they went to the movies, he always made sure they arrived before six p.m. when the price changed.

A former president of South Shore Country Club recalled that Seubert would arrive at the club in his chauffeur-driven Cadillac carrying his sandwich in a paper sack so he wouldn't have to buy lunch at the club after playing golf. He would never buy a drink until the other golfers shamed him into bringing his own whiskey and keeping it in his locker. But even then he wouldn't buy a set-up; he would get ice out of the water cooler.

This attitude carried over into his management of the company. A few weeks before January 1, 1945, when Edgar F. Bullard was to step up to president of Stanolind Oil and Gas Company, Standard's wholly-owned oil and gas exploration and production company, Seubert, who coincidentally would retire as Standard's chief executive officer on that date also, called Bullard in and said:

"Now, young man, you're taking on a very important position. But there are two things you have to watch out for in managing this important branch of our activity. In my experience, the two most important things to watch are the purchasing department and the expense accounts of the executives."

Here was the case of a man who was charged with the responsibility of going out and finding new oil, and he was supposed to look first at the purchasing department and expense accounts of executives!

The fact is that Seubert was not comfortable in situations where cost and value were not the same thing. In a refinery or a service station, cost and value are related. If a refinery unit or station burns down, the owner can duplicate it at a known cost. This can't be done in the oil exploration part of the business. Cost and value are not the same. Hundreds of thousands of dollars or even several million dollars may be spent drilling a single well. The well may discover a new oil or natural gas field—or it may be a dry hole.

Seubert started out boldly enough toward increasing Standard's pipeline transportation system, and, more important, its domestic oil and natural gas resources. Within a year after Seubert had been named chief executive officer, Standard in 1930 bought the remaining 50 per cent interest in Sinclair Pipe Line Company for $42.5 million and changed the name of its now wholly-owned pipeline system to Stanolind Pipe Line Company. The system was situated in the heart of the midcontinent and extended from Houston to Chicago (later built to West Texas fields) and from Wyoming to Chicago. Standard now was near its goal of independence from others for crude oil transportation to its refineries. Being a common carrier, the system also transported crude oil for others—at one time serving more than 50 refineries directly or through connecting carriers.

As new oil fields were discovered and production increased, Stanolind built new lines and increased capacities of others by looping or adding pumping equipment, or both. For a number of years, it was known as the longest pipeline system in the world with more than 14,000 miles of pipelines in 11 states. In 1955, an Interstate Commerce Commission report showed that the system (its company name was changed to Service Pipe Line in 1950) had become first in the nation among more than 90 U.S. pipelines when it pumped 111,438,050,000 barrel miles—barrels handled times distance travelled. It held that record for years. In 1965 it pumped 156,127,372,000 barrel miles.

Standard also boosted its domestic oil purchasing capability in 1930 when it acquired for $30 million the remaining 50 per cent interest in Sinclair Crude Oil Purchasing Company, one of the largest crude oil purchasing operations in the U.S., and changed its name to Stanolind Crude Oil Purchasing Company.

Perhaps Seubert rode the momentum Stewart had created. The Stewart period had seen Standard acquire Dixie Oil Company in 1919, Midwest Refining Company in 1920, 50 per cent interest in Sinclair Pipe Line Company and in Sinclair Crude Oil Purchasing Company in 1921, and Pan American Petroleum and Transport Company beginning in 1925.

In 1929, the same year that saw Stewart's downfall and Seubert's designation to replace him as Standard's chief executive officer, Dixie Oil, having already grown considerably in acreage and production, acquired 500,000 acres of prospective oil and gas leases in Kansas and Oklahoma from Amerada Petroleum Corporation, and on November 1, 1929, moved its headquarters to Tulsa from Shreveport.

Acquisition of Mc-Man Oil and Gas Company came in 1930 when Standard—for 300,000 shares of its stock—bought the highly successful company with production in Oklahoma and substantial holdings in Texas, including production in the important Yates field in Pecos County.

A large share of credit for the ensuing growth through discovery of new fields, increased production from existing fields, and acquisitions over the next several years was due to certain strong oil field personalities who had come into the organization. These executives had emerged through Midwest Refining and Dixie Oil and focused the much-needed expertise of the oil and gas explorer and producer on Standard's growth. They were Alonzo W. Peake, Frank O. Prior, Edgar F. Bullard, and Albert L. Solliday.

Peake was a 1912 Stanford University graduate whose first job had been as a California oil field roustabout. He joined Midwest Refining in 1916 as a field superintendent. Prior attended Stanford, dropped out for World War I service, and received his degree in mechanical engineering in 1919. He went to work for Midwest Refining as a roustabout in the Salt Creek field in 1919 and met Peake, who had advanced to superintendent of the gas department at the company office in Casper, Wyoming, that same year. According to Prior, the two became better acquainted when Prior got up nerve to bum a ride "with the boss" (Peake) to see a friend in a Casper hospital. While Peake and Prior hadn't known each other during their Stanford days, it turned out that Peake had known Prior's hospitalized friend.

About a year after that ride in Peake's big Cadillac touring car, Peake was appointed chief engineer with six departments reporting to him, including a new mechanical department. He named Prior head of that department. When Peake was made president of Dixie Oil Company in 1928, he brought Prior down from Casper with him.

Bullard, a 1921 Yale University graduate, was chief geologist with Dixie. He had come to the company by a rather unusual route. After attending Phillips Exeter Academy, he majored in geology in Yale's mining engineering course. Although he had prepared himself for a career in mining, he found upon graduation that there were no jobs available. But, while spending an afternoon at New York's Saratoga racetrack, he became acquainted with Colonel Stewart who arranged for Bullard to take a job with the recently acquired Dixie Oil Company. Bullard soon became enamored of not only the exploration and production business but the Southwest. He remained a confirmed bachelor.

Solliday, the son of a Watertown, Wisconsin banker, earned a degree in geology from the University of Oklahoma. He joined Dixie in 1923 as a temporary draftsman, but soon moved into geological field assignments. He quickly showed special aptitudes for land negotiations, and these talents were to play a key role in his career. He gained a reputation for being able "to smell a good deal from a bad one a mile off."

On December 12, 1930, Standard incorporated a new subsidiary, Stanolind Oil and Gas Company with general offices at Tulsa, and on January 1, 1931, consolidated into it the properties of Dixie Oil, Mc-Man Oil and Gas, and the Texas and Oklahoma properties of Midwest Exploration Company (a subsidiary of Midwest Refining Company). Uniting these units in a single exploration-and-production-oriented subsidiary created for Standard a domestic oil and gas production nucleus—a major step with far-reaching consequences for Standard's future growth and profit.

Peake was elected a director and vice president for production of Standard in 1929 and was to be Standard's general office advocate for aggressive expansion of oil and gas resources. Prior became the first president of Stanolind Oil and Gas, Bullard was named director of exploration, and Solliday became superintendent of the land department.

On July 1, 1931, Stanolind Oil and Gas acquired Southern Crude Oil Purchasing Company, one of many subsidiaries of Standard's Pan American Petroleum and Transport Company. Steps were taken immediately to bring to an end a troublesome episode that involved Dixie Oil prior to the consolidation. Dixie Oil had held substantial interests in Southern Crude's net daily average oil production of about 7,400 barrels and in promising leased acreage. Certain members of Southern Crude's management were suspected of being involved with a drilling contractor in illegal kickbacks and in selling, or themselves using, confidential company information on drilling prospects. These practices were not unusual in the oil industry during the first two decades of the century. But they were not condoned by the management of Dixie Oil in the late twenties, by the new Stanolind Oil and Gas, or by its parent company.

Southern Crude was Stanolind Oil and Gas Company's first major acquisition. Following it, in 1932, Stanolind Oil and Gas acquired field properties of Midwest Refining Company that hadn't been included in the properties of Midwest Exploration Company absorbed by Stanolind when it was organized.

Twenty or so other producing and nonproducing properties were purchased during the depression years. As a result of acquisitions, the operating territory of Stanolind Oil and Gas grew from its original relatively small holdings in Kansas, Louisiana, Michigan, and Oklahoma, with smaller acreage in Alabama, Arkansas, and New Mexico. Southern Crude added more West Texas production, and Midwest Refining properties extended the territory to Colorado, Montana, New Mexico, and Wyoming.

Under the impact of the depression, Standard's earnings dropped drastically—from $78 million in 1929 to $16.5 million in 1932. No saving was too small to make. Advertising expenditures were halted temporarily. Company airplanes were sold. Directors, who were formerly furnished cars, were told to buy their own. Support for the Whiting refinery band was discontinued. Seubert, who had little patience for the slow nature of research, demanded a list of chemists to be fired as surplus.

Business was so bad in the fall of 1932 that even general office employees were mobilized to act as salesmen. For three weeks before Christmas, employees were asked to go out and sell Christmas coupon books in $5, $10, and $25 denominations to friends and relatives.

With so little demand for gasoline because of the depression, and with too much oil production in the late 1920s, the discovery of the great East Texas field in 1930 compounded the oil surplus; the price of crude oil dropped as low as 10 cents a barrel. Most of Standard's refineries were operating at about 50 per cent of capacity, and in 1932, two small refineries, one in Michigan and one in Wyoming, were closed.

Price-cutting small companies became more than nibblers in the scramble for a share of the market, resulting in reduced sales by Standard and other established marketers. Some price cutters sold gasoline below posted retail prices direct to motorists from tank cars spotted on railroad sidings—one of the worst forms of competition Standard faced, and others sold motorists cheap gasoline designed for lighting, heating, and cooking in rural areas but which worked satisfactorily in low-compression automobile engines. Major dealers offered all sorts of inducements to protect their share of the gasoline market. It was hard for a motorist to buy gasoline without being offered a premium: candy, cigarettes, ash trays, dolls, chinaware, cigarette lighters, and a host of other items.

With an excess of oil on the market, domestic producers were soon pressuring Congress to enact a tariff on imported crude oil and refined products in order to force up their prices and to give domestic producers both a price increase and greater access to markets. For Standard, the tariff would have affected crude oil imported from Venezuela and Mexico by Pan American Petroleum and Transport Company. It would also have applied to refined products imported by Pan American from a 110,000-barrel refinery the company had built in 1928–29 on the Caribbean island of Aruba to process crude from its Venezuelan properties.

Standard saw itself forced out of importing operations if the tariff were adopted. It had two options: either develop additional refining and marketing outside the tariff wall, and some moves were made in that direction, or sell Pan American Petroleum and Transport properties except those in the continental United States.

It had been Stewart's intention while he was chairman to make Standard a worldwide enterprise, and with the Pan American Petroleum and Transport purchase he had gone a long way toward doing so. But Seubert was not Stewart and 1932 was not 1927.

In May, 1932, the board of directors voted to sell the company's foreign interests to Standard (New Jersey) for $47.9 million in cash and 1,778,973 shares of Jersey stock, making Standard (Indiana) the owner of seven per cent of Jersey stock and the largest single stockholder in that company.

In an exchange offer in 1969, Standard (Indiana) distributed its remaining holdings of the Jersey stock to its shareholders on the basis of seven-eighths of a share of Jersey stock for one share of Indiana stock, and placed the 1,653,016 of its own shares received in its treasury account.

The decision to sell Pan American Petroleum and Transport's foreign interests was one of the most controversial in the history of Standard. Some have believed that Stewart was forced out and Seubert put in his place not so much because of Stewart's questionable participation in the Continental Trading Company-Mexia oil deal but because Standard (New Jersey) was feeling the hot breath of competition by its one-time subsidiary, and the eastern interests thought Seubert would be more likely to make a deal than would Stewart.

There is nothing in the record to support this belief; it was probably kept alive for a time by the fact that Seubert was noted for checking his decisions with the Rockefeller interests and New York bankers. Others have strongly believed that such a scenario would have been ridiculous. On the other hand, it is demonstrably true that if Standard (Indiana) had carved out a share of what then was a limited world market, the principal losers would have been Standard (New Jersey) and the Royal Dutch/Shell Group.

The positive side of the transaction was that the two anticipated negative events soon occurred. Less than a month after consummation of the sale, Congress passed a tariff effective in June, 1932, which removed oil from the free list. The tariff imposed a duty of $1.05 per barrel on gasoline, $1.68 per barrel on lubricating oil, and 21 cents per barrel on crude oil, fuel oil, and other liquid derivatives. East Texas crude oil was then selling at only about 42 cents a barrel. Since gasoline was selling in bulk in Baltimore for only five or six cents a gallon and the billing price was tied to the price of gasoline in the retail market, it was obvious that Pan American Petroleum and Transport would have had a big financial loss in the U.S. market after paying the new tariff. Then in 1938, Mexico expropriated all foreign-owned petroleum properties in that country.

Seubert found it difficult to accept the standards by which oil explorers and producers made judgments. After a lifetime of dealing with ledgers and accounts subject to audit, he lacked confidence in decisions involving millions of dollars which might be based on no more than a recommendation of a subsidiary which, couched in the jargon of the oil fields and buoyed by the optimism of the explorer, seemed to him less than sufficient. Prior, the oil field expert, once said that the only word Seubert knew was "No."

But with the treasury strengthened by the cash infusion from the Jersey deal, the oil field experts—Peake, Prior, Bullard, and Solliday—pressured Seubert into oil field investments whose value would be counted not only then but well into the future. Four yardsticks measure the success of their aggressive efforts: Acreage held under lease and reservation, wells drilled, drilling expenditures, and net domestic production of crude oil.

At the end of its first year of operations (1931), Stanolind Oil and Gas held 29,541 producing and 921,043 nonproducing acres. The totals jumped to 56,471 and 1,039,625 producing and non-producing acres respectively in 1932 with the acquisition of additional Midwest Refining properties and some other properties. The number of producing acres climbed steadily from then on as did the nonproducing acres, except in 1933 and 1934 when nonproducing acreage dropped below one million.

The number of wells drilled was impressive especially for a depression economy; drilling expenditures indicated that Stanolind was allowed a sizeable allocation of Standard's total discretionary spending dollar.

In 1932, Stanolind Oil and Gas spent $3.9 million to drill 243 gross wells compared with $2.3 million for 128 gross wells in 1931. After cutbacks in 1933, drilling expenditures and number of wells drilled resumed a steady climb to a peak in 1937 when drilling costs for 1,061 gross wells (900.16 net) totaled $33.4 million. Drilling activity declined just prior to and during World War II, then began climbing again although the number of wells drilled annually didn't top 1,000 again until 1955.

These efforts were ultimately reflected in Stanolind's growing net domestic crude oil production. In its first year (1931) Stanolind produced 7.2 million barrels (13 per cent of Standard's total refinery runs). By 1945, Stanolind's net production had climbed to 61.5 million barrels, 52.5 per cent of refinery runs. It would continue to grow through 1976, when it peaked at 198.7 million barrels, 53 per cent of refinery runs. (In 1976, operations in Canada and overseas added another 112.4 million barrels to Standard's worldwide production).

After three early years of negative profits, Stanolind Oil and Gas earnings were 9.46 per cent of Standard's net earnings of $18,949,680 in 1934. In 1945, they were 40.19 per cent of Standard's net earnings of $50,340,476, and two years later, in 1947, they were 60.25 per cent of net earnings of $89,094,558.

It was during the depression years, difficult though they were for corporations and rank and file citizens alike, that Stanolind Oil and Gas laid the foundations for funding Standard's subsequent return to foreign oil operations.

Contrasting with Seubert's guard over the cash-on-hand column, Peake, Prior, and Bullard knew that information itself was often money and that information not acted upon could often be opportunity missed or money lost.

The discovery in 1934 by Stanolind Oil and Gas Company of the Hastings oil field near Houston, Texas, one of Standard's most significant finds, was a dramatic example of the need for both speed and ingenuity in using information provided by torsion balance surveys and seismograph crews. When word reached Edgar F. Bullard, then a Stanolind Oil and Gas vice president, that a seismic crew had found indications of a major geologic structure near Hastings, it was a holiday weekend and all the offices and banks were closed. But because Bullard was aware that other companies were also active in the area, he knew he had to move quickly.

He immediately sent George W. Clarke, then head of the land department, to Houston where Clarke rounded up all the reputable land brokers he could find, and persuaded authorities to open the courthouse on San Jacinto day—a holiday marking the final victory in the war for Texas independence—so that oil leases could be recorded.

Knowing that farmers would want cash for oil leases they sold to Stanolind, he appealed for funds (since banks were closed for the holiday) to such places as a company installation in Wyoming and the Whiting refinery to send whatever money they had on the premises. The move was a wise one; once the purchase of leases began, the price went from one dollar to $5,000 an acre in two days. However, Standard's early start enabled it to take a dominant position in the area, which became one of the company's major oil fields.

Purchase of the Yount-Lee Oil Company properties on August 1, 1935, stands out as the most significant addition during this period. Based at Beaumont, Texas, Yount-Lee Oil was one of the largest independent oil producing companies on the Gulf Coast. At the time of the purchase, it had average net daily oil production of 18,942 barrels. Properties included acreage in the great East Texas field, at Spindletop, and in the Hackberry field in southern Louisiana. Through Stanolind Oil and Gas, Standard paid $42 million in cash for the Yount-Lee properties. This purchase enabled Stanolind to increase its daily average production to 68,965 barrels in 1936 and moved it into fourth place among producing companies on the Gulf Coast.

On another front, during the last half of the 1930s, a refining innovation emerged in the industry which some contemporary authorities viewed as the first major revolution in the refining of crude oil and the production of gasoline since Standard developed the Burton-Humphreys high-pressure, high-temperature cracking process in 1913.

The process was known by the name of the French engineer-industrialist Eugene P. Houdry who had discovered in 1927 that a gasoline he produced in his laboratory by a catalytic cracking method was superior to racing quality gasoline then available. Vacuum Oil Company licensed the process and persuaded Houdry to bring his laboratory from France to its Paulsboro, New Jersey, facilities in 1930. Houdry and his associates and Vacuum formed Houdry Process Corporation a year later, then Vacuum's interest waned after it became Socony-Vacuum Oil Company and Houdry's experimental results proved less than hoped for.

2. The natural gas processing plant at the Hastings field near Houston, Texas, as it appeared in 1957, ten years after its completion.

Soon finding another supporter in Sun Oil Company, Houdry moved his equipment to Sun's large Marcus Hook, Pennsylvania, refinery and laboratory. Following successful pilot plant development and operations, the three investors in the Houdry Process Corporation—Sun, Socony-Vacuum, and Houdry—agreed to balance their financial and technical contributions since Sun's had outdistanced Socony-Vacuum's.

Socony-Vacuum then decided to build a small commercial unit to test the process thoroughly before starting a larger unit. As a result of the shorter construction time required, in June, 1936 at Paulsboro it brought on stream the first commercial Houdry catalytic cracking unit. Sun installed its first commercial Houdry unit, larger than Socony-Vacuum's, in April, 1937 at Marcus Hook.

At the 1938 annual meeting of the American Petroleum Institute, A. E. Pew, Jr., a member of Sun's founding Pew family and vice president in charge of manufacturing, reported:

"An outstanding feature of these catalytic operations (the Sun and Socony-Vacuum Houdry units then operating) is their ability to produce aviation gasoline. It is believed ... that the manufacture of aviation gasoline by this process (seven million gallons in 1937–38) represents the first commercial application of a synthetic process for aviation-fuel production."

Although the industry had achieved numerous technological advances since the Burton-Humphreys thermal cracking process had been introduced, the Houdry catalytic process offered unique advantages. Scientists, operators and economists of other oil companies soon were analyzing the feasibility of licensing the new process. At Standard, the study was conducted under the direction of Max G. Paulus, vice president and director of manufacturing, with the analysis taking place in the Whiting research laboratory's process design department then headed by Robert C. Gunness. Standard and other companies concluded that the license fee was too high.

To develop a competing catalytic cracking process that would not infringe the Houdry patents, Standard (Indiana), Standard (New Jersey), I. G. Farbenindustrie, and M. W. Kellogg Company (a large engineering and construction firm specializing in the petroleum industry), organized Catalytic Research Associates in October, 1938. They were soon joined by Anglo-Iranian Oil Company, Limited, Royal Dutch-Shell Company, The Texas Company, and Universal Oil Products Company.

In early 1939, President Edward G. Seubert departed from his prepared remarks at a pre-annual meeting press briefing to comment on Catalytic Research Associates, prompting one financial writer to describe Seubert's comment as a disclosure coming "in an expansive moment of unaccustomed loquacity. The normally reticent Mr. Seubert would not be talking at all unless he felt reasonably sure that he has something and unless the new process is somewhere near ready to go," he added. The new process resulting from the work of the Catalytic Research Associates, was a fluid catalytic cracking process announced by Standard (New Jersey) in 1940 and demonstrated for news media in February, 1941.

Standard (Indiana)'s contributions to development of fluid catalytic cracking included three key inventions: The "bottom draw-off concept" by F. W. (Fred) Scheineman, an engineer at Whiting; the "aerated catalyst standpipe" by Vanderveer Voorhees, an inventor and patent attorney in Standard's Patents and Development department (later named Patents and Licensing department); and the "internal cyclones" by Robert C. Gunness, then in charge of chemical engineering design of processing units at the Whiting laboratory.

47

The technology which Seubert hinted at in his surprise disclosure at the press conference in 1939 was indeed remarkable, and Standard's scientists had contributed significantly to the revolution in refining technology.

In 1942, the emphasis of the Whiting research laboratory quickly shifted to projects related to the war. Research expenditures increased from about $1.3 million to more than $3.6 million by 1945—all directed toward the objective of finding new and more efficient ways to refine crude oil and to provide higher-quality products that new war machines required. Stanolind's research efforts at Tulsa were also altered to emphasize war work. Standard filed 862 United States patent applications, many of them subject to war-time secrecy restrictions, and obtained 661 patents during the war period.

Based on laboratory experience and a small pilot plant, Standard inaugurated the world's first commercial hydroforming unit in the fall of 1940 at its Texas City refinery. This flexible new process, producing high yields of aromatics and high-quality aviation gasoline base stock, substantially increased aviation gasoline and toluene production. Based on the data obtained, new plants were designed for construction by the company at its Whiting refinery, by the government at its Baytown, Texas, ordnance works, and elsewhere.

A new fluid catalytic cracking unit at Wood River designed for high grade motor fuel production was modified to make blending stock for 100-octane gasoline. One under construction at Texas City was modified to operate at high temperature instead of low to produce additional butylene for the manufacture of butadiene for synthetic rubber and aviation gasoline components.

To further increase production of toluene and aviation gasoline components, new alkylation, isomerization, catalytic cracking, and related units were built at Whiting, Wood River, Salt Lake City, and Texas City. The isomate unit installed at the Whiting refinery in 1944 was the first commercial plant to isomerize light naphtha for aviation gasoline. A new superaviation fuel with a performance rate of 115–145 compared with 100–130 rating of pre-war aviation gasoline was announced in 1944.

Midway in the war, most of a $90 million refinery expansion program impelled by the urgency of the military conflict had been completed, and a plan to expand the staff and build a new research center at Whiting had been approved.

48   When German submarines began to take a heavy toll of

Allied shipping in the summer of 1941, Standard and other members of the oil industry began playing a role in what had become the Battle of the Atlantic. This involved getting oil supplies to East Coast ports. Pan American Petroleum and Transport Company was called upon in most of 1941 to contribute about 20 per cent of its ships to carry military oil products from the Gulf of Mexico to Atlantic coastal ports.

Besides supplying huge quantities of toluene, high octane aviation gasoline, 91-octane aviation gasoline for transports and trainers, and an all-purpose gasoline for tanks, trucks, jeeps, half-tracks, and boats, Standard shipped large quantities of navy diesel fuel and lubricating oil, white oil and petrolatum for medicinal use; a new lubricant to protect metal against swift corrosion in the tropics, and special greases for airplane equipment which would function from 60 degrees below zero to equatorial heat.

As an outgrowth of research to find lubricants to meet all kinds of weather conditions, Standard's scientists created a new, heavy-duty, all-weather motor oil, Stanolube HD. Standard assigned its entire output of this product to the armed forces. After the war, Stanolube HD evolved into Permalube and Super Permalube motor oils sold to the public at service stations.

The imposition of gasoline and tire rationing, the slowing down of civilian motoring, and the lack of manpower forced the closing of 150 of the company's bulk plants and almost 5,000 of its retail service stations. Conservation became the theme of the company's advertising—as was to be the case during the gasoline shortage in 1979. The wartime slogan was "Care for your car for your country." Thousands of copies of a booklet entitled "Twenty-Five Ways to Save Fuel Oil" were distributed.

Defense preparations and the advent of World War II had a great impact on Standard, as they did throughout the nation. In 1940, anticipating future national defense needs, the government formed the National Defense Advisory Commission and selected Standard's best known scientist, Robert E. Wilson, then president of Pan American Petroleum and Transport Company, to be in charge of the Natural Gas and Petroleum Section of the Raw Materials Division. Wilson's credentials included his World War I service as a major in the Chemical Warfare Service.

As the nation shifted from a defense to a war basis, President Franklin D. Roosevelt created the Office of Petroleum Coordinator for National Defense, and the Petroleum Industry War Council was set up to advise and counsel with the coordinator. Wilson resigned from his other war-related assignments, and he and Edward G. Seubert were appointed with 78 oil company executives as members of the council.

Wilson, Seubert, and Peake served on several of the council's standing committees. Bruce K. Brown, then a Standard director and general manager of research and development, was given leave of absence to act as special consultant on aviation gasoline. In July of 1942, he became an assistant deputy petroleum coordinator in the Office of Petroleum Administration for War. These men were among many Standard executives who served in the home-front war effort.

The shortage of manpower during the war changed the nature of Standard's work force. By the end of the war, 7,713 employees of Standard and its subsidiaries had been granted military leave to enter the armed services. To offset the shortage of labor, more women were employed, some in technical work but many others in heavy manual labor. By the end of 1944, about 5,000 women were employed by Standard and its subsidiaries; they constituted 15 per cent of the total work force.

Had it not been for problems caused by the war, Seubert would have retired in 1941, but the board asked him to remain as president past his normal retirement date. On January 1, 1945, with the war nearing a conclusion, Seubert stepped down. The choice of his successor and the conditions which surrounded it were to create a division within the company that endured for almost 15 years.

Divided Authority at the Top

5

At the time of Edward G. Seubert's retirement as president and chief executive officer, Standard, rather than being a unified operation with central direction, actually consisted of three power centers which tended to operate independently of each other. Standard's general and sales offices were in Chicago, Pan American Petroleum and Transport Company was headquartered in New York, and Stanolind Oil and Gas Company was headquartered in Tulsa, Oklahoma.

Local autonomies and local personalities often held sway and, if it could be said that any one local autonomy—with its personalities—was to have a unique and major role as Standard grew, the choice would go to Stanolind Oil and Gas, the exploration and production subsidiary.

Tulsa was then known as "The Oil Capital of the World," and Standard had other subsidiaries headquartered there from time to time: the pipeline company, the crude oil purchasing company, and the gas products company. But the exploration and production subsidiary was the most influential.

It was so influential that it often was referred to simply as "Tulsa," as were the others, with less audacity, when the topic was theirs. And "Tulsa" could be described accurately as defiant of "Chicago," as the general office was referred to. This defiance was embedded in the conflict between the personalities in Stanolind Oil and Gas, who understood exploration and production thoroughly but were dependent upon Chicago for operating and growth funds, and those in Chicago, who, in the opinion of many key executives, displayed too little knowledge of Tulsa's area of expertise and its importance to Standard, yet held the purse strings.

The exception in Chicago was Alonzo W. Peake, who had

been a major factor in exploration and production through the Seubert years as vice president for production in Chicago for Standard. In Tulsa were Peake's long-time associates Frank O. Prior, who was president, and Edgar F. Bullard, executive vice president, of Stanolind Oil and Gas.

Peake was the sole interface between Tulsa and Chicago and had been for years. Rigid rules controlled communications between Chicago and Tulsa. All written communications, for example, had to go through Peake's office before being sent on to Prior or Bullard. Telephone calls (which could not be monitored) were frowned upon.

Because of his accomplishments in executive positions as well as his extensive oil field operating experience, Peake had hoped that he would succeed Seubert as president and chief executive officer. But when Seubert retired at the end of 1944, Standard's board of directors reestablished the office of chairman and designated Robert E. Wilson, president of Pan American Petroleum and Transport Company in New York since 1937, as chief executive officer. The board then elected Peake president. When Wilson was picked, there was the equivalent of an oil field explosion in Tulsa and Chicago. Peake flew to Tulsa, where he met with Prior and Bullard to decide whether the three of them should quit. They conferred for several days and decided Peake would return to Chicago to negotiate for independent authority to run at least exploration and production with no interference from Wilson.

When Peake arrived in Chicago to negotiate, he laid a firm plan of organization before Wilson: Peake, as the new president of Standard, would stake out his claim to head company operations; Prior would come to Chicago from Tulsa to take Peake's place as Standard's vice president for production; and Bullard would be named president of Stanolind.

Peake had some good cards; the major stockholder interests could not have been happy with the prospect of losing three key executives in a very profitable part of the company. Wilson, realizing there was no real alternative, drafted and signed a letter accepting Peake's terms. Today, it reads more like a letter of abdication than an agreement between a chief executive and a nominal subordinate.

The agreement stated that Wilson would act as chairman. However, the major operations of the company would come under Peake. The key paragraphs of the letter from Wilson to Peake were:

"You are to have the direct responsibility for and immediate direction of, the principal operating departments, namely, production, pipe line, refining and sales, of the company and its Stanolind and Utah subsidiaries, and also the closely affiliated departments of advertising, traffic, lake and river transportation and purchasing.

"I am to have direct responsibility for and immediate direction of the financial, accounting, tax, legal, public relations, stockholder relations, research, development and patent activities of the company and its subsidiaries, and over all the activities of the Pan American subsidiaries" (meaning Pan American Petroleum and Transport Company which included among its numerous subsidiaries The American Oil Company).

"It is understood that neither of us is to be 'insulated' from the departments or subsidiaries under the immediate direction of the other, and that each is free to secure desired information direct from any department of the company, but that we will refrain from giving directions to those under the other's jurisdiction . . ."

Wilson summed up the impact of this arrangement in a memorandum to the board of directors: "In general, the pattern of the organization will be that the 'staff' departments will report primarily to me, and that the 'line' or operating departments will report primarily to Mr. Peake . . ." Although Wilson officially was chief executive officer, he and Peake each were to report independently to the board of directors—a most unusual arrangement.

Although Wilson's public appearances (he was an inveterate public speaker) accounted for an increased visibility and improved public image somewhat reminiscent of Stewart's efforts to inform the public about the company, divided authority could not work to the company's benefit. Samuel K. Botsford, assistant corporate secretary during the period, summed it up as well as anyone in an interview with Paul H. Giddens, author of the company's official history published in 1955.

"A divided management could not accomplish anything but a divided result," Botsford told Giddens. Over a decade, Botsford said, "it created a cancer within the company. I think the image of Standard (Indiana)—in community life and in public life—was enhanced . . . but within the company, I think we lost ground because we drew further apart in our objectives; we never really accomplished what we should have . . ."

Peake was a tough, hard-nosed operator who knew every phase of oil exploration and production. Wilson was no match for

53

him. To the end of his life, even after serving as chairman of Standard, Wilson still referred to himself as a chemical engineer rather than as a business executive. This self-appraisal may have been correct. Later Peake was to remark to John E. Rouse, a production and manufacturing official with Standard and its Stanolind exploration and production subsidiary, that when Wilson was named chairman, "They ruined a darned good research man to make a hell of a poor executive."

Wilson's research credentials were excellent. He was a graduate of the Massachusetts Institute of Technology where he served on the faculty as associate professor of chemical engineering before joining Standard in 1922 as assistant director of research. His service in two world wars was related to chemical engineering and applied research—in uniform in World War I as a major in the Chemical Warfare Service, in World War II home-front assignments with the federal government, and as one of four managing directors of the General Aniline and Film Corporation, a German property seized by the U.S. government.

High awards Wilson received included the Chemical Industry Medal in 1938 for distinguished work in the field of applied chemistry; a National Association of Manufacturers citation in 1940 as a modern pioneer for his work in cracking and conservation of hydrocarbon vapors; the prestigious Perkin Medal for applied chemistry in 1943; the Lord Cadman Memorial Medal of the British Institute of Petroleum; the Northwestern University Centennial Award; and the Washington Award for Engineering. He was active in leading professional chemical societies, and had published 70 or more technical papers. With 89 patents in his name, Wilson was a leading authority on cracking, motor fuels, and lubricants.

He was recognized as an expert technical witness in patent litigation. One example is the role of Wilson in a U.S. government antitrust suit against Standard and certain other members of the so-called Patent Club. In hearings conducted in October, 1925, before Charles Martindale of Indianapolis, appointed by the court as special master in chancery to take evidence, Wilson acted as Standard's expert technical witness. Ralph H. McKee, professor of chemical engineering at Columbia University, was expert technical witness for the government.

McKee attempted to impeach the validity of the defense of Standard and its codefendants and in doing so led Martindale to conclude that McKee's testimony in favor of the government's position was beyond understanding by the court. Martindale then adopted for the government the testimony of Wilson as being more reasonable and accurate.

It was a tradition in Standard for innovative scientists with doctorates in chemistry or chemical engineering—such as William M. Burton, Robert E. Humphreys, M. G. Paulus, Walter G. Whitman, Carl C. Monrad, Ernest M. Thiele, and others—to play leading roles in keeping the company in the forefront of industry technology. Whether to identify himself with this tradition or to satisfy a desire to be accepted by his peers in the academic community, Wilson always insisted that he be referred to as "Doctor" Wilson. If anyone failed to remember it was "Doctor," the caller would be reminded of the omission by Wilson's secretary. It was something of a shock then for the assistant corporate secretary of the company, Botsford, to learn one day that "Doctor" Wilson, despite his research accomplishments had not earned a doctor's degree at all. Over time, Wilson was awarded 10 or 12 honorary doctorates, but he had completed academic requirements for only a master's degree at M.I.T., possibly because service in World War I interrupted his program.

Wilson's early management experience as contrasted with his principal orientation in research may explain his reluctance to bring Standard back into the international arena. Oil exploration and production abroad or domestically was not his forte. In 1935, he had transferred from his position in Chicago as a Standard director and vice president in charge of research to New York as vice chairman of the board of Pan American Petroleum and Transport—only three years after Standard (Indiana) sold to Standard (New Jersey) the overseas interests it had acquired by purchasing controlling interest in Pan American Petroleum and Transport. Perhaps this sale influenced Wilson throughout his career.

But after World War II, when the great economic expansion began in Europe, Asia, and in the U.S., the very large resources of oil found in Saudi Arabia, Iran, Iraq, and Kuwait took on real value. By the early fifties, companies with stakes in foreign oil production were making money and lots of it. Prior and others urged Wilson to get Standard involved. Wilson, however, had no stomach for engaging in the oil business outside the United States. He was quoted as saying that holding Jersey stock, of which the company had a large number of shares at the time as a result of selling its overseas interests, was a very comfortable way of engaging in foreign activities.

The tone of the corporate management outside the board

room during the Wilson years may be illustrated in part by the customs—reaching back to the Stewart regime—imposed at Red Crown Lodge, a converted fishing camp on Trout Lake in northern Wisconsin.

Colonel Stewart had purchased the lodge for Standard in 1922 as a setting for executive get-togethers. He espoused a philosophy that executives who played together worked better together. With his authoritarian manner, he dominated the highly-structured recreational activities he set up. For baseball, he assigned the positions. The prevailing wisdom held that the assigned second baseman had better be on second base at 2:15 when the game started or else his career would be jeopardized.

Stewart's practices were modified by his successors—depending on their personalities. Morning (and sometimes evening) meetings were added to the schedule where presentations were made on important facets of the company's business. Outdoor sports were limited to afternoons, and participation in organized activities became optional. Nevertheless, a trip to Red Crown Lodge often would be remembered for the extracurricular and inconsequential.

One executive recalled that Wilson barred anyone from the dining room who didn't wear a tie and coat. Further, he required the assembled executives to stand and sing the Standard Oil "fight song," which some unknown bard had composed in the middle of the LaFollette Committee investigations of the oil industry in the 1920s. The lyrics, if they may be called that, were sung to the tune of "Tammany" and went as follows:

> Standard Oil, Standard Oil,
> Turns the darkness into light;
> Makes the customers feel all right.
> Standard Oil, Standard Oil,
> Curse it, damn it,
> You can't do without it,
> Standard Oil!

Peake was cut from a different pattern. Despite his Stanford degree, he still talked and looked like a typical hand in the oil fields where he had gotten his start as a roustabout. In his earlier years, he chewed tobacco; later, when he moved to company headquarters in Chicago, he chewed cigars—without bothering to light them. This led to the presence throughout the general office of brass spittoons in areas where Peake might be expected to appear. In his own office, the spittoon was located in the center of a six-foot piece of circular carpet to protect the regular floor covering from the times he missed the target. Needless to say, it was changed rather often.

As can be imagined, he was a rugged-looking man with a craggy face. He was absolutely open and direct; so open that sometimes it was embarrassing. There was no subterfuge; he loved to tell off-color stories, of which he had a considerable repertoire, and could get away with telling them in company where another kind of a man might have had his face slapped.

Everybody in the company who knew Al Peake liked him. They respected him because he was a "people man" and knew instinctively how to win people's loyalty and affection. Unlike Wilson, he was not much at making a speech, though he would if he had to. But he was a man who knew how to live and work with people and he was superb at that. This was to be demonstrated toward the close of his career in his negotiations with Jacob Blaustein, a major minority interest holder in Pan American Petroleum and Transport; there could not have been two people more different in taste and background, but Al Peake's knowledge of human nature more than offset that difference.

Peake had another attractive trait. Where some of his associates might say, "I did it," Peake would always say, "We did it." He was also noted for his prodigious memory. Bullard said Peake could remember the exact depth of a well for months after it had been drilled, and could recall 20 years later specific wells in the Rocky Mountain area where he had done his early work. But everything was retained in his head. Bullard claimed he had never seen Peake write a single memorandum.

The modest nature of Peake was perhaps best illustrated when he retired from the company. He simply pasted a scribbled sign on his office door with the words 'gone fishin,' shut the door, and left.

Prior was a different kind of a manager—hard-driving, sometimes bullying in his relations with people. He, too, was uncomfortable speaking in public; even making a talk to a group of 40 or 50 employees was a tremendous chore for him.

Prior's intensity is reflected in a story surviving to this day: Francis J. Keleher, later to be Stanolind's treasurer, and a group of others were working on purchase of the Yount-Lee oil interests in 1935 and had been going day and night for more than a week. Sunday evening, Keleher called Prior and told him, "The guys just have to have some food and some time off," and took the negotiating team to dinner.

Just as they sat down and had ordered their first drink, a

waiter came over and inquired which one was Mr. Keleher. When Keleher identified himself, the waiter said, "You'd better get on the phone. There's a wild man on the other end." When Keleher got to the phone, it was Prior, who demanded, "Where the hell have you been; we're wasting time."

Prior was quick in his judgments. If he liked a person, he would be loyal to a fault and keep that individual on the staff long after his usefulness may have ended. But, if he disliked someone, then the knife was sharp and quick. One never knew what Prior's reaction might be. If it suited his mood, he would berate someone for a matter which did not seem to be all that important.

Bullard was a great believer that the best form of management was from the "bottom-up." He preferred not to impose any ideas downward in the organization. His strength was in allowing people to develop through their own initiative and letting that initiative be tested in the projects they recommended.

Toward a Common Purpose

6

The agreement for divided authority between Wilson and Peake had been signed on December 20, 1944. Throughout their succeeding years, Peake, as president, and Prior, as executive vice president and Peake's principal confidant, tended to bypass Wilson, as chairman, and to set their own course, striving all the while to overcome Wilson's resistance to introduction of a more modern management structure, improved methods of procedure, and elimination of operating matters from the agenda of the board of directors.

Nevertheless, progress was made during the late 1940s and the 1950s. Exploration in Canada, which Stanolind Oil and Gas began in late 1947, was enlarged. Stanolind Oil and Gas undertook exploration outside continental North America (but limited in the beginning to the Western Hemisphere), a step toward reentry into the international oil arena and one which Wilson generally resisted. A subsidiary was organized to consolidate the beginnings of a chemicals business which in a few years would grow to major proportions.

As his retirement in 1955 approached, Peake began to deal in a definitive way with a long-standing minority interest dispute which had troubled Standard's management for nearly a quarter of a century. The dispute was between Standard and the Baltimore, Maryland-based Blaustein family whose patriarch father had founded The American Oil Company. The foundation for the dispute was laid in June, 1923, when the Blausteins entered into a 10-year gasoline supply contract with Pan American Petroleum and Transport Company and in return sold 50 per cent interest in American Oil to Pan American Petroleum and Transport. At the time, Pan American was controlled by the Edward L. Doheny

3. A 1951 photograph of Robert E. Wilson, (left) chairman of the board and chief executive officer (1945–1958); Alonzo W. Peake, (center) president (1945–1955), and Frank O. Prior, then executive vice president (chairman of the board and chief executive officer 1958–1960). In the photo, Mr. Wilson is presenting service pins to Mr. Peake and Mr. Prior.

family of California. When Standard, having acquired Pan American Petroleum and Transport beginning in 1925, sold that company's foreign properties to Standard (New Jersey) in 1932, it arranged for the Jersey company to supply American Oil's gasoline requirements through 1933—a development that concerned the Blausteins.

 The Blaustein saga was an American success story. Louis Blaustein came to America from Lithuania while still in his teens.

Like many immigrants, he became a peddler, travelling from farm to farm in eastern Pennsylvania. Later, he moved to Baltimore where he opened a wholesale grocery store. As was often done at the time, he also sold kerosene, sometimes called coal oil. Seeing the loss incurred as kerosene dripped out of leaky wooden barrels in which the jobber delivered it to the Blaustein store, Louis suggested that the jobber mount a steel tank with a spigot on a dray wagon for deliveries. The jobber liked that, and he subsequently hired Louis.

Later, Louis worked 18 years for Standard (New Jersey). When the Jersey company wanted to send him to Germany to organize that company's activities there, he resigned and set up his own organization, The American Oil Company. The company consisted of Louis, his son Jacob, a small tank wagon and a horse and the driver, and it sold kerosene to retail outlets. Soon, it opened a drive-in gasoline filling station, one of the first. The Blausteins incorporated The American Oil Company in 1922 and marketed gasoline through a subsidiary, Lord Baltimore Filling Stations, Inc.

Louis Blaustein believed that innovation was the only thing that would enable a small oil company to survive. Chief among the innovations he introduced—the development that really made the company—was an antiknock gasoline. In the early days of the automobile, gasoline was of low octane. As car engines were improved by increasing compression ratios, this low-octane gasoline caused them to knock because of the fast rate of ignition of the gasoline.

The Blausteins conceived the idea of mixing benzol, a volatile by-product of steel mill coke oven operations, with the gasoline they were selling. They hired a chemist, and, by a process of trial and error, finally hit on a mixture that would burn more smoothly than any gasoline then being sold. It was the first unleaded antiknock gasoline. They called it Amoco, promoting it with the slogan, "Feed your car Amoco Gas, and you'll think it's on a diet—it requires so little." With this strategy, the Blausteins built American Oil into a thriving marketer, competing successfully with the majors. But they were buying most of their raw gasoline supply from Standard (New Jersey), their biggest competitor.

Pan American Petroleum and Transport Company had ample supplies of crude oil and refined products, but a weak gasoline marketing organization. The Blausteins saw that an alliance with

Pan American—preferably an ownership alliance—would bolster Pan American Petroleum and Transport's marketing capabilities and, of prime importance to the Blausteins, assure a gasoline supply for American Oil. Such an alliance also could help Pan American Petroleum and Transport expand its business of selling fuel oil. It was with this in mind that the Blausteins in 1923 sold 50 per cent interest in American Oil and Lord Baltimore Filling Stations to Pan American Petroleum and Transport, and contracted with Pan American to supply American Oil's gasoline needs at a favorable fixed margin until year-end 1933.

When Standard (Indiana) sold Pan American Petroleum and Transport Company's non-U.S. oil properties and operations to Standard (New Jersey) in 1932, the Blausteins feared that American Oil's marketing operations would be prejudiced, especially since American's product supplies would again be coming from the Jersey company, its principal competitor.

Prolonged negotiations ensued, and in February, 1933, a "definitive agreement" was signed which provided for the reorganization of Pan American Petroleum and Transport Company and of American Oil Company. The agreement set forth certain steps that would be taken to make Pan American a fully integrated domestic oil company. Under the agreement, the Blausteins exchanged their remaining American Oil stock for stock in Pan American. The agreement was signed by the Blausteins, Standard (Indiana), Pan American, and American Oil and Lord Baltimore Filling Stations, Inc.

But as the years passed, the Blausteins came to believe that the terms of the "definitive agreement" were not being carried out. In a suit brought to trial on December 4, 1939, the Blausteins alleged that Standard (Indiana) had broken the letter and spirit of the "definitive agreement" of 1933, in regard to building a refinery, buying crude oil properties, and otherwise proceeding to develop Pan American Petroleum and Transport as an integrated domestic company capable of fulfilling American Oil's needs. Among properties whose production the Blausteins claimed should go to the integrated company were the South Houston and Hastings fields which Stanolind Oil and Gas had discovered. Crude oil from these fields produced higher antiknock gasoline than crude from some other fields, a feature that was particularly attractive to the Blausteins because of their market for this product. In essence, the Blausteins alleged that Standard (Indiana) had preempted corporate opportunities for its own benefit to the detriment of Pan American Petroleum and Transport stockholders. It was a classic example of minority stockholder claims that a partially owned company was being run for the benefit of parent company shareholders at the expense of minority interests.

The controversy finally was settled by an agreement negotiated by Peake and Jacob Blaustein. Pan American Petroleum and Transport was merged into Standard on August 17, 1954. The Blausteins exchanged their interests in Pan American Petroleum and Transport for Standard stock, American Oil became a wholly-owned subsidiary of Standard, and Pan American Petroleum and Transport became a 100 per cent rather than 78 per cent owned subsidiary of Standard. As a result, the Blaustein family interest became the largest single stockholding in Standard with 4.3298 per cent of Standard shares outstanding on September 2, 1954, the date of the transfer.

One of the final sticking points in reaching the agreement was whether Jacob Blaustein, the son of Louis, who had been active in American Oil since boyhood and at one point had been president of American Oil and executive vice president of Pan American Petroleum and Transport, would be elected a member of the Standard board of directors. The contract called for Jacob's going on the board for one year, following which he could be re-elected or not, just as any other director.

Jacob faithfully attended almost every weekly board meeting even though he disliked flying and had to commute by train between Baltimore and Chicago. He always brought with him a long yellow pad on which he took voluminous notes; what he did with them after the meeting remained a mystery to his fellow board members.

Following the amicable conclusion of the Blaustein lawsuits, and the 1954 merger into Standard of Pan American Petroleum and Transport Company, Peake retired as president on May 3, 1955, and was succeeded by Prior. Standard was soon ready for another major step which Peake and Prior had envisioned in streamlining the corporate structure to increase operating efficiency and reduce overhead costs.

Effective February 1, 1957, Standard consolidated nine subsidiaries along functional lines into four operating companies.

Pan-Am Southern Corporation was liquidated and its refining and marketing assets were transferred to American Oil Company for continuation of the operations in six south central states as a division.

The oil and gas producing properties and operations of Pan American Production Company, one of the subsidiaries of American Oil since the 1954 reorganization, were transferred from American Oil to Stanolind Oil and Gas Company, and the Stanolind name was changed to Pan American Petroleum Corporation.

American Oil Pipe Line Company, another American Oil subsidiary, was merged into Service Pipe Line Company. (Service Pipe Line, prior to 1950, was named Stanolind Pipe Line Company.)

Crude oil purchasing operations of Pan American Production Company and Pan-Am Southern Corporation were assigned to Stanolind Oil Purchasing Company, and the name of the combined operation was changed to Indiana Oil Purchasing Company.

Amoco Chemicals Corporation, which Standard had incorporated on September 12, 1945, as a sales unit, was chosen as the vehicle for the assembly of all of the company's chemicals activities into a single organization. Consolidated into Amoco Chemicals were a wholly-owned subsidiary, Indoil Chemical Company, formed in 1948 to market chemicals from petroleum; the synthetic fuels and chemicals research activities of Stanolind Oil and Gas, including its Hidalgo Chemical Company; Pan American Chemicals Corporation; and chemical activities and properties of Standard, American Oil, and American Oil Company (Texas).

Utah Oil Refining Company, which manufactured petroleum products and sold them in five western states and which had become a wholly-owned subsidiary of Standard after Standard acquired outstanding Utah Oil minority share holdings in 1956, wasn't affected by the 1957 reorganization. Nor were Tuloma Gas Products Company, a wholly-owned subsidiary which Standard formed in 1954 to market liquefied petroleum gases, and Midwest Oil Corporation, an exploration and production company operating in the U.S. and Canada in which Standard then held a substantial stock position. Utah Oil merged into American Oil Company in 1960, and Tuloma into American Oil in 1968. It was not until 1977 that Midwest Oil Corporation merged into Amoco Production Company (the new name chosen on February 1, 1971, for Pan American Petroleum Corporation) and was liquidated, closing a decades-long history.

The history of Midwest Oil Corporation began in 1911 when a Colorado Springs, Colorado, investment firm incorporated

Midwest Oil Company. Its original business was to acquire interests in the Salt Creek, Wyoming, oil field but later became a full fledged operating oil exploration and production company. Standard acquired its original stock holding in 1920 and over the years bought additional shares of Midwest Oil Company stock and later, shares of Midwest Oil Corporation. The latter was formed in 1951 by a merger of Midwest Oil Company and two other oil producing firms.

By early 1971, Standard held slightly more than 51 per cent interest and, as a result of redemption of minority interest shares by Midwest Oil, Standard increased its holdings to 68 per cent by the end of the year.

From a geographic standpoint, the operations of Midwest Oil Corporation and Standard's principal exploration and production subsidiary, Amoco Production Company, were similar and in some locations were competitive. As it had with other duplicative subsidiaries, Standard proposed to merge and consolidate functions of the two to simplify the organization and reduce costs. However, four minority stockholders in Midwest Oil Corporation sought an injunction in United States District Court at Denver in September, 1971, to block the proposed merger.

While the litigation was pending, Standard withdrew its merger proposal and issued voluntary exchange offers which resulted in the increase of Standard's ownership position to 95 per cent in 1972. Finally, in 1973, under terms of settlement of the lawsuit, Standard was positioned to acquire the remaining 5 per cent minority interest. After this was accomplished, operations of Midwest Oil Corporation were merged in 1977 into Amoco Production Company.

The dual status of Standard—fulfilling the roles of both parent company and manufacturer, distributor, and marketer in its 15-state Middle Western territory—also was unaffected in the 1957 reorganization. It was not until December 31, 1960, that Standard completed turning over operations to subsidiaries and became exclusively a parent company. But it was in the 1957-1960 period that the task of modernizing Standard's antiquated operating organization—not much changed from horse and wagon days—was taken up in earnest.

Robert C. Gunness, who had been elected one of two executive vice presidents on September 24, 1956, (John E. Swearingen was the other) and assigned to direct and coordinate the parent company's manufacturing, sales, and supply and transportation departments, summed up the problem in a speech at a 1957 management conference. Gunness titled his speech: "A Penny and a Half is Not Enough."

To illustrate his thesis, Gunness provided each executive at the meeting with an envelope containing one full penny and another which had been cut in half. When the managers opened their envelopes, they were told this penny-and-a-half represented the one and half per cent rate of return in 1957 on each dollar the parent company had invested in its Middle Western refining, distribution, and marketing operations.

In his analysis, Gunness noted that the company was 68 years old and rightfully proud of its pioneering work in the Midwest. However, he also reminded his audience that ideas that made very good sense when they were originated no longer added up to efficiency.

One example he cited was Standard's bulk plants—about 5,000 of them—located at railroad sidings throughout rural areas and small towns of the Midwest to receive shipments from refineries. Because they were built during earlier times, they were located literally on a horse-and-wagon basis, permitting a driver with a wagon and team to cover his territory. With modern roads and transportation, the need for such close bulk plant spacing was gone, but the bulk plants continued to exist as in the past. Gunness illustrated the folly of this costly tradition by describing one territory where a competitor with four bulk plants was selling almost half as much gasoline as Standard which had 298 such installations.

Assignment of personnel also drew strong criticism. In one territory, Standard had more than 100 employees; its major competitors each had 12. The parent company was demonstrably less efficient in utilizing people than its own subsidiary, The American Oil Company. Adjusting his comparison to reflect sales volume, Gunness found that American—then a separate but wholly-owned marketing subsidiary—could do its job with 18,100 people; to produce the same sales volume, Standard's marketing component had 28,400 people on its payroll, a situation that "often makes poor use of good people," as Gunness put it.

The livelihood of this large number of people had to be considered. It was painful to shut down a bulk plant where someone had not only been working for the company for 20 years or more but also was the company's representative in the community and its affairs. Human considerations as well as good business sense made the cutting back a slow affair; it took almost 20 years to reduce the number of these plants by half, relying heavily on normal attrition. Finally, in the late 1970s, the company was able to get out of direct sales to the farm market entirely by selling the remaining petroleum bulk plants to the operators, generally on very favorable terms. The net effect was to modernize Standard's distribution system to reflect current realities.

The company's refineries also reflected historical rather than contemporary patterns. They had been built when practically all bulk transportation of finished products was by rail, and the company endeavored to supply a full range of products—not just the most profitable. Market volumes and freight costs made it prudent to have comparatively small refineries strategically located in the sales territory. By the post World War II period, however, products were being transported more efficiently by water, pipeline, and truck. Larger refineries were essential if costs were to remain low to take advantage of the economies of scale. As Gunness expressed it, the changes were essential although expensive.

It was projected that by 1970 almost 90 per cent of the company's capital investment (in refining) would be for facilities built since 1955.

An Emerging Leadership

7 ————————————————————————

In reminiscing about his career with Standard, Frank Prior once recalled some thoughts he had before he became president upon Peake's retirement in 1955: Wilson would retire as chief executive officer in 1958. Since Prior was only two years younger than Wilson, this wouldn't leave Prior much time to implement changes he felt were necessary, and to build the organization he would need if he were elected chief executive officer.

"I had to have some young people to build on over the years. I couldn't be president until Peake retired and that left me only two years to build the organization I needed. Due to Wilson's peculiarities, I couldn't accomplish much between 1955 and 1958 except to train some younger people."

The skill with which Prior identified these younger people is evident in the fact that among them were two future presidents of the company, Robert C. Gunness and George V. Myers, and a future chairman, John E. Swearingen.

Swearingen had started out to be a civil engineer. When he found that one of the requirements of that profession was an ability to do free-hand sketches and drawings, and his self-appraisal told him that he couldn't draw anything—even a straight line—he switched to chemical engineering in his freshman college year.

In 1934, when young Swearingen was enrolled at the University of South Carolina, the depression was at its worst. His parents had limited means. His father had been blinded in a hunting accident at the age of 13, but despite this handicap he went on to become a teacher and served several terms as the elected State Superintendent of Education.

A measure of the senior Swearingen and his determination

not to consider his blindness a handicap is the fact that, although blind, he regularly shaved himself with a straight razor. He would say, "I'm not handicapped; I just can't see." John's mother always referred to her husband as "Mr. Swearingen," the custom among genteel southern couples during the period.

Being genteel and a school teacher could also mean limited income. Money was hard to come by; college meant tight budgeting even though tuition was only $150 a term. A scholarship enabled John to finish at the University, but after that he wanted to do graduate work at an institution with broader opportunities in the field of chemical engineering.

When he discussed his proposed plans with Professor James E. Copenhaver, the two men worked out a list of about 15 schools where John might apply for a fellowship which would enable him to do graduate work. Professor Copenhaver said he would sign the letters of recommendation to those schools if John would type the letters. That was a bigger chore than it might seem since John's typing was by the hunt-and-peck system. Finally, however, the job was finished and the letters were sent off.

His letters produced responses from the Armour Institute of Technology in Chicago, Stanford University, the University of Virginia, and others. But the one that appealed to him most came from Carnegie Tech at Pittsburgh (now Carnegie-Mellon University). At the time, Carnegie Tech was one of the two or three leading schools for chemical engineering in the country. There were two outstanding professors at Carnegie Tech: Warren McCabe, who had come from the University of Michigan, and Carl C. Monrad, also a Michigan graduate, who had worked for a time at Standard's research laboratory in Whiting.

When he received his master's degree from Carnegie Tech, Swearingen had offers from several recruiters, including ones from Atlantic Refining Company, Gulf Oil Corporation, and U.S. Rubber Company. He finally decided on Standard Oil Company (Indiana), principally because Monrad recommended it and because it offered him $25 a month more pay. He joined Standard on June 14, 1939, as a chemical engineer at the research laboratory in Whiting, Indiana.

Swearingen vividly recalls getting off the train in Chicago at the 63rd Street station, which wasn't much of a place even then. He had a big steamer trunk which he somehow managed to wrestle down the stairs and drag with him to the bus stop where he had been told he could get a bus for Whiting.

69

When he arrived at Whiting, he had only $20 in his pocket which was to last him two weeks to his first paycheck. Fortunately, there was a company-operated lunchroom called the "bunkhouse" where all the refinery supervisors and technical people from the research laboratory ate and where one could get a huge lunch for 25 cents.

The cook's name was Lena, and she could make an apple pie Swearingen defied anybody to surpass. The food was served "family style," and everybody would go in, gobble their food in 10 or 15 minutes, and then be on their way.

Whiting, then as now, was an industrial community. It was June and it was hot; the air was full of fumes from steel mills and refineries in the area. The laboratory was in an old building that had been remodeled about 1910. It had no air conditioning, and it was right next to the railroad tracks. When the Broadway Limited or the Twentieth Century Limited thundered by, the whole building shook.

A small group was working there at the time—only about 150 people. To young Swearingen, it was an exciting and interesting place; he was meeting people he had only heard about before, including Ernest W. Thiele, assistant director of research, who had done some pioneering work on distillation with Swearingen's former professor, Warren McCabe.

At the laboratory Swearingen became increasingly interested in the economics of refining processes. His interest continued during the war as he advanced from the position of chemical engineer to group leader. He had been involved in the decision to develop a catalytic cracking process instead of licensing the Houdry process at an exorbitant fee, and in a number of ensuing innovations that contributed to production of the vast amount of improved and new products required by the war and later the needs of the post-war world.

At the end of the war, scientific management planning, economic studies, and effective cost controls were gaining attention in the refining business. Moreover, the war experience had broken down many of the secrecy bugaboos surrounding technical and cost information. One of the biggest problems, since the refinery produced many products, was deciding how much of the total refining cost should be assigned to each product. The problem is the same as butchering a hog. One of the things produced is bacon. But how much of the cost of the hog is bacon and how much of the cost is ham or pork chops? The company's premise was that the primary product of the refining process was gasoline and that the cost of other products was related to the cost of gasoline or the cost of converting the other fractions to gasoline.

The group at Whiting, which had been engaged in the pre-war cost studies, began to take a look at some other economic factors that might have an impact on the growth of the company. There was little forward planning in the company, nor much interest in new methods of economic evaluation, so the young scientists were more or less plowing virgin territory when they began to investigate things of a larger dimension than those related to process design and other refining operations.

Also, research, as an important function in itself and not limited to laboratory work on crude oil refining or product improvement, was at last emerging. Ground was broken in 1945 for a new research center at Hammond, Indiana, near the Whiting refinery, and it was dedicated in 1948. Joseph K. Roberts, a chemical engineer who had joined Standard in 1928 as a group leader at the Whiting laboratory, was now general manager of research, reporting directly to Robert E. Wilson, the research-oriented chairman of the company.

Burton had advanced to president, and Humphreys to vice president for manufacturing in the later years of their careers. With these two men the scientist-to-top-executive tradition had been forged, then reinforced by the advancement of Wilson to chairman. Roberts subscribed to it, and his ambition was to advance to the chairman's position when Wilson retired.

It was Swearingen and members of his group who, in this atmosphere, began to ask themselves such questions as how to measure the economic impact of different alternatives, the procedures for doing so, and the impact of interest and taxes on investments. Although the company was not in the international oil business at the time, they also tried to educate themselves about that.

None of these questions had been addressed on anything more than a sporadic basis before. Perhaps the idea of investigating these dimensions emerged now and not before because of the priorities and the nature of the oil business in each of rather well-defined preceding periods.

In Standard's case, there had been first the period between 1889 and 1911, characterized by the building of the refinery at Whiting—near to Chicago and a rail transportation system; construction of two more refineries at Wood River, Illinois, and

Sugar Creek, Missouri, and the marketing surge westward into the rapidly developing Middle West. Next was the period between 1911 and 1918 when the Burton-Humphreys high-pressure, high-temperature cracking process doubled the amount of gasoline that could be produced from a barrel of crude oil, responding to the proliferation of the gasoline engine-powered automobile and farm tractor and compounded by urgent World War I demand for oil products.

It was much the same in this regard during the 1918-1929 period; the thrust was principally expansionary, even worldwide —a larger organization to serve more markets, manufacture of products the company already knew how to make but in larger quantities, and securing its own crude oil supply and pipeline transportation system. All required forward planning of a sort, but not of the type called for in later times.

The decade of the so-called great depression which followed —1930 to 1940—had its own list of steps forward by Standard. All of these steps occurred in a tight-fisted atmosphere of caution in making investments deemed by many members of Standard's management (except for the incumbent chief executive officer and his adherents) as the result of pure penury. It was in this period that Carl C. Monrad, who would be one of Swearingen's professors when Swearingen was working for his master's degree at Carnegie Tech, was doing pioneer work in the development of costing methods for petroleum products at the Whiting research laboratory.

The technological advancements in refining during the 1940-1950 period—much of which was preoccupied by World War II —may have highlighted the need for economic analysis. The more advanced processes and products developed for wartime necessities, as well as conventional items, demanded that attention be paid to the total cost of each fraction produced from the barrel of crude oil. It was in this period of new questions that a more sophisticated function of economic analysis joined refinery planning as a major necessity.

Some of the memoranda Swearingen wrote from studies performed by the research group he headed at Whiting found their way to the desks of the company's principal officers in Chicago. At about this same time, Standard's exploration and production arm—Stanolind Oil and Gas Company—sought approval of Standard's board of directors to build a plant in southwest Kansas to produce gasoline from natural gas for which there was no ready market. The investment required was expected to be about $150 million, a huge sum of money at that time. A high-level discussion ensued as to the price projections for gas, gasoline, and fuel oil.

Incredible as it may seem today, the only analyses done in the entire company on these price projections were the memoranda Swearingen and his group had prepared at Whiting, one of which tried to examine the relationship between crude oil prices and fuel oil prices. Prediction of crude oil prices and fuel oil prices was important in any economic evaluation of a refining unit because fundamentally, what the new catalytic technology did was to convert fuel oil to gasoline. The gasoline price was determined primarily by crude oil price, but the fuel oil market was influenced by alternative fuels—coal and gas. The principal concern of Standard was the differential between fuel oil price and crude oil price and not the absolute levels.

Paul R. Schultz, one of the young men with whom Swearingen had worked at Whiting, had, by this time, been transferred to Stanolind's headquarters in Tulsa. Schultz suggested that Swearingen be brought to Chicago to give his opinion in the matter. So Swearingen, still a cub engineer in the research department, was asked to come down to tell the board of directors about the relationship between crude oil prices and gasoline prices. It was a strange way to operate.

Shortly thereafter, Standard's general manager of research, Joseph K. Roberts, offered Swearingen the job of head of research at Texas City for Pan American Refining Corporation, an affiliated company. The Texas City research organization was only about one-fourth the size of the one in Whiting, but there was a substantial salary increase tied to the offer.

Before Swearingen could make up his mind, John E. Rouse, then director of production and manufacturing for Stanolind Oil and Gas, called Swearingen and offered him a job in Tulsa working in the manufacturing department for Jay H. Forrester.

These offers did not go unnoticed; Prior, who at this time was Standard's vice president for production, then offered Swearingen a job as his personal assistant. Swearingen was not unaware that the three jobs offered him came from three men who represented different factions in the company, so the decision was a difficult one. It was even more so since Prior, if he had desired, could have blocked any one of the moves.

Finally, Swearingen told Prior that he did not want to come

to work in the general office as his assistant. Although Swearingen had been with the company only eight years, he understood the deep-seated importance of the exploration and production end of the business. For this reason, he wanted to become acquainted with that part of the operation and learn more about it. To Prior's credit, he encouraged young Swearingen to take the job in Tulsa, and without Prior's support and interest, there's no doubt that many of the opportunities which subsequently came Swearingen's way would not have opened up.

Swearingen was just 28 years of age in 1947 when he transferred to Stanolind Oil and Gas, the subsidiary that operated much as an independent fiefdom from its headquarters in Tulsa. The experience during the war years at Standard had been valuable for Swearingen (scientists and others with technical specialties were deferred from military service). The research department had, in effect, become the front edge of the manufacturing department in converting refinery equipment from peacetime purposes to the production of military needs. It was the only department capable of handling the highly technical details of such a shift.

Bolstered by this background, Swearingen, after his arrival in Tulsa, received some rather extraordinary and unexpected assignments. One of these was to teach him quite a lot about making pig iron, not the usual part of a learning curve in an oil company.

Immediately after the war, pipe was in short supply for drilling wells—or for any other purpose. Brown & Root Company of Houston was doing a good bit of construction work for Stanolind at the time. To get more pipe for Stanolind, George Brown came to Rouse in Tulsa with a proposal to buy and rehabilitate an old blast furnace at Chester, Pennsylvania.

The plant was at least 50 years old and had not been operated since the 1920s. But Brown & Root thought it could put the blast furnace back into operation, make pig iron, sell the pig iron to a steel maker for conversion into ingots, and then sell the ingots to a pipe maker to produce pipe for drilling wells. In retrospect, it was a complex deal, even on paper.

A commitment was made to buy the plant; Stanolind owned three-fourths, and Brown & Root one-fourth with the responsibility for supervising construction. Things seemed to go well for a few months. Then Stanolind began receiving wires almost weekly with the same message: "Send another $100,000." After a few of these, Swearingen was sent to Chester in the fall of 1947 to find out what was happening, when the project would be completed, and what it would finally cost.

Swearingen knew nothing about the blast furnace business, but he was forced to learn fast. When he got to Chester, the place looked like an anthill. The rehabilitation job had been contracted to a company headed by a man named Brassert, who had been Andrew Carnegie's steel-maker at the turn of the century. So by 1947, he was a very, very old man, indeed. The people on the job had a poor idea of what they were there to accomplish or when, with the result that costs were totally out of control. It was obvious to Swearingen that Stanolind should get out of the project if it possibly could.

After putting out a few lines, Swearingen made a handshake deal with some steel operators one of whom was David Thompson, a man with a million dollars who had had experience in blast furnace operations. They were to buy the plant, operate it, and supply Stanolind Oil and Gas with enough pig iron to meet the conversion contract and let the company get out whole. Swearingen went back to Tulsa elated—but the contract didn't arrive.

After waiting about three weeks, he went back to Chester to see what had happened. It developed that Thompson, the man with the money and experience, had suffered a heart attack, and the others wouldn't proceed without him. Then, in early 1948, the bottom dropped out of the market for pig iron, and the product couldn't be given away. So the blast furnace ran only a few days—and Swearingen still has a souvenir of what he says is some of the most expensive pig iron ever produced.

After that experience, Swearingen continued to work for Rouse, a fiery-tempered but able man who early in 1948 had been elected vice president of operations at Stanolind Oil and Gas. In Tulsa, an exploration meeting was held every morning where new information and drilling reports, which might confirm or alter earlier judgments, were evaluated. Although Swearingen was a newcomer with no special skills to add, he asked Rouse if it would be possible to sit in on these meetings as part of learning about the company. Rouse finally agreed—if John would agree not to say anything during the meeting. Swearingen kept his promise, sitting in on these meetings for more than a year, all the while advancing his education about the exploration and production end of the business.

On January 1, 1950, Swearingen was transferred to Oklahoma City as division manager of Stanolind's Central (Mid-

Continent) division. He was only 31 at the time, and it did not take any imagination to anticipate what the older hands thought of this kid from the Chicago research staff running their operation. His challenge came the first morning he was in the chair at the daily exploration committee meeting—and the result of it was to have a great effect on his future actions.

V. G. (Vic) Hill, the division exploration superintendent, and T. L. (Pat) Regan, the production superintendent, brought in a proposition to support the drilling of a well in Seminole County, Oklahoma. An independent operator was drilling a well next to a Stanolind lease, and the company was to pay part of the cost because the well would not only test his lease but Stanolind's as well. The request was for Stanolind to pay $10,000 of the $50,000 cost of drilling the well; further, the two superintendents reported that the drilling had already started, and they had made an oral commitment to pay Stanolind's share.

When Swearingen looked at it, he said, "Well, if he's going to drill it anyway, why do we have to pay him anything?" The others argued that they had made a commitment, and Swearingen argued they had no authorization to do so. Using a pretext to avoid making a decision, he put the matter over until the next day. After the meeting broke up, he thought it best to call George W. Clarke in Tulsa, who was then director of exploration, and get his reaction to the deal.

"George," Swearingen said, "I may not understand this, but I don't really know whether we should make this contribution or not because the man's going to drill the well anyway for his own account. What do you think I should do?"

George's response was short. "Who's the manager in Oklahoma City?" he asked. "I am," Swearingen replied. "Then you decide," Clarke said, and hung up. Swearingen says it was the best lesson he ever had in his life.

The next day, Swearingen accepted the recommendation of his colleagues and approved the deal. He now says the reason should have been obvious to him—that's the way business is done in exploration and production, on a handshake.

After that incident, Swearingen took the position he would make his own decisions and not ask others to make them for him. He took the attitude, "Well, if you don't like it, you can get another boy. But I'm going to do it my way; I'll tell you what I've done, but I'm not going to ask you to take on my job." He once said he wished all of Standard's executives could have an experience similar to his with Clarke.

Swearingen's tenure in the Southwest was to be brief. On February 1, 1951, he was transferred back to Tulsa as an executive assistant, and was elected a member of the Stanolind Oil and Gas Company board of directors on May 9. He served on that board until August 1, 1951, when he returned to Chicago as Standard's general manager of production.

The factions which existed in the company at the time were well illustrated by the nature of Swearingen's leave-taking. Edgar F. Bullard, then head of the Stanolind subsidiary, took him aside and said, "Well, John, I've selected you to go to Chicago. I was asked to go to Chicago myself, but I didn't want to go. No matter what they tell you in Chicago, I want you to understand you are my representative there."

A year later Swearingen was elected a director of Standard. In 1954 he was named vice president for production and a director, in 1956 executive vice president responsible for coordinating activities of six of the principal subsidiaries with the parent company, and on March 19, 1958, he was elected president as Prior moved up to replace Wilson as chairman.

Shortly before Wilson retired, the company formulated a statement of principles on "Corporate Citizenship." It read in part:

"Every corporation is, by law, a person in the courts. It can sue and be sued. But a corporation ought to be a meaningful person in a sense much broader and more meaningful than that. It should be a person in the sense of being a good citizen of the community, alert to its responsibilities . . .

"We have acknowledged that we should share in the giving of time and effort, as well as of money, to movements for civic betterment. All who work for Standard have been encouraged to participate actively in such movements . . . . Thousands of our people, from directors to beginning junior clerks, have participated and are doing so now.

"Basic as these responsibilities are, however, a corporation has obligations even more basic. To its customers, it must furnish good products at fair prices. To its employees, it must provide the conditions, opportunities, and rewards that promote and recognize loyal and efficient service. To its stockholders, it owes a fair return on their investment and a constant endeavor to protect and enlarge their property. To suppliers and all others with whom it has business relations, it has a responsibility for considerate and ethical dealings. Finally, to society as a whole, it owes a fair accounting of its activities, and the articulate expression of its views and philosophy with the end in view of making available an adequate basis for evaluative judgment."

It was a step in getting employees to understand that Standard was a single company with a single purpose and that everyone should work together. In expanding on this theme later, Swearingen focused on the "one-company" theme inherent in the statement on corporate citizenship. "That has been one of our problems, to make sure that people understand we have only one group of shareholders; we're all in the same canoe, and if the canoe goes over Niagara Falls, we all go over together," Swearingen said. "We've got to paddle in the same direction. At one time different parts of the company would even fight each other more than they would fight a competitor; that was stupid."

With these plain-spoken views on building a common enterprise, John E. Swearingen, president, became chief executive officer when Prior retired as chairman on August 25, 1960. The position of chairman was left vacant. A new era in the history of the company had begun. And for John Swearingen, the words of George Clarke—"You decide"—had taken on a new meaning.

The Transition

One of the things Swearingen had reason to be grateful for after he became chief executive officer was that Peake brought about the settlement of the Blaustein matter before he retired in 1955. Jacob Blaustein had become one of the most active board members and his support had assumed increased importance. Jacob often voted "No" and was not afraid to put his knowledge of the oil business and oil marketing in particular against that of the other directors.

Swearingen's relationships with Jacob Blaustein were colored by the difference in their ages. Swearingen was only 39 when he became president in 1958 and 41 when he became chief executive officer upon Prior's retirement in 1960. In Jacob's eyes, Swearingen was a youngster and he was not at all certain that Swearingen could be trusted with the responsibilities of running such a big company.

Consequently, the big problem Swearingen had in dealing with Blaustein was to maintain his own independence and position as the elected head of the company. This resulted in many long hours of conversation where, in effect, Jacob wanted to be president of the company without the title. Swearingen's philosophy was to trade Blaustein a rabbit for a horse any time he could. In other words, if the matter were not consequential, he would give in to Blaustein; if it were a matter of substance, he would hold his ground. In later years, Jacob Blaustein became a strong supporter of the young chief executive.

Almost one month to the day after Swearingen became chief executive, a long-awaited step in the functional restructuring of the corporation was authorized at a special shareholders meeting on September 29 to become effective on December 31, 1960. On that date, a new era in Standard corporate history began as

Standard became exclusively a parent company. The responsibilities of the parent company as they were defined in the 1960 Annual Report were:

    to provide guidance for policies, planning, and programs of the consolidated enterprise;
    to oversee and handle the company's business and financial affairs;
    to coordinate operations among all subsidiary companies;
    to evaluate performance, organization, and personnel.

The parent company's own refining, marketing, and transportation operations, and its subsidiary, Utah Oil Refining Company—holdover situations from the 1957 consolidation of functions—were merged into American Oil Company, and American Oil Company now became the single marketing arm for refined products in the United States, with the responsibility also for manufacturing (refining) and a large portion of the company's transportation system. The name American was introduced on service stations nationwide except in the 15-state midwestern territory where American Oil continued to protect its exclusive use of the Standard name by marketing through a Standard Oil division.

A modernized version of the red, white, and blue Torch and Oval emblem that had evolved over a number of years would continue to carry the name Standard in the Midwest, signifying the Standard Oil division of American Oil, but in other areas the name American would appear. The names Pan-Am, in the south, and Utoco, in the west, were eliminated.

American Oil introduced its new nationwide status and trademark in the biggest advertising and sales promotion campaign in Standard's history. Becoming a marketer—and advertiser—coast to coast for American Oil was a "Big Step," the very words used in ads and commercials across the country.

The name Standard and the right to use that name exclusively in its midwestern territory were assets Standard (Indiana) had when it became an independent enterprise in the 1911 dissolution of the Standard Oil Trust/holding company organization. Through the years, various others of the former Standard Oil Trust companies tried to invade this Standard (Indiana) territory with their own versions of the Standard name. Standard (Indiana) went to court dozens of times through the years to protect its right to sole use of the name in its 15-state midwestern marketing territory when other Standard companies sought to use the name or variations of it. In every instance it won.

4. The 80-story Standard Oil Building near Chicago's lake front is headquarters for Standard Oil Company (Indiana)'s world-wide operations. The company's general office has occupied about half of the building since it was completed in 1973. Remaining office and commercial space is leased to others.

5. Standard (Indiana) dedicated its Amoco Research Center at Naperville, Illinois, in 1971 upon completion of the first phase of this multimillion-dollar complex. Laboratory and service facilities are provided for research in chemical products and processes, new and improved petroleum products and processes, and specialized areas such as molecular biology, energy conversion and storage, and synfuels chemistry.

6. The original buildings of the Amoco Production Company Research Center at Tulsa, Oklahoma, were completed in 1953, providing modern quarters for research that began a quarter century before. Expanded over the years, the center houses facilities for scientists and technicians specializing in oil and natural gas exploration and production.

7. The natural gas processing plant at Whitney Canyon field, Wyoming, was brought on stream in October, 1982, with Amoco Production Company as operator for itself and partners. The plant has design capacity to process 270 million cubic feet of natural gas daily and yield daily gross production of 12,600 barrels of NGL, 200 million cubic feet of dry gas, and 1,200 long tons of elemental sulfur. It also will process 6,000 barrels daily of condensate collected at producing wells for direct pipeline shipment.

8. Snow blankets the Anschutz Ranch East field in this 1980 photo. The field is one of 24 Western Overthrust Belt fields of the 26 discovered in Wyoming and Utah by the end of 1982 in which Amoco Production Company held interests.

83

9. The Salt Creek oil field, shown here in a 1983 photo, is one of five major oil fields in Wyoming operated by Amoco Production Company, the state's largest oil and natural gas producer. Appearance of the field in modern times is in sharp contrast with that of the early 1920s. (See photo on page 25.) Discovered in 1908, the field's cumulative production has been estimated at 543 million barrels, about 56 per cent net to Amoco.

10. The discovery well for Morganza field in the prolific Tuscaloosa Trend in Louisiana, one of five major fields discovered by Amoco Production Company in the Trend, where drilling peaked in 1980.

11. Welders work on a platform being installed on Matagorda Block 623 offshore
Texas in the Gulf of Mexico. Amoco Production Company drilled three natural gas
discoveries on the block in 1980–1982. The platform in the background also is on
Block 623. A wildcat well Amoco drilled on offsetting Block 622 indicated additional
substantial natural gas reserves.

12. An Amoco drilling and production platform in the North West Hutton oil field. The field is in the United Kingdom portion of the North Sea 80 miles northeast of the Shetland Islands. The sea here is 470 feet deep. From seabed to top of drilling derricks the platform is 840 feet high, about the same as a 70-story building.

13. Vibrator trucks of a seismograph crew traverse sand dunes in the desert of Sharjah, United Arab Emirates. Amoco Sharjah Oil Company discovered the Sajaa field with large natural gas and condensate reserves. Amoco holds 100 per cent working interest in the field and in a 600,000-acre concession area in Sharjah. Additional wells were drilled, gas processing and other facilities were installed, and the first shipment of condensate was exported in August, 1982.

14. These drilling and production platforms in the Gulf of Suez are representative of facilities used to discover and bring on production 22 oil fields in the Gulf from 1975 through 1982. Four of the fields are major in magnitude: El Morgan, July, Ramadan, and October fields. Amoco Egypt Oil Company conducts operations in Egypt jointly with the Egyptian government oil company.

The most celebrated of these cases came in 1935 when Standard (New Jersey) attempted to introduce the brand name "Esso" into the Midwest. The judge ruled that "Esso" clearly was a phonetic equivalent of the letters "S.O." and therefore the Jersey company couldn't use it in Standard (Indiana)'s marketing territory. The former Standard Oil Company (New Jersey) is, of course, legally able to do business in the Midwest under its current name "Exxon," which has no overtones of the name "Standard."

"American" seemed to be a suitable name for use outside the 15-state Standard territory until motorists starting speeding along interstate highways at 65 to 70 miles per hour and more. The company found the name too long (eight letters) for motorists to read quickly. It needed a shorter name that people could easily identify. The Torch and Oval had already been established as the common trademark, and having a company name identified with it was important. The word "Amoco" (five letters) was chosen for use everywhere except in Midwestern marketing operations where the name "Standard" had to be continued in the trademark although it also was an eight-letter word.

The Blausteins had coined "Amoco" from the name American Oil Company for the gasoline they marketed along the East Coast in the early days. Over time, Standard incorporated "Amoco" into the names of a number of its products and most of its subsidiaries. Among the first of the subsidiaries to have Amoco in their names were Amoco Chemicals Corporation (1945), which became prominent after Standard's scattered activities in chemicals were consolidated in 1957, and Amoco Trading Corporation (1958). Pan American Petroleum Corporation, which had replaced the name Stanolind Oil and Gas Company in 1957 for the U.S. exploration and production subsidiary, was changed to Amoco Production Company on February 1, 1971. After January 1, 1973, when Standard changed the name American Oil Company to Amoco Oil Company, all major subsidiaries worldwide had the word "Amoco" in their names.

Some challenges facing Standard in 1960 were made easier to deal with because of the accomplishments of Peake and of Prior in developing candidates for top executive positions, eliminating important minority interests in certain subsidiaries, and in consolidating major operating functions. But it was clear that there were a number of things the company should do now. The company was a large, segmented, diffused organization, and thought it was big enough to do anything it wanted to do. Yet, it always seemed to fall back on the strategy of "that's the way we've always done it."

Solutions to problems are found by people, and Swearingen was fortunate in having able associates in responsible positions throughout the company. Near him in the corporate organization were two executive vice presidents who also had been among those Prior had looked upon as "young people to build on over the years."

One was Robert C. Gunness who received a B.S. degree in chemistry and physics from Massachusetts Agricultural College, earned a doctorate in chemical engineering at Massachusetts Institute of Technology, and for two years served as an assistant professor in that MIT department. He joined Standard's Whiting research staff in 1938 as head of the process design group. He soon made a reputation as a specialist in distillation and heat transfer, and contributed to the development and design of new processes including fluid catalytic cracking. He was named manager of research for Standard in 1947, and assistant general manager, manufacturing in 1952. Elected to Standard's board in 1953, he became general manager for supply and transportation in 1954. Then, in 1956, Gunness was named an executive vice president.

The other executive vice president was George V. Myers, who had been hired in 1953 from Westinghouse Air Brake Company to be financial vice president of Stanolind Oil and Gas. He was elected a director of Standard in 1956, vice president-production in 1958, then executive vice president in 1959.

The two executive vice presidents were well suited philosophically and temperamentally for the vital roles they had in the task ahead. With a large organization such as Standard it was very difficult to change course abruptly and say the company would no longer do things the way it had been doing them for 50 years. The important point now was to recognize that transition would not come instantly but that every effort should be made to assure that as it came about it would be effective.

To begin with, it was necessary to get the various segments of the company to communicate with each other. To accomplish this, Swearingen set up task forces in 1961 to consider a future course for exploration and production, refining and marketing, foreign operations, chemicals, and financial controls and accounting—in other words, the entire corporation. To assure fresh viewpoints, each task force was tailored to compel a radical departure from long-standing custom. Thus L. William Moore, who was in charge of refining and marketing as president of American Oil, was a member of the task force on exploration and production; executives from exploration and production were assigned to sit down and contemplate the problems of marketing. To many, at first, Swearingen's strategy was obscure. To them, the make-up of the task forces was strange; what did marketing people know about exploration, and vice versa? But the task forces not only produced penetrating analyses of the condition of the company that led to acceptance of company-wide planning, they also opened up communications, let a substantial number of people see opportunities, or lack of them, in other parts of the company, and got the input of the people who were going to have to implement plans.

The basic facts at which these task forces were looking were summarized in a Consolidated Planning Report issued in July, 1961, which reviewed Standard's historical performance and compared it with that of other oil companies. The report suggested that if Standard's rate of return on invested capital were to equal or exceed that of the rest of the industry in the future, a redirection of effort would be necessary. The report emphasized three points:

First, greater efficiencies in operations were necessary, particularly in the use of capital.

Second, the company's crude production should be increased to provide a greater portion of its refinery runs.

Third, significant improvements in the areas of financial control, personnel development, and research and innovation should be made.

A top executive group put the task force reports together in a preliminary 10-year plan for 1962–1971, which called for definitive shifts in the company's investment policies and strategies and which the board of directors approved in principle in April, 1962. The preliminary plan began with a statement of basic goals and strategies to achieve those goals: "Standard's fundamental goal is to so organize and direct its human and fiscal resources that it can, as quickly as possible, earn no less than a 10 per cent return on borrowed and invested capital," the plan stated. "The best way to attain this goal is through the finding (or acquiring) and producing of as much crude oil and natural gas as can be readily and profitably converted into dollars."

The preliminary 10-year plan was candid. "Until our corporate house is in order," it asserted, "our primary concern is to economically increase our production of crude oil and efficiently monetize it. . . . Other activities must be supporting or provide a significant hedge; when they are neither, they are diversionary and should be avoided or abandoned."

The plan also contained these descriptive comments: "There has been a regrettable characteristic of many years standing within our company of making plans and forecasting earnings on the assumption that, in the interim, our competition is not going to do anything. A small group will be established to follow the history, present activities, and plans of other oil companies. This group will also be responsible for following the political and economic climate in various countries overseas." In the decade of the 1970s, the second part of this assignment was to assume critical importance as the company's holdings were threatened by political turbulence in the Middle East.

The plan telegraphed a determination to break down the baronies and fiefdoms in various parts of the company. "Specific provisions are being developed for rotation of personnel among all parts of our business," it declared, "a step that should assist materially in breaking down compartmentalization and in resolving the troublesome problem of communication."

This need for better communication led to still another step —a series of field trips by Swearingen, Gunness, and Myers in which company goals were outlined to employees much as Colonel Stewart had done 40 years earlier. An extract from one of these speeches gives a flavor of the plain talk Swearingen felt was necessary at the time. These were the main points:

"First of all, we are a $3 billion company, and we intend to act like one. We must engage in activities which take advantage of our size.

"Second, we are determined to emphasize marketing in all of our operations.

"Third, we have definite ideas on further integrating all our domestic operations:

In production, we want to become more self-sufficient.

In manufacturing, we intend to become more automated, to drive unit costs down and build efficiency up.

In marketing, we will keep our prices competitive, but not necessarily the lowest or highest.

In research, we are going to emphasize new directions which can lead us to technological breakthroughs we can exploit commercially.

"Fourth, we want to live within our means financially. We will continue to pay dividends at approximately one-half of net earnings.

"Fifth, we expect to continue our efforts to establish a position in the oil business abroad—in production, in refining, and in marketing.

"Sixth, we want our employees to know and understand that our company offers opportunity to those who are capable and willing to work."

As planning continued, Standard in 1964 prepared to mark its 75th anniversary. The anniversary seemed an auspicious time to call top management together and see what the company was doing and why. Thus, it was that on February 12, 1964, the first Senior Management Conference was held with approximately 200 principal officers and managers of the parent company and subsidiaries present. The 1963–1972 plan, based on the preliminary plan 1961–1971, had just been distributed and the conference was an opportunity to expand people's thinking about the other fellow's problems as well as their own; all worked for one company—Standard—regardless of whether they were attached to a subsidiary or the parent company. "This concern for the company as a whole becomes more significant as we move further toward decentralization," Swearingen said. "We are dedicated to the proposition that in a company of our size, operations must be decentralized in order to be effective."

Another of the purposes of the conference was to get the executives to see planning as an on-going process. Lawrence A. Kimpton, former chancellor of the University of Chicago, had come on Standard's board in 1958 and in 1960 joined the company full-time with responsibility for coordinating planning efforts. He put it this way:

"There is no such thing as *the* plan ... there is only the continuous process of planning. Nonetheless the results of each planning go-around are of great value. The knowledge of our company, its strengths and weaknesses, grows; our policies and our problems become more sharply defined; and we begin to possess a real mastery over our environment rather than being at the mercy of it."

In this connection, the conference emphasized the distinction between developing a plan and making a forecast. The plan represented the program of what the company intended to do; the forecast represented what it expected might happen. The plan represented the company as being something dynamic which could be controlled; the forecast was a reaction to what might happen in the surrounding business environment. So, in addition to planning, control budgets were set up on a two-year basis to provide a check against the realities of the outside world as the executives attempted to implement the plan.

Great emphasis was put on getting individuals to make executive decisions. Swearingen often said he abhorred the phrase, "corporate decision," for there really is no such thing. At the genuine decision-making level, there are only decisions made by human beings, either singly or collectively, he said, paraphrasing Dr. Edward Teller, who once remarked that the most inert material he had ever worked with was the human mind—with one exception, and that was a group of human minds. Hopefully, when the first Senior Management Conference was concluded, Standard had begun overcoming that particular obstacle.

Cost-cutting was essential and much of it started at the top, not at the bottom, as the executives absorbed the implications of the task force studies and ensuing planning. The subsidiaries had grown, merged, and remerged through the years; each had its own multi-member board of directors. This situation created confusion with respect to levels and degrees of authority. Subsidiary boards of directors patterned themselves after the parent company's board, including parallel perquisites such as company cars, airplanes, and office furnishings. They sought to emulate the parent board in other respects as well, acting independently to a degree in seeming disregard for the fact that only a parent company board answers to stockholders.

Swearingen decided the only way to cure that was to reduce each subsidiary's board to the legally required size consisting of a president, another officer, and a general counsel. This further emphasized the policy espoused by Prior that authority should be delegated to individuals and not to committees where lines of authority, responsibility, and accountability weren't clearly defined. Swearingen grew up under this regime in Standard, and always subscribed to it.

Because Swearingen had spent his entire career with Standard, however, he sensed a danger that, in exercising his new authority, he might become too parochial. Therefore, he decided to look around to see what other companies were doing. Since he didn't think other oil companies were paragons then, he really wasn't looking to pattern his program after theirs. Rather, he chose to visit such companies as DuPont, Eastman Kodak, and Xerox, where the chief executives were quite helpful to him.

DuPont had a highly sophisticated management system, and Standard subsequently adopted many of its principles. Standard also developed its own planning with the help of such outside consultants as Hay Associates in the area of organization and administration, and Price Waterhouse and Company in accounting and controls.

Another strong influence on Swearingen was a small book by Frederick R. Kappel, then chairman of American Telephone and Telegraph Company, called *Vitality in a Business Enterprise.* The book was based on the McKinsey Foundation lectures Kappel gave in 1960 at Columbia University's Graduate School of Business in which he laid down a challenge to managers of large business enterprises:

". . . every consideration of how to manage comes down ultimately to the people involved. How does a business get, hold, and help develop people who are capable of sustained competence and creative, venturesome drive, and who will have also a strong feeling of ethical responsibility? Only as we succeed in this shall we succeed in maintaining and increasing business vitality."

When it came to people and finding individuals with vitality, the accounting department of Standard was a great challenge; it was trying to use 1920 style management for 1960 style problems. Former chief executive officer Seubert, who had little formal education but who worked his way up in the organization from the position of clerk, had established a hiring pattern in the accounting department that survived for nearly half a century.

Instead of hiring bright, young people just out of college with accounting degrees and MBAs, the accounting department continued to hire people qualified only as clerks who, with few exceptions, had no college degrees; what emerged at the top was what had come in at the bottom. Moreover, there had never been a budgeting and control process suitable for a company with annual revenues that flirted with the two-billion-dollar mark through the 1950s. The company didn't seem to realize fully that columns of numbers balanced to the penny failed to tell how the company was getting along.

Another former chief executive officer, Wilson, on January 1, 1952, had hired as financial vice president, David Graham, an Englishman who had worked for a number of U.S. companies, including the Weyerhaeuser Company. Graham was elected to

Standard's board of directors in 1952, the same year as Swearingen. As financial vice president, he enjoyed meeting with investment bankers, deciding what securities to buy or sell for the company's pension funds, or trying to outguess the stock market. But when it came to the nitty-gritty of redoing the whole accounting and financial control system and dealing with the organizational and hiring problems related to modernizing the department, he had little interest.

Graham resigned as financial vice president and director on February 28, 1962, and went to work for Hornblower and Weeks, a stockbrokerage and investment advisory firm. There he could do what he liked doing, and enjoyed great success. This left the problem of finding a replacement. Swearingen didn't want anyone from another oil company; rather, he was looking for an experienced financial person from a major company outside the industry. Given this mandate, and failure to find a suitable candidate by one executive search firm, a second reported back that "The man you want is L. Chester May, who is now treasurer of the American Telephone and Telegraph Company and whose superior is just two years older than he."

Swearingen had come to know, as well as admire, the AT&T chief executive officer, Fred Kappel, after reading his series of lectures and serving with him on the board of The Chase Manhattan Bank. When Swearingen called on Kappel to ask for permission to talk to May, Kappel was cordial—and confident. "Look, John," he said, "there are a lot of people working for me you could come after and do me a favor. But Chet May is not one of them. I want to tell you here and now, you can't get him. Therefore, I have no objection to your talking to him." Swearingen got in touch with May, who, it became evident, saw his career at AT&T blocked because of the age of his immediate superior. He agreed to join Standard, and was elected vice president, finance, on March 1, and a director on May 2, 1963.

May brought in strong people at competitive salaries in accounting, data processing, and financial management from within the company and from outside, emphasizing career growth potential. Uniform data processing replaced uncoordinated equipment and manual operations. The computer organization grew from near nothing to over 1,200 people by the time May retired on April 5, 1976. The management information system became one of the most advanced in the U.S.

Standard's bond rating was raised from double "A" to triple

"A" as May worked to provide financing for expanding operations. The investment community's view of Standard as stodgy and uncommunicative was overcome. Standard soon earned high marks in investor relations.

Another shift in top management was to result in the appointment of Jack M. Tharpe as general manager of employee relations. Tharpe had started with the company in the personnel department of the Indianapolis marketing division in 1941 and had joined the then-titled "Industrial Relations Section" in 1947. After a stint as an administrative assistant to Prior, he had moved to the Employee and Public Relations department of Stanolind Oil and Gas Company in Tulsa. In 1962, he was named manager of employee and public relations in that Tulsa subsidiary.

But Tharpe's real objective was to head the employee relations department for the entire company. To this end he kept a notebook of the things he wanted to do if the time ever came when he had a chance to organize and run the department his way.

Tharpe had come to know Swearingen after Swearingen transferred to the general office, and Tharpe was working as Prior's assistant. Tharpe was constantly lecturing Swearingen on the subject of personnel relations when the two of them were between assignments from Prior.

One day, Swearingen turned to Tharpe and asked, "Why are you giving me all these lectures?" Tharpe replied, "Because some day you'll run this company, and I'd like to have one guy run it who knows something about the people end of our business." Swearingen, not even a vice president then, sternly replied, "Don't you ever say that again."

Despite Tharpe's aspirations and closeness to Prior, Standard in 1956 hired as its personnel director J. Howell Turner, who had been a member of Industrial Relations Counselors, Inc., an organization formed by the Rockefeller interests to provide consulting services in the industrial relations field, principally to the Standard Oil companies but also to anyone else who chose to employ it for that purpose.

Tharpe recalls he had been so determined to get the job in Chicago that he had only rented a house in Tulsa, fully expecting he would return to Chicago. When word of Turner's hiring came through, he tore up his notebook of ideas, built himself a house, and told Swearingen, "I've never been so hurt in my life as I am over some other guy filling my job. That job's mine. I love this company and I love the people in it and I think I understand it."

After Swearingen took over as chief executive, he had reason to remember these conversations. Major consolidation of subsidiaries along functional lines and continuing modernization had resulted in an employee force of 38,000 people in 1963 doing the tasks that in 1956 had required 52,000 on the payroll. But the approaching major program of cost cutting and further modernization would include additional reductions and reassignment of personnel in refining, marketing, and in some other functions with difficult and complicated labor union negotiations over matters such as eliminating antiquated work rules that restricted management's flexibility to manage. To preside over this serious "people" situation, Swearingen turned to Tharpe when Turner left the company. On March 1, 1965, Tharpe moved into the job of which he had dreamed.

Events justified Swearingen's confidence. Tharpe played a key role in softening the impact of reductions and subsequent increases in the work force and in orchestrating changes in its makeup brought on by new and more sophisticated technology and evolving social conditions. With major capital investments in automated equipment, more modern machinery as well as growth, there was over the years a net increase in the number of employees to just over 47,000 at the end of 1978. Still, even with expanded operations, fewer people were employed at the end of 1978 than in 1956.

Two other changes in this period were also of some significance. The first dealt with the practice of outside directors remaining on the board well into their seventies, contrasting with the mandatory retirement age of 65 for employee directors established by the examples of Wilson, Peake, and Prior. The problem was one of getting the outside directors to vote, in effect, for their own compulsory retirement. This was accomplished by putting a "grandfather" clause in a board resolution adopted on February 19, 1963, establishing retirement age for outside directors at 70 but exempting the outside directors then serving. Outside directors serving in 1963 were Jacob Blaustein, president of American Trading and Production Company, and Homer J. Livingston, chairman of The First National Bank of Chicago. Blaustein and Livingston died in 1970 at ages 78 and 66 respectively.

The second change involved the relationship of the head of Standard with the Rockefeller interests and bankers in New York. The practice of seeking their informal blessing on top management matters had survived Seubert and continued on through the

1950s with Wilson and Prior. Swearingen recalls that shortly after he went on the board of directors in 1952, Wilson, Peake, Prior, and he made the rounds in New York to meet the heads of the big banks which held in trust substantial amounts of Standard stock. Swearingen was, of course, the junior man who was being looked over.

When Swearingen became chief executive officer, he decided to end this practice. He had nothing against New York bankers as such; in fact, he subsequently served on the board of the Chase Manhattan bank for more than 20 years. But he was determined that the New York bankers were not going to run Standard. He wasn't going to go down there. He was going to run Standard the best way he knew how; if they didn't like it, he expected he would hear from them in due course. As it turned out, he never really heard from them.

Building or Remodeling?

9 ━━━━━━━━━━━━━━━━━━━━━━━━━━━━━━

In January of 1965, *Forbes* magazine began an appraisal of Standard with this view of the task of management:

"Basically, there are only two major kinds of management tasks. One involves taking a small company and building it into a large one. The other is taking a big company and improving its profitability. The first can be described as a building job. The second is a remodeling job. John E. Swearingen has what is essentially a remodeling job."

Forbes, in its customarily candid way, then went on to outline some of the problems the company was facing. The appraisal was reminiscent of the challenges which had been given to Standard's task forces in 1961 and of the priorities which had been decided upon after those task forces had rendered their reports.

After acknowledging the fact that Standard was "huge" and the fifth largest corporation in the oil industry as well as the 13th largest in America, *Forbes* went on to say, "But Indiana Standard has its problems."

None of these problems was new to Standard, but it is useful to look at them as they were seen by an outside observer.

As *Forbes* saw it, "Among the top half-dozen oil companies, it (Standard) alone lacks a big market in crude outside the United States. When things get really rough in the U.S., such internationals as Standard Oil Company (New Jersey), Texaco, Gulf and Socony Mobil can count on foreign operations for up to half of their profits. But only 8 per cent of Indiana Standard's assets are located overseas and its foreign profits make up a small percentage of the total.

"Furthermore, Indiana Standard is at a disadvantage even in the U.S. It produces enough crude to supply only about 50 per cent of its refinery needs. It owns reserves that could supply more, but . . . prorationing . . . keeps Indiana Standard from producing more oil in Texas [where it owns substantial reserves] and also keeps up the price of the crude it must buy from other producers.

"Yet Indiana must sell refined products in a market where prices have fallen to the lowest level in 15 years. As a result, in 1963 it made only 6.7 per cent on invested capital, compared with 9.5 per cent for the industry as a whole."

What the *Forbes* article was not able to reflect was the mandate Swearingen had given the task force committees in October of 1961:

"It seems to me we have two principal questions to answer," he said:

"(1) What can be done to introduce economies into our present business and improve its income?

"(2) What changes in emphasis in our capital spending program will produce improved long range results?

"We are embarking on a new era in our whole company's affairs," he told the group. "I know that we can set a goal for ourselves and devise a plan for reaching it. We will be better off for having done so even if we fall short, than if we had no plan at all. But, I do not expect to fall short . . ."

The plan, which took form as the first 10-year planning effort in the history of the company and emerged in April of 1962 after the task force studies were completed, began by taking note of Standard's inferior performance in comparison with the rest of the industry.

"If Standard's rate of return on invested capital were to match the industry's in the future," the authors of the report observed, "a redirection of effort would be necessary, involving essentially a three-pronged program. First, greater efficiency of operation, particularly in the use of capital; second, the company's crude production should be increased relative to its refinery runs; and third, significant improvements in the areas of financial controls, personnel development, and research and innovation should be made."

Thus the *Forbes* author in 1965 was only giving recognition to goals that Standard had already set for itself. The author was able to quantify at least part of the efficiency with which these goals were being pursued. "Since 1958," he wrote, "while its prices have dropped 6.5 per cent and its wage levels have risen 20 per cent, Indiana Standard has increased its earnings by 55 per cent."

Nowhere was the increase in efficiency more dramatic—or more needed—than in the performance of the refining and marketing operations of American Oil Company. The Task Force Planning report had called for "a drastic change in American Oil's business philosophy." The result was that *Forbes* could report in 1965 that there had been a 14 per cent increase in gasoline sales with 13 per cent fewer stations.

Swearingen felt it was time to reorganize the executive structure to reflect the new operational realities and provide a better balance between centralized financial and policy control and decentralized operations. His proposal was adopted. Swearingen was elected chairman on September 1, 1965, and Robert C. Gunness, then one of two executive vice presidents, was elected president of the parent company. George V. Myers continued as executive vice president and Richard J. Farrell, Frank C. Osment, John E. Kasch, and Blaine J. Yarrington were elected vice presidents of Standard.

Two years later, in 1967, a further modification of the organization seemed to be indicated. An "Office of the Chairman" was established, consisting of Swearingen, Gunness, and Myers. Delegation of responsibility among members of the office and formalized reporting relationships among the executives reporting to the office were changed as conditions changed. Individual reporting executives were not restricted as to their reporting relationships. In 1974, when the office was abolished, the chairman formally assumed direct responsibility for nonoperating functions such as finance, law, public affairs, and office of the corporate secretary. The president, reporting to the chairman and chief executive officer, was for the first time designated chief operating officer with direct responsibility for subsidiary and parent company operating functions.

In a memo explaining the reorganization on October 11, 1967, Swearingen outlined its purpose as one of defining the relationship between the parent company and subsidiary companies and "accountability being clearly centered in individuals rather than in boards, committees, or other groups."

The company, through a series of moves, made it clear that there was to be a much sharper definition of responsibilities. Autonomy for the subsidiaries within a well-defined budgeting and monitoring system made for initiative and vigor. Operations were clearly in their hands. Each top manager was now functionally responsible for planning, coordination, guidance, control, and evaluation within his field, but acting for the corporation as a whole.

As Swearingen had told the first Senior Management Conference when he convened it in 1964, "Standard is an integrated oil company. This means more than production, refining, and marketing of oil. An integrated company means that we are all in this process together and whatever our operating responsibilities, we share a common concern for the total enterprise."

Following the 1967 reorganization, the company convened the second conference of its senior management officers in February of 1968 to evaluate progress, to measure results against the 10-year plan, and to outline goals for the future. In opening the 1968 meeting, Swearingen recalled the themes of the 1964 conference in these words:

"We believe that meeting served a useful purpose in trying to bring into focus two principal points: First, that we were in fact a single company rather than a loosely bound aggregation of affiliated activities and that our future lay in developing further a spirit of dedication to the company as a whole; second, that our company was not doing as well as it should, that we had set a number of objectives to improve the performance of the company, and that to realize these objectives would demand superior performance from everyone in the company."

The initial comparisons reflected what had, indeed, been a superior performance. Between 1961 and 1967, Standard's earnings had almost doubled, rising from $154 million to $282 million, an annual growth rate of 11 per cent compared to 10 per cent for 16 other major companies. Overall, Standard had more than met its target of an 8 to 10 per cent per year increase in earnings—a rate of growth above that of the industry as a whole.

The goal of a 10 per cent rate of return on borrowed and invested capital was to be more elusive but was clearly within reach. It had continued to grow from its earlier figure of 6 per cent; in 1967, it had reached 9.2 per cent.

There was a continuing pressure for better coordination of activities. F. Cushing Smith, a vice president of Standard, in discussing the consolidated 10-year plan, emphasized that one of the purposes of the 1967 reorganization had been to achieve a higher degree of integration within the company. As part of this effort, he noted several specific studies which were then underway. They involved a comprehensive look at the future of the company's domestic marketing operations, a long-range domestic

103

manufacturing study, a major planning program to reassess the future of overseas operations, increased attention to personnel recruiting and development, and the establishment of a new group to investigate the possibilities of diversification.

Despite the new aggressiveness and the record of performance, there were storm clouds on the company's horizon. One of these was the continued worsening of the United States balance of payments in foreign trade which had led to imposition of restrictions on flow of funds for foreign direct investments in January of 1968.

"Our nation's balance of payments problems are serious," Swearingen told the conference, "and they are likely to get worse. If the present regulations do not bring about a substantial reduction in the outflow of capital funds from the United States, new regulations will surely be drawn to accomplish this purpose. We are going to have to scramble to complete the projects we now have underway—such as bringing North Sea gas to shore in Britain, exploiting our gas finds in the Netherlands, expanding our oil production in Egypt, developing new oil fields in Canada and the Persian Gulf of Iran, and completing our Madras and Belgian projects."

Swearingen also warned about the possibility of a change in the basis for international monetary exchange rates as the amount of obligations that existed in the form of dollar claims against the United States continued to exceed the nation's ability to redeem them in gold. "The root of the problem," he said, "is the question of whether the U.S. government can balance its budget, balance its foreign exchange, and retain the confidence of the world through sound internal fiscal policies." Although he avoided the position of predicting the worst would happen, he said "there is enough chance, however, of a recession or depression in the making that we should not be oblivious to the possibility."

There were other contingencies to be anticipated, including an inflation rate stimulated by the guns-and-butter program of President Lyndon B. Johnson, the tumultuous effects of an age of social protest, and a dampening of economic activity through wage and price controls.

Still, the chairman was optimistic and spoke of further moves toward consolidation. The general office of American International Oil Company (the overseas operating subsidiary), for example, had been moved to Chicago, although there was no room to accommodate it at the 910 South Michigan Avenue headquarters building.

Swearingen hinted that a solution to this problem was soon to be found. "Not the least of our problems is where everyone could be housed if the headquarters of all of our companies were brought to Chicago," he said. "We are presently working on the question of how best to unify our activities so that everyone—customers, investors, and the general public—understands and recognizes that we are in fact a single, strong company rather than unrelated organizations, or at best, an aggregation of loosely bound affiliates."

Swearingen concluded the conference on an optimistic note, citing Vince Lombardi's philosophy about being mentally prepared to win. "We have developed a momentum and forward thrust through which we can realize our true potential—and we must maintain it," he said. "The expansionary phase on which we are now embarking represents a determination to break out of a static mold, and a willingness to accept the risks which are a necessary part of such an undertaking.

"Our intention is to return this company to the front ranks of the petroleum industry. Mediocre efforts are going to have to be replaced by a norm of superior performance in all of our activities. And I am convinced that we need to develop a new attitude toward our opportunities—let us say we need to develop the habit of winning."

Domestic environmental factors affecting Standard's business were summed up by Swearingen as he introduced the third Senior Management Conference on April 27, 1970. Among these factors he included: further attempts at regulation and control by government of business in general and the oil business in particular; higher taxes on the oil industry; threatened deficits in the federal budget caused by urgent social needs and high defense spending; a high rate of inflation; and money for new investments high in price and short in supply. There were enough uncertainties clouding the long-term outlook for the domestic oil business that the company felt compelled to press forward on diversification into overseas oil, chemicals, and mining.

In their letter to shareholders dated March 1, 1971, and published in Standard's annual report for the year 1970, Swearingen and Gunness underlined the importance of reversing the trend of declining domestic production and increasing dependence on foreign oil. "This trend must be reversed if the future needs of the United States for reliable energy supplies are to be met," they wrote. "The situation demands a clear national policy that our security requires increased domestic production of oil and gas, and adequate economic incentives to find and develop the needed new reserves."

Changes in economic relationships throughout the world contributed to a sense of instability and increased the difficulty of making long-range plans. The Soviet Union had become the world's largest steel producer, surpassing the output of the United States for the first time. Moscow became a billion dollar U.S. grain customer, altering the economics of American agriculture. The European Common Market was enlarged to include Britain, Denmark, and Ireland—establishing a competitive trading bloc larger than the United States. The stirrings of monetary instability and an awareness of the weakness of the dollar resulted in two devaluations by the United States within a 14-month period.

Faced with such uncertainties, Standard executives had reason to be grateful for the self-imposed financial discipline which governed their operating plans. Throughout the previous decade, they had devoted an extraordinary amount of attention to how the business should be financed. Analyses and forecasts by the financial department permitted the company to anticipate its cash requirements at any time. By maintaining a top credit rating, the company was able to raise additional funds at minimum cost.

Swearingen continued to press for better planning in order to anticipate and deal with the rapid rate of change when he opened the fourth Senior Management Conference on March 21, 1973. "From past experience," Swearingen told the conference, "we have found that we have been largely unable to predict radical change in any truly meaningful way. Our forecasts of the future—economic, political, technological—have been notably faulty at precisely those points where predictions would be most useful. In general, we are not very successful at forecasting turns—sharp deviations from past experience. If we are to be successful in the future, it is imperative that we develop and adopt a strategy which will ensure corporate success even under rapidly altering socio-economic conditions."

The socio-economic conditions to which he referred included sharply increased government regulation of the industry. This had led to the establishment on February 1, 1973, of a department of Law and Public Affairs headed by Richard J. Farrell, vice president and general counsel, concurrently with the consolidation of the major subsidiaries' public relations departments into a single department in Chicago. Farrell described the genesis of the department in these terms:

"During much of the past decade, while most of us were concentrating almost exclusively on performing our economic function to the best of our ability, American business in general and the oil industry in particular, have been engulfed by a tidal wave of disenchantment with the established institutions of our society. This has been followed by successive waves of expectation that corporations can and will alter their behavior to meet a growing number of new demands of society. . . .

"At the heart of the problem are basic value changes born of the increasing affluence enjoyed by most citizens. The success we have enjoyed in our traditional role of satisfying public needs and desires for goods and services has led to new desires and new expectations related to improvement in the overall quality of life and satisfaction of nonmaterial personal goals. Even in our own corporate household, we are conscious of changes in the attitudes of employees toward work and their concept of company loyalty."

Farrell went on to sound a warning about the conditions under which the oil industry and Standard would have to operate in the future. "Realistically, I believe that the extent and nature of the government control over the operations of a competitive market in the oil and gas industry will hinge on our ability to generate public understanding of the extent to which law and regulation have interfered with the development of adequate reserves. More important, it will hinge on our ability to supply the energy needs of the nation as fully and effectively as we have in the past or to explain more effectively why we can't. Finally, it will hinge on our ability to develop the quality of communication with government that will assure that those regulations and laws that are promulgated actually achieve their objectives without disrupting business operations or damaging the economy."

It was painfully apparent that production of oil and gas was not keeping up with demand and that the oil companies were living off their reserves. George Myers reported at the 1973 conference that while industry reserves were equal to approximately 14 years of production in 1961, production increased faster than additions to reserves and 10 years later proven reserves in the industry amounted to just nine years at the then-current rate of production. Standard was in a slightly better position than the rest of the industry although its oil reserves had dropped from 22 years' supply to 14 years'.

Myers observed that "the alarming aspect of this comparison is the fact our company, along with the rest of the industry, has been increasing production of oil and gas and is really reporting profits by a process of asset liquidation. It is certain that the cost of replacing these assets will be greatly in excess of their original cost. Moreover, it is probable that the overall cost of replacement may exceed the current selling price." His prediction in this regard was to prove too modest.

During the 1960s, the company had moved away from historic avoidance of capital debt and had financed its rapid expansion in part by utilization of outside financing and borrowing. This represented an increase in debt from 12 per cent of capital in 1965 to 25 per cent of capital in 1970—a level that the company thought prudent to regard as a maximum.

The implications of this were further spelled out by Swearingen. "One major strategic factor in our situation is clear and unmistakable: we are a crude-short company and we are likely to continue to be one for the foreseeable future. . . . Among other things this means that our corporate progress from this point on is going to depend increasingly on our entrepreneurial abilities and skill in managing our assets.

"In our own company, we find our refining facilities running at or above our rated capacity. For the first time in 25 years, we have been forced to allocate supplies of heating oil to customers and a similar pinch may be shaping up in gasoline as we move into the peak driving months. . . . For some time to come it appears our refined products sales will be supply-limited rather than market-limited—a situation unlike anything most of us have experienced in our careers."

But the real shock was to come later that year when war broke out again between Israel and Egypt on October 6, 1973, followed by the ban on oil exports to the U.S. by Arab oil-producing countries October 19-21. The ban was in effect until March 18, 1974. The Organization of Petroleum Exporting Countries (OPEC), which had been formed in 1960, doubled prices abruptly and unilaterally in December, and boosted their prices more in following months. The people with the oil had wrested control of it from the people with the markets. The industrial nations of the world were staggered by the economic impact of these additional costs, and Third World countries suffered a severe setback in their efforts to improve their share of the world's economic resources.

The Most Valuable Resource

10

As the company grew during the sixties, the need for managers with technological training and administrative skills grew proportionately. To meet this challenge, a company-wide plan of career training and development was designed and instituted to assure that Standard would be able to draw future executives from within its own ranks as well as to maintain the necessary number of highly qualified employees in the professions. This manpower planning system sought to forecast both long-range and short-range manpower needs. Short-range projections were translated into recruiting goals.

Standard's efforts to recruit and train a cadre of future managers and executives came at a time when the perception of business and the careers it offered were at one of its historic low-points. An article in the February, 1966, issue of *Fortune* magazine reported, for example, that of Harvard's 1,091 bachelor degree candidates in 1965, only 51 said they planned to enter corporate life. Perhaps 12 more, with backgrounds in fields of technology, would join a company after graduation. American Oil recruiters estimated that only 3 per cent of the men and women they interviewed on college campuses would ever go to work for the company.

Lawrence A. Kimpton, familiar with student attitudes as a former chancellor of the University of Chicago, sought to paint a different picture of a business career. "For young people who have the necessary intellectual capacity, the determination, and the vision called for," he said, "there are very few careers in life which can match the opportunity to be found within today's corporations."

Extra funds and manpower were allocated to an effort given

109

the appropriate name of Manpower Selection and Development. Intensive campaigns were organized with the goal, in the words of a company publication, of "developing the image of the company as a progressive, innovative, forward-looking organization that offered real creative opportunities to talented people."

Jack Tharpe was sensitive to the climate of the time. "I suppose to an industrial organization," he told a management conference, "social change in the employment field can most easily be related to what has in some quarters been categorized as the 'psychology of entitlements,' *i.e.*, entitlements to an education, a well paying job with the quality of life the prospective employee expects, medical care, a decent place to live, and (in the case of) minorities to a certain percentage of professional and managerial jobs."

Such concerns weren't limited to the domestic part of the organization. Standard's growth overseas presented a unique and constantly changing set of problems in meeting the company's manpower requirements and in assuring proper recognition of the particular needs of overseas employees—both expatriates and nationals of the host country. As Tharpe observed, "Our expatriate employees are more likely than not to be in a location where the cultural, social, and economic climate is strange to them. How to establish personnel policies and practices that are fair to both the expatriates and the company is an endless and complex task."

Recruiting goals continued to be as they had been outlined in 1962:

"First, we must recruit into our organization the best individuals with a talent for leadership that we can find. Second, we must provide opportunities for individuals to develop managerial competence on the base of their primary technical skills. Third, we must enlarge the managerial competence of our outstanding employees so that they can be prepared to assume broad responsibilities and exercise sound judgment on matters affecting major parts of the company's business."

In 1970, Gunness observed that manpower planning was assuming increased importance. Among the problems he anticipated were those reflecting a differing set of standards as new recruits joined the company. "Young people, impatient with established procedures, many with negative attitudes toward business, and with little sense of company loyalty, will have to be accommodated into our system," he told a group of executives. He also emphasized the need for increased manpower planning as he observed that "many of us in this room today will retire in the decade of the 1970s and will have to be replaced with competent managers."

One method of assuring that these managers would be in place was the program of intercompany transfers to broaden experience. Candidates for promotion were drawn from throughout the entire company. Attesting to the value of that practice, Gunness cited one instance in which the selection system identified 65 individuals within the company who were well-qualified to fill a certain position for which a subsidiary had considered advertising for a replacement.

Recruiting and hiring policies had to be developed and managed against the background of social unrest which swept the country during the 1960s. The civil rights movement had come of age; the assassination of President John F. Kennedy on November 22, 1963, was followed by the assassination of Martin Luther King, Jr., on April 4, 1968; hearts of large U.S. cities were torn by riots; the Vietnam war engendered protests and bitterness.

The inner-city riots resulted in new demands being placed on American business and industry. In Detroit, president James Roche of General Motors stood on the roof of his company headquarters and watched fires rip through the heart of the city; within hours he was to recruit a group of his peers from the Detroit business community to form a New Detroit Committee to deal with some of the unsatisfied needs which had led to the riots. In Chicago, the Urban League formed a Business Advisory Council to provide an exchange of views between business leaders and the black community.

Standard's efforts to eliminate discrimination in hiring practices had been among the earliest and most aggressive of major American corporations. But progress was painfully slow. In 1942, the company had eliminated from employment forms and active employee records all reference to nationality, race, color, or creed. In the early 1950s, it adopted a broad policy of nondiscrimination and received a special citation from the Commission on Human Relations of the city of Chicago. The citation came a bit too early as the company struggled to translate its policy into practice. Despite memoranda of instruction to supervisors, the total number of blacks and other minorities in the company's 40,000 plus work force stood at only 628 in 1965.

The civil rights movement of the 1960s also had an impact on other facets of the company's operations. One of these was the existence of segregated rest rooms at some service stations. Abolishing them not only flew in the face of local custom in some communities, it even required a defiance of local laws which had not yet been struck down by the United States Supreme Court. Further complicating attempts to deal with the problem was the fact that most of the service station operators were independent businessmen; in reality, they were customers of the company and not employees subject to its jurisdiction.

Despite these complications, the company did not equivocate in facing up to the problem. On October 1, 1963, a memorandum went to all department heads stating:

"Segregated facilities at service stations or at other company locations are in conflict with company policy. Discourtesy of any kind in our dealing with Negroes and any other customers is also a serious policy violation."

At many plants there were employee clubs, which, while independently operated by the employees themselves, still received company contributions toward their support. When one of these was found to have a "whites only" policy, the company notified all the clubs to eliminate discriminatory clauses in their bylaws or face the loss of company funds.

In 1965, a major initiative was taken by the company in the area of equal employment opportunity when it published a statement dealing not only with the number of minorities who should be employed but the level at which they should be employed. It foresaw the need not only to have more members of minorities on the payroll but also to ensure that they had an opportunity to progress within the company and to obtain positions at a higher level and of greater responsibility. The statement laid out objectives which continue to govern much of the company's operations.

Over the next few years, with the firm support of South Carolina-born Chairman John E. Swearingen, the company struggled to put into practice the principles enunciated in the 1965 policy statement. One of the hurdles was that Standard consisted for the most part of highly technical departments. As most minority employees were being recruited at lower entry levels, they could not be advanced unless they had a technical background qualifying them for the specialized work that constituted most of Standard's activities, or went "through the chairs," in an internal training program such as had been traditional in the past.

After a few years, the company found that the normal

promotional process could not be applied to minorities if they were ever to move in any numbers into positions of greater responsibility. As Standard strove to deal with these problems, Swearingen suggested to President Robert C. Gunness that Gunness head up an Urban Affairs Task Force to structure more formal and long-term ways of dealing with these external forces and pressures.

A Department of Urban Affairs was established in June of 1969, in response to a major Task Force recommendation. The Task Force subsequently presented management with a list of some 40 recommendations. The Task Force said to management, "What we must do is work into the fabric of the company fixed objectives for the achievement of social goals." Extensive planning went into the transition as managers were given not only a set of goals for sales and production but for a specific level of minority hiring and promotion as well. The same standards were applied to minority purchasing since the company was aware that many minority businessmen were familiar with manufacturing but that few were experienced in marketing. Standard recognized its own economic stake in urban areas which were changing racially and in many cases deteriorating. The company's gasoline marketing was heavily represented in some of these areas. The city of Chicago was an example. Many of the 1,264 Standard service stations were situated in neighborhoods where social unrest was the norm.

When the purchasing effort started, Blaine J. Yarrington, then president of American Oil, stated the objective bluntly: "This isn't going to be a public relations effort. This is going to be real minority purchasing." The Task Force came late to this process. But, if the Task Force came late to the battle, it also had before it a classic case of evolution without progress. Originally, in 1961, a black consultant from Washington, D.C., had been hired to undertake the task of trying to identify minority suppliers from whom the purchasing department might buy goods and services. He was paid a fee of $25,000, and at the end of a year, Standard had increased its minority purchases from zero to $25,000—the amount of the fee for the consultant.

A black analyst in Standard's purchasing department was more successful, and minority purchases went from nothing to almost half a million dollars a year between 1961 and 1966. By 1970, the amount had reached only $600,000. The company was convinced, however, that this was only a miniscule part of the opportunity. To correct the situation, each location in the company in 1971 was asked to provide management with a dollar figure of what it would spend the following year with minority-owned enterprises.

The results indicated progress. Every location in Standard exceeded its goal in the first year; during the decade of the '70s, the program showed a cumulative annual increase of 40 per cent per year. In 1980, purchases from minority businesses were more than $116 million.

Outside the company, through Yarrington's leadership, Robert Stuart, chairman of the National Can Corporation, agreed to head a National Minority Purchasing Council in cooperation with the National Association of Purchasing Managers and the United States Department of Commerce. Soon, that organization had more than 1,000 corporate members and was organized into some 37 regional councils around the country. Members were spending more than $2 billion per year with minority suppliers.

Dealing with discrimination was only one area of concern. In some areas, growth seemed constrained only by availability of engineers and scientists having expertise unique to the field. In electronics, for example, Ray Stata, chairman of Analog Devices, Inc., in which Standard acquired 15 per cent equity interest in 1977, said "sales of U. S.-made electronics have risen six-fold in 20 years, but the number of engineers and scientists who can design such products has only doubled."

The severe strain on the supply of experienced people also was apparent in oil and gas exploration and production. The number of graduating engineers was too small. Exploration and production technology was advancing rapidly, so rapidly that even experienced engineers needed periodic updating. Newly hired engineering graduates needed company-provided classroom instruction in addition to on-the-job training. The situation improved during the late 1970s, but Swearingen, noting that there still remained a good deal of catching up to do, said that the oil industry should lend a hand. Standard, he said, was making equipment grants to engineering schools, and engineering faculty grants to encourage young graduates to earn advanced degrees and pursue academic careers.

In the areas of exploration and production, Standard offered new graduates who joined the company on-the-job training supplemented with intensive classroom courses. Standard established an Exploration Training Center and a Production Training

Center in Tulsa in the 1970s to coordinate and intensify formal and informal instruction for explorationists and engineers. More than 5,000 men and women annually were given specialized instruction at these centers.

In accepting the Western Society of Engineers' Washington Award for 1981, Swearingen told the group "Today we stand on the brink of what could well be a second industrial revolution. Engineers, along with scientists, will be responsible for providing the timely and abundant supplies of energy that will fuel that revolution."

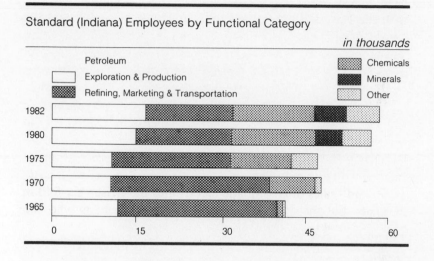

Standard (Indiana) Employees by Functional Category

The implications for manpower utilization in a company such as Standard, operating worldwide, were particularly relevant in the late 1970s and early 1980s when competition for trained and skilled explorationists and engineers had become as intense as the search for oil itself. In particular, large subsidiaries, such as Amoco Production, were constantly losing trained personnel to smaller companies or wildcatters who could promise the recruit a "piece of the action." Operating on a worldwide basis after the consolidation of domestic and foreign exploration and production in 1981 also eliminated a rigidity within the company which had sometimes caused young explorationists and others to be reluctant to switch from one subsidiary to another. Under the new structure, all personnel changes would be administered by a single organization and assignments anywhere would be on the same

115

promotional and reward basis. Similar benefits became available by consolidating manufacturing and marketing in Amoco Oil on a worldwide basis.

Still, manpower demands seemed insatiable. In 1980, Standard hired 1,400 professional and technical employees, a 39 per cent increase over 1979. In selecting these new recruits, Standard personnel managers had as their mandate increasing the total representation of minorities and females in the work force, and assuring these employees they had equal opportunity for promotion into positions of greater responsibility when deserved. Of the engineers hired during 1979–1980, 11.5 per cent were from minority groups, and 10.5 per cent were females. Of those hired with geology or geophysics degrees, 19.5 per cent were females and 5.5 per cent were from minorities; both percentages exceeded the national representation of those groups in these disciplines.

The human element also was a factor in the construction of a new 80-story international headquarters office building for Standard at the northern edge of Grant Park in downtown Chicago. As the company had grown, its offices had spread to 12 locations in the Loop area in addition to the officially designated headquarters location at 910 South Michigan Avenue.

The building at 910 had originally been an eight-story warehouse. When Standard bought the building for its corporate headquarters in 1918, an additional 12 stories were added, making it a 20-story building. The original steel that was set for the warehouse dictated the size of the offices, which, in Richard J. Farrell's words, "all looked like either football fields or bowling alleys."

Up until World War II, the company had shared the building with the Continental Assurance Company (now CNA) and the Sanitary District of Metropolitan Chicago. As the company's operations expanded, the tenants found other homes, but the additional space was not enough to contain the corporation's expanding activities.

The easiest and most prudent way to centralize the many activities related to headquarters' operations seemed to be to acquire the surrounding land and build a tower adjoining the 910 Building; then the older building eventually might be torn down. This was attractive not only to the company, but to the city; the area around the building was substantially deteriorating and a new office building would have provided an anchor for the south end of Michigan Avenue. In preparation for such a project, the company acquired most of the surrounding land, including the site of the old St. Mary's church. The parishioners had moved from the area and Cardinal John Patrick Cody was eager to select a more central location in the Chicago Loop.

With one exception, all the needed property was acquired, and that exception was ultimately to result in a dramatic change in Chicago's skyline. In the middle of the Michigan Avenue block stood a small building owned by an elderly lady who ran an antique store and published a small magazine. She simply wouldn't sell, even though Standard executives beat a path to her door with offers that eventually reached two and a half times the building's appraised value.

John Swearingen himself called on her and, in his best South Carolina manner, tried to talk the lady into selling. The owner, who was then about 75 years old, listened patiently. Finally, she said, "Mr. Swearingen, my tenants are only paying me $1.50 per square foot rent. If I moved out of here into a higher cost building, I don't know what would happen to my tenants." Faced with such resolve, Swearingen decided there was no alternative but to look elsewhere.

A committee under the chairmanship of Farrell, then general counsel and later vice president, law and public affairs, began a site study in which it looked carefully at 14 different locations from the south to the north end of Michigan Avenue. Eventually, the group settled on a site on the Illinois Central Railroad property, next to the Prudential Insurance Company's Mid-America headquarters building which had been erected in 1955. Protracted negotiations resulted in the purchase of the site.

A committee headed by Farrell received 59 submissions from architectural firms around the world. Of these, 19 firms were chosen for further consideration. Edward Durell Stone, the architect who had done the General Motors Building in New York, the New Orleans Trade Center, the National Geographic Building in Washington, and other notable buildings in the U.S. and elsewhere, was selected. A joint-venture firm was formed in which Stone would do the design drawings and Perkins and Will Corporation, a major Chicago-based firm, the production drawings. Turner Construction Company was named general contractor, and ground-breaking ceremonies were held in 1970.

Standard also put its own expediters and inspectors on the job. The skills available from the research and engineering departments of Standard proved to be invaluable in design and construction innovations.

For Standard, the construction of a building was more than a matter of architecture, design, and materials. The general contractor and subcontractors on the Standard Oil Building were told that the goal was to have 30 per cent of their workforce from minority groups. Gunness told them, "We expect you to have a better record on hiring minorities on this job than any other job you have ever done." As a result about 34 per cent of the labor force during construction consisted of members of minority groups.

When the building at 200 East Randolph Drive was finished and employees began moving to their new offices in late 1972, it was the second tallest building in Chicago at 1,136 feet, and fourth tallest in the world.

The new building became the location of Standard's international headquarters. With adequate office space under one roof, Standard brought together boards of directors and specialized staffs of its major subsidiaries and merged duplicative staffs into single departments by function to serve the total company. For the parent company, Standard, and Amoco Oil, Amoco International, and Amoco Chemicals, it was a move from separate buildings in Chicago to the new structure. For Amoco Production, it was a move of some 700 miles from Tulsa, Oklahoma.

The 80-floor, marble-clad Standard Oil building structure is surrounded by large open-air space. Waterfalls on the east and west sides and in the plaza on the south, a multitude of shrubs and honey-locust trees, as well as flowers changed with the seasons, add to the building's appearance. A reflecting pool, opposite a 190-foot long waterfall in the plaza, contains a "sounding sculpture" by the renowned sculptor, Harry Bertoia. More than 6,000 pieces of art—originals and reproductions—by more than 1,700 artists from more than 80 countries and including over 300 Chicago artists were hung in hallways and offices. The building became a showpiece of the Chicago skyline.

"Getting the Lead out"

11

The engine of an average automobile of the teens and early '20s knocked and lost power during acceleration and when climbing hills, causing motorists to press manufacturers for autos providing the pleasure of knock-free power drivers wanted to enjoy behind the steering wheel. Auto makers vied with each other to respond by increasing engine compression as far as available technology allowed. Increasing compression improved power and performance but worsened the knocking problem. Whether knocking was caused by carbon deposits in engines or by the chemical composition of gasolines was hotly debated in research, manufacturing, and marketing circles of gasoline and automobile manufacturers.

First honors for solving the engine-knock problem went to marketers Louis Blaustein and his son, Jacob, who achieved antiknock qualities by adding benzol to gasoline that American Oil sold along the U.S. East Coast. But Standard had to look for another way because benzol was not available in the quantities needed to make the Blaustein type of antiknock gasoline.

That other way emerged in 1923 when Thomas Midgley, Jr., then employed by General Motors Chemical Company, found that the problem was caused by the chemical composition of gasoline instead of carbon build-up in engine firing chambers as some argued. With suggestions from Robert E. Wilson, then assistant director of research for Standard, Midgley found that a small fraction of tetraethyl lead added to gasoline all but eliminated the knock. Standard became the first major marketer of leaded gasoline.

Standard's first sale was made in 1923 at a Richmond, Indiana, service station. Midgley devised a small unit called an

119

"Ethylizer" which was installed atop the gas pump, and the attendant made one turn of the crank for each gallon of gasoline he put in the car.

Wilson saw the commercial possibilities of the new anti-knock product and suggested Standard become a partner in its manufacture and sale. However, he was rebuffed by the president of Standard, William M. Burton, who told him "Standard is not interested in a sideline of this kind." Within two months, General Motors made an agreement with Standard (New Jersey) for just such an association in what was to become the Ethyl Corporation. When Standard's chief executive officer, Colonel Robert W. Stewart, heard rumors of the arrangement, he rushed to New York to try to get in on the partnership. He was too late; from that point on, Standard paid tribute to Standard (New Jersey) for the use of tetraethyl lead, just as the latter had been forced earlier to pay Standard (Indiana) for use of the Burton-Humphreys cracking process.

It was a great opportunity that Standard had missed. No one thought then about air pollutants from auto emissions. Neither did anyone think that one day in the future the use of lead-free and low-lead gasolines would be mandatory to stop this source of air pollution. Tetraethyl lead was comparatively cheap, supply was available, only small quantities were needed to produce gasolines that worked well in high compression engines, and Standard and its competitors saw no reason not to use it.

The revolution in the refining of crude oil and production of gasoline embodied in the fluid catalytic cracking process and hydroforming of heavy naphtha to produce aromatics utilized in producing high-octane aviation gasolines during World War II accelerated the octane race in automotive gasolines. In both of the years 1954 and 1955 Standard reported to its stockholders that octane ratings of its gasolines reached "the highest point in our history," and there were further increases in succeeding years. Gasolines of various octane ratings were laced with additives such as de-icers, and seasonal and geographic formula changes were made to assure satisfactory startup and performance characteristics regardless of temperatures and altitudes. Through it all, while continuing to promote the use of aromatics and tetraethyl lead additive to improve octane ratings and performance elsewhere, Standard religiously supported successful marketing of the unique unleaded antiknock gasoline sold in the expanding East and South marketing territory—first under the original American

15. The service station of the 1920s was called a "filling" station. This one was at the corner of Thirteenth and Lafayette in St. Louis, Missouri. In addition to gasolines and motor oils for cars, kerosene for lamps and stoves was also sold at such stations. A photo of a 1982 service station is on page 222.

Oil name and later under that subsidiary's new name, Amoco Oil Company.

Standard marketing officials recognized the advantages of offering the public a product that was unique, as had the Blausteins of American Oil, even though, because of the high manufacturing cost, it had to be sold to the motorist at a higher price. But production of unleaded antiknock gasoline was resisted by Standard's manufacturing department. Making higher octane antiknock gasolines without tetraethyl lead would require heavy capital investment as well as greater manufacturing costs to produce the aromatics that came to prominence for aviation fuel during World War II. But aromatics now were valuable in the manufacture of Amoco Chemicals products. Finally, making higher octane antiknock gasolines without tetraethyl lead cost more and intense price competition at the service station made that point extremely important.

Another strong argument used against the manufacture of unleaded gasoline by Standard's manufacturing and marketing departments was that Standard's market share in the Middle West was several times greater than American Oil's market share in the East and South. While a small proportion of the total motoring population in the East and South was willing to pay a premium price for unleaded gasoline, there was an unanswerable question as to whether a much higher proportion of motorists in the Middle West could be induced to pay a similar premium. For all these reasons there was even debate about discontinuing production and sale of unleaded gasoline in the East and South.

It was the one issue at Standard board meetings on which Jacob Blaustein was emotional. Unleaded antiknock gasoline had been the pride and joy of the Blausteins, father and son, ever since they developed it and began selling Amoco Gas in the early 1920s. Jacob strongly resisted proposals to drop it and his views prevailed. The unique unleaded gasoline was continued in the East and South.

Although Standard and the industry possessed the know-how for production of unleaded antiknock gasolines, switching was uneconomic as long as leaded gasoline was a viable product. Amoco Super Premium marketed in the East and South remained the nation's only unleaded gasoline until 1970.

In the final years of the 1960s, the automobile stood indicted as the largest single contributor to air pollution in the country. Massive research by the automobile industry, with the assistance of oil companies, resulted in development of devices that were expected to virtually eliminate automotive emissions as a major air pollution contributor. But the new devices wouldn't be totally effective until lead-free gasoline was available generally because the key emission control device, a catalytic converter to be installed in auto exhaust systems, would be ruined after a few miles if it ran on leaded gasoline.

Standard paved the way in 1970 for introduction of the catalytic converter when it became the first company to market a lead-free regular grade gasoline nation-wide. Marketing of the unique 100-plus octane Amoco Super Premium lead-free gasoline continued in 25 Eastern and Southern states and in the District of Columbia. The experience over more than 50 years of Standard's American Oil Company in manufacturing and marketing lead-free gasoline stood the company in good stead from the standpoint of technical competence. But making lead-free gasoline available nation-wide required a commitment of more than $100 million in capital spending by Standard in 1970 and 1971 to expand refinery equipment for aromatics production and blending, and installation of service station facilities to handle three grades of gasoline—a leaded premium, a leaded regular, and a lead-free regular.

Expanding sales of unleaded gasoline nation-wide took on aspects of a highly coordinated military operation. Nineteen task forces were formed to get the new fuel manufactured and available at all service stations. The Planning and Engineering department secured early approval of $33 million for an additional Ultraformer at the Whiting refinery—essential to the production of unleaded gasoline in the quantities which would be required. At some service station locations, the company was able to utilize new tanks installed over the preceding 10 or 15 years in anticipation of the possible introduction of a third grade of gasoline. When the third grade turned out to be lead-free, some of these already were in place. For new pumps required to handle this third product, American Oil and one other company pre-empted the entire 1970 production of two of the largest pump manufacturers in the country.

At the end of the year, Blaine J. Yarrington, who had been elected a director of Standard and president of Amoco Oil on March 1, 1970, said, "In all my years with the company, I can't think of a time when we responded as swiftly and confidently to an opportunity as we did this spring to the issue of unleaded gasoline. Once convinced that the real way to take pollution out of exhausts was the catalytic converter—and that this would mean no more lead in gasoline—we really did get the lead out, in more ways than one."

There was some consumer resistance to the new regular grade lead-free gasoline. For one thing, it cost more than the regular grade common for so many years. Then too, there was the inertia born of long-established habit. Even in the East and South the motorist tended to be either a confirmed user of Amoco Super Premium lead-free or satisfied with leaded lower grades. But American Oil obtained some 90 million gallons of federal government business in 1971 after an executive order was issued which required the use of unleaded or low-lead gasolines in government vehicles able to use one or the other.

Sales of unleaded fuels increased and in July, 1974, government regulations were adopted which required most service stations to market lead-free gasoline. Beginning with 1975 models, most vehicles would have emission-reducing catalytic converters which required the use of unleaded gasolines. In 1976, 31.6 per cent of all Amoco gasoline sold was lead-free while the industry average was 20 per cent. A new Amoco Premium lead-free gasoline was introduced in 1977 and, in the face of intense competition, the company continued to be the nation's Number 1 lead-free marketer with an 11 per cent share.

The use of lead-free gasolines became the norm for motorists across the nation. Automobile manufacturers designed gasoline tank receptacles which would only accept smaller-diameter nozzles on lead-free pumps at service stations. Only older vehicles could accept larger nozzles dispensing leaded gasolines.

The U.S. oil industry average retail price of regular grade gasoline in 1952 was 20.04 cents a gallon; in 1962 it was 20.36 cents, an increase in the decade of 32 one-hundredths of a cent. But the motorist paid more. There had to be an explanation. There was: taxes. In the same ten-year period, state and federal taxes on gasoline increased to 10.28 cents a gallon from 7.32 cents. The average price, including taxes, that the motorist paid at the service station was 30.64 cents a gallon in 1962, up from 27.36 cents in 1952.

Rising pump prices of gasoline evolved into a political issue. By 1974, the average service station price, then including 12 cents in taxes, rose to 52.41 cents a gallon. "Divestiture" became a popular word among populist politicians who somehow believed that if oil companies were allowed to engage only in one function, such as refining, and not in another concurrently, such as marketing, the oil industry would be more competitive and prices to consumers would go down.

In the late 1960s, Amoco Oil saw its contribution to the company's earnings slipping drastically. Standard had put heavy reliance on the loyalty of service-oriented customers. Independent marketers, however, were gaining an increasing share of the market. Price conscious customers skipped the amenities and looked for the lowest price at cut-rate service stations concentrating on high volume, low-price, gasoline-only operations.

As price competition increased at the service station, Standard approached the problem warily—in part because of a long and arduous legal battle with the government dating back to the depression. That battle had its origin in Detroit in the 1930s when Standard's competitors offered a reduced price for gasoline to some of the company's best wholesale customers.

When several of these customers switched suppliers to get the better price, Standard agreed to match any part or all of the reductions offered by its competitors. The result was a complaint from the Federal Trade Commission, issued on a chill November day in 1940, that this constituted unfair price discrimination and amounted to unlawful injury to competition. The commission contended that Standard should not have reduced the price to these particular wholesalers or it should have reduced the price to everyone in the area to whom the company was selling, including all retailers.

In their reply, Standard's lawyers pointed out that neither of these two courses was reasonable. Unless Standard met the competitive prices it would lose its customers. If the prices had been lowered to everyone, the company would not only be losing money; it might be in danger of being accused of destroying competition by setting the price too low.

The case finally got to the United States Supreme Court which ruled in 1951 that Standard was correct—that meeting competition in good faith is an absolute defense to a charge of price discrimination. This was Phase One of the dispute, which had taken 11 years to resolve.

The FTC was not a willing loser, however. After the Supreme Court ruling, the commission charged that the company had not acted in "good faith" in meeting the competitor's price. The climb back to the U.S. Supreme Court started all over, and again the Court ruled in favor of Standard—but it was not until 1958. It had taken 18 years of legal action to establish the right of a company to meet a competitor's price.

Faced with continuing price competition from independents, Standard and other major companies were forced to reexamine their traditional ways of marketing gasoline. For years, almost 75 per cent of the market had been served by large numbers of small dealer-operated stations, each providing a great variety of services, but enjoying a relatively small volume of gasoline sales at each location.

It was the kind of service Americans expected from their corner grocery store; however, this kind of service suffered from the same pressures which ultimately sealed the fate of most Mom and Pop groceries—mass merchandising techniques and the cost and price advantages of the supermarket approach.

The independent marketer and large jobber, who bought directly from the refinery, used his own tank trucks, and marketed through his own service stations, did not have the large capital resources of the major companies. But he saw that with the supermarket approach a few stations—later to have self-service facilities also—could be located in areas of highly concentrated population. And, by means of lower prices based on volume and cost advantages, he could lure customers away from the brand-name stations.

In Standard's case, a 1960 task force had recommended that the company emulate the independents by converting to large, high-volume stations when new construction was being considered, sacrificing total geographic distribution for concentrated coverage. West Coast stations should be closed down, the report said, along with outlets in the Southwest where the company had initiated operations only a few years before.

L. W. Moore, president of American Oil Company, outlined a parallel problem to the 1964 Senior Management Conference. He reported that the marketing and refining segment of the company, as represented by American Oil, amounted to 38 per cent of the total capital employed by Standard. Yet its rate of return was only 5.1 per cent on an investment base of more than one billion dollars. Thus, if Standard were to achieve its goal of a 10 per cent rate of return, the profitability of this sector, representing more than one-third of total investment, would have to be improved.

Gasoline Retail Outlets Served by Standard (Indiana)

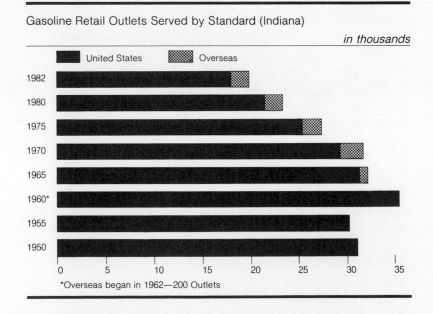

in thousands

*Overseas began in 1962—200 Outlets

Moore pointed out that more than 80 per cent of gross profit was then being generated in sales channels which accounted for only 45 per cent of volume; putting it another way, 55 per cent of sales were contributing only 20 per cent to profits.

As Moore saw it, the dealer was key to this problem. He cited the fact that in 1963 alone, 200 service stations closed for lack of personnel to run them. Annual dealer turnover was running at a fearsome 15 per cent. To correct the situation, a joint project was formed between the marketing and employee relations departments to explore means for improving dealer selection. In the training area, the company began working with the University of Chicago to study training needs, techniques, and programs to improve the training not only of dealers but of agents and salesmen.

Changes were also effected in the basic marketing organization, with greater authority being given to regional managers. A long-range national marketing strategy was established which set objectives for each region so that specific investments and operating plans could be made.

Inherited and traditional ways of doing business were identified as a heavy burden. A study by the financial department showed that selling and administrative costs were running about 50 per cent higher at Standard, expressed as a percentage of income, than the industry average. In an effort to increase productivity and reduce some of these costs, a new accounting center, using high-speed and high-capacity equipment took over marketing accounting for the Chicago region. At the same time, American Oil undertook the first major overhaul of basic accounting procedures in more than 40 years.

Policy changes were not confined to improving return-on-investment of existing facilities. Investment policies also were changed. Investment in new stations was reduced from $35 million a year to $25 million, following the corporate strategy that dollars should be invested where they would produce the greatest return. The $25 million figure also represented an absolute minimum if the company were to remain competitive.

As Standard developed its marketing strategy to meet changing conditions and competition, it did not neglect its own heritage. The company felt that car-care service was a rule in which Standard was seen with confidence and that this customer loyalty should be encouraged and preserved. Research identified three types of customers: the full-service customer who always wants the best; the price customer who doesn't care about anything but the lowest price; and the "switchers" who might buy for price one time but who might want expert car service at another. The switchers were the target for new stations which were to be large multi-pump layouts with or without self-service facilities, car washes, and service bays. The remaining stations would be full-service car-care outlets where the company's reputation for quality care could be maintained.

The closing of large numbers of smaller stations was undertaken by many major companies. The process accelerated and the total number of stations in the U.S. decreased dramatically from the all-time high of 226,459 in 1972. The industry closed stations at a rate of approximately 10,000 per year to 193,000 in 1975 and 171,000 in 1978. Many of these stations were simply abandoned and became eyesores in the community. Recognizing that such eyesores were not good for the industry, Standard in 1968 announced a six-point plan for dealing with its own closed stations, including maintaining them if they were temporarily closed, or removing them when it became clear they were to be permanently abandoned.

Processing Crude Oil

12

The general public tends to picture the oil industry simply as a series of service stations tending to the needs of motorists. That it also supplies heating oils, special lubricants, and large amounts of fuel to basic industries—such as steel—and raw materials to some —such as textiles—is known by few outside the industry.

In the petroleum industry, refining and processing are synonymous with manufacturing. But, unlike lumber, steel, and many others, these are manufacturing processes in which the raw material is seldom, if ever, seen. Crude oil—as well as natural gas—is produced through a pipe in the well, then transported through an arrangement of piping and valves at the wellhead to pipelines and automatic measurement facilities and storage tanks. From these it moves principally by pipeline, tanker ship, or barge—some by rail —to refineries or gas plants where manufacturing into petroleum products useful to man takes place. And when a finished product of petroleum is sold "on the street," the purchaser may never see it. Or it may be in a form—such as a plastic cup, a transparent food package, or a clothing item—that is in no way related in the customer's mind to its crude oil or natural gas origin.

Inherent in this manufacturing and product management is a high degree of automation—computer controls coupled with sophisticated electronic monitoring and recording devices— which enables the refiner to process crude oil into thousands of products on a continuous basis without being touched by human hands.

In the case of crude oil, the percentage of each product yielded from a barrel fluctuates according to the properties of the oil being refined and the seasonal product most in demand. During the oil shortages of 1978–1979, the public was constantly made aware of different product supply requirements imposed on the oil companies by the Department of Energy to shift production from more gasoline to more fuel oil or vice versa, or to increase or decrease deliveries from one area to another.

Petroleum in its natural state is composed of many thousands of hydrocarbon molecules that vary in size, weight, and pattern. The first processing step at a refinery is to sort out or separate these molecules according to boiling point. Fractional distillation takes place in a pipestill, or fractionating tower, where heat and pressure cause lighter components, or fractions, to turn to vapor and rise in the tower. They are condensed and drawn off at different levels through pipes leading from the side of the tower. Gasoline, a light hydrocarbon, is drawn off at the top of the tower, and kerosene, a slightly heavier hydrocarbon, is drawn off at a lower level. Heavy oils are drawn off near the bottom. Even though some of these components are then almost ready for market or transfer as feedstock for petrochemical plants, most require additional processing before they leave the refinery. These refining steps include catalytic cracking, catalytic reforming, alkylation, desulfurization, dewaxing, treating, and blending.

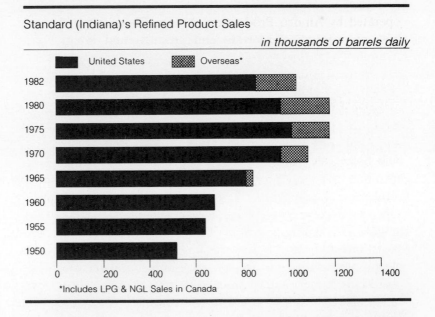

Standard (Indiana)'s Refined Product Sales

in thousands of barrels daily

United States   Overseas*

*Includes LPG & NGL Sales in Canada

The result of this sophisticated and technical process, largely computer programmed and controlled, is a myriad of products. An abbreviated listing includes:

130

Gasolines—in several octane ranges, including aviation fuel.

Jet fuel and kerosene—similar to gasoline but somewhat heavier.

Liquefied petroleum gas—bottled gas for heating, cooking, and crop-drying. Also used as a petrochemical feedstock.

Heating oils—for home furnaces.

Diesel fuels—for trucks, buses, some automobiles, and locomotives.

Industrial fuels—heavy fuels for firing boilers in factories and ships.

Lubricating oils—a wide variety for different types of machinery and automotive engines, transmissions, and differentials.

Greases—many types for special purposes.

Waxes—for candles, waxed paper, and coatings for food product containers.

Coke—solid industrial fuel and electrodes.

Asphalt and road oils—for industries, highways, parking lots.

Agricultural chemicals—such as ammonia fertilizers that bring more crop yield per acre.

White oils and petrolatums—for medicinal purposes.

From refinery-produced chemical feedstock and from liquefied petroleum gases extracted at natural gas processing plants operated by Amoco Production, Amoco Chemicals produces a host of products. Important end products and intermediates include:

Bottles, structural foam products, crates, pallets; antifreeze; carpet backing and yarn; grain, cement, vegetable and other types of bags; self-hinging packages, appliance parts, medical equipment; tires; sports equipment, automobile interior components and front ends; molded rubber goods; caulks and sealants; pleasure boat hulls, bathtubs, industrial tanks and pipe; appliances, furniture, toy, and houseware components; foamed plastics for food packaging; polyester fibers and films for apparel, recording tape, food packaging; thermoplastic engineering resins; water soluble and high-performance paints; high-temperature molded parts and decorative and protective coating; high-performance electric wire insulation; solvents and agricultural chemicals.

Many refinery and chemical plant processes have been developed, patented, and licensed to competitors by Standard as the result of work by scientists employed at its research centers. Others are joint-effort developments with other companies in which Standard scientists contributed in leading roles. Still others are purchased technologies.

The volatility and flammability of the fluids a refinery processes make fire and explosion continuing potential hazards and demand that safety be a first priority. A disastrous explosion and fire occurred on the morning of August 27, 1955, when a vessel at Whiting exploded, sending steel fragments into the air and down over the adjoining neighborhood. A three-year-old boy was killed and his brother injured as they slept in their bed. Walter Rhea, assistant general foreman of the light oil division, suffered a fatal heart attack while enroute to fight the fire. Fortunately, these were the only casualties.

Extinguishing the fire which followed the explosion required eight days. More than 200 men received first aid treatment at the refinery hospital and 140 others were treated at other hospitals and first aid stations in the area.

Despite the spectacular nature of the fire, efforts of company firefighters prevented serious destruction of refinery facilities. Operations were resumed within three months. The fluid hydroformer that exploded was a total loss but most of the units suffered no damage. New units were constructed, substantially modernizing and increasing the capacity of the refinery.

As the characteristics of the crude oil entering the refinery system changed over the years, Standard adapted its refining facilities accordingly. At Texas City, for example, no foreign crude oil was processed prior to 1972. Then, because of a decline

Standard (Indiana)'s

Net Crude Oil & NGL Production vs. Refinery Runs

in thousands of barrels daily

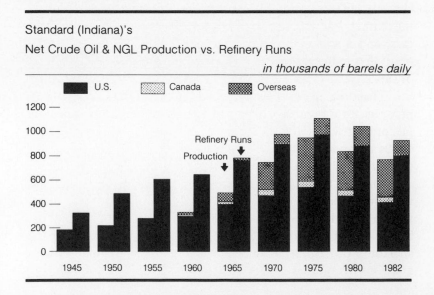

in U.S. oil production and continuing growth in product consumption, the refinery started processing foreign crude in increasing amounts. In 1980 foreign crude oil averaged more than 50 per cent of Texas City's input and over 30 per cent of Standard's total U.S. refinery crude oil charge.

The declining quality of the foreign crudes necessitated a modernization program at Texas City to switch half of the refinery's capacity from medium-sulfur crude oil to heavy- and high-sulfur crudes. Estimates were that 80 per cent of the world's known oil reserves were in the medium- to high-sulfur range. Additionally, prices were lower than those for low-sulfur "sweet" crude oils which were also less plentiful. To be competitive, refineries able to process lower-quality oils were essential.

Alterations of refinery processing capabilities were also mandated by the federal government's required phase-down in the tetraethyl lead content of gasolines. As lead-free gasoline demand increased with the growth in the number of vehicles using only that type of fuel, Amoco Oil in 1979 began a multi-million dollar expansion of gasoline upgrading capability at five of its refineries.

Conservation, the increase in the number of fuel-efficient cars, and consumer resistance to higher gasoline prices forced other adjustments in the manufacturing and marketing approaches of the company. Historically, it had always been difficult for the oil industry to match advance estimates of demand with the construction of refinery capacity. As recently as 1978, refineries in the United States were operating at almost 90 per cent of capacity, and new refineries were being planned to serve a growing market. But with higher prices, smaller and more fuel-efficient cars, and a softening of the economy, demand lessened to the point that refineries in 1981 were operating at only 68.5 per cent of capacity.

Theodore R. (Ted) Eck, Standard's chief economist, saw no prospect for a reversal of this reduced consumption of gasoline. He predicted gasoline consumption would decline during the 1980s by about 30 per cent from its peak in 1978 and refinery capacity by about 20 per cent from its peak in 1981.

Another factor in the picture was that the OPEC countries were finally beginning to realize their dream of greater participation in the "downstream" operations of refining and marketing. Saudi Arabia committed $10 billion to such projects, and the sheikdom of Bahrain, with financial support from Saudi Arabia and Kuwait, another oil-rich country, was building a $400 million

133

petrochemical complex. "OPEC is firmly set on the road toward greater involvement in refinery operations," declared a report from the OPEC secretariat in Vienna. "OPEC countries aspire to progress from the relatively simple technological state of raw material production and exports to the more complex one of processing these materials and exporting goods with a high technological content . . . and increase export earnings."

The products of these OPEC refineries would obviously be competitive with the overseas refineries belonging to United States companies as well as in export markets for American refined products. Faced with declining demand as well as the certainty of increased competition, oil refiners in the United States were forced to close their least economic refineries. Some of these refineries were not equipped to handle the lower grades of crude being imported and would have required millions of dollars of additional investment to remain viable.

In evaluating its own situation, Standard in early 1981 decided to close down its Wood River, Illinois, refinery, and in 1982 closed refineries at Baltimore, Maryland, and at Sugar Creek, Missouri. The two largest refineries—at Whiting, Indiana, and Texas City, Texas—had been modernized. These, with refineries at Salt Lake City, Utah; Casper, Wyoming; Mandan, North Dakota; Savannah, Georgia, and Yorktown, Virginia, were expected to provide sufficient capacity to meet future product demand.

Standard (Indiana)'s Refinery Capacity

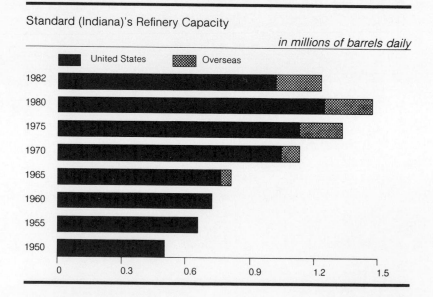

in millions of barrels daily

Over the years, Standard had closed down refineries at Zilwaukee, Michigan; Laramie and Greybull, Wyoming; Superior and Destrehan, Louisiana; Neodesha, Kansas, and El Dorado, Arkansas. All were older, smaller plants that had become technically obsolete and therefore uneconomic and non-competitive. So refinery closings were not new to Standard. In each case— including the 1981 and 1982 shutdowns—Standard found jobs for affected employees in other operations, allowed early retirement benefits to be paid or gave generous severance allowances.

OPEC, the Embargo, and Controls

13

In October, 1973, Arab oil exporting countries imposed an embargo on oil shipments to the United States and certain other countries in retaliation for those nations' support of Israel. America's imports of Arab oil amounted only to 5 per cent of domestic demand, but product shortages materialized across the country.

The ensuing energy "crisis" focused the attention of the general public, the Congress, and regulatory bodies on oil more sharply than ever before. Oil and natural gas are part of the country's store of natural resources, but the embargo—with its subsequent "long lines" at gasoline service stations and sharp price increases—raised questions about the husbandry of those resources. Should government become more involved?

Earlier, government control was limited essentially to the prorationing of the amount of oil and gas which certain states would permit to be taken from the ground. Five states adopted measures to prevent wasting these natural resources in periods when capacity for production exceeded consumer needs.

In the years after World War II, however, the advantages of overseas lower-cost, higher-yield wells had changed the nature of the world oil business. For example, where once Standard's profits had run neck and neck with those of Gulf, Texaco, Mobil, and Standard Oil of California, Standard (Indiana) in 1958 found those companies earning twice what Standard did, largely because of their overseas operations, particularly in the Middle East.

Oilfields in the United States were not as prolific as those in the Middle East, and so their operating costs were substantially higher. But it was clear that the U.S. price of oil could not be insulated from foreign competition any more than could the prices of lead, zinc, copper, wheat, wool, steel, textiles, automobiles, T.V. sets, or anything else.

The cost advantages of overseas operations were soon reflected in a sharp rise in the amount of oil imported into the U.S. In 1955 and 1956, imports were increasing by more than 10 per cent each year. As U.S. production declined and exploration was reduced, the country was faced with the specter of a domestic oil industry so enervated that the ability of the United States to be self-sufficient in time of war or national emergency was seriously in doubt. As usual, when Washington sensed a crisis, it turned to controls rather than to a rational analysis of the problem.

In 1957, voluntary oil import controls were announced by the U.S. government and were complied with by most of the industry. Although Standard, with its largely domestic base, was responsive to the idea of import controls, it found itself at a disadvantage because of the historical reference points on which the import quotas were based.

Because the company had no history of imports of any consequence, Standard was limited in the amount of lower-priced foreign crude oil and products it could bring in. On the other hand, for companies like Exxon, Texaco, and Standard Oil of California, with crude oil from the Middle East, and the output of refineries in the Caribbean which were processing crude from Venezuela, there was a distinct advantage. Those companies had a history of importing foreign oils.

In 1959, the voluntary controls were made mandatory. With the imposition of mandatory controls, Standard pointed out the unfairness to a company such as Standard, which had traditionally emphasized production within the United States and had only recently become an importer. Refiners with long records as major importers east of the Rockies were given quotas for the last half of 1959 that averaged 10.4 per cent of their refinery needs; Standard, by contrast, received a quota that was only 5.1 per cent of its crude input requirements.

After almost a decade, the results of this bias were described by Swearingen to an industry association in April, 1968. He began by emphasizing the support of his company and himself for some kind of import controls. "While our individual views of the most effective means of control may vary," he said, "we in the industry know that certain restrictions are necessary to preserve a strong domestic producing and refining complex for the nation's security. The largest energy-consuming country in history cannot afford to rely on overseas oil lifelines which can be severed overnight by political disturbances in some other part of the globe.

"However," he said, "there has been a gradual, but persistent erosion of the oil import program over the nine years of its existence—an erosion that has reached serious proportions. This has resulted from the granting of a growing list of exceptions to favored companies, individuals, or special groups of importers on grounds having little relation to domestic security.

"These exceptions have included such things as proportionately greater allocations to small refiners than to large refiners; allocations to customers of the oil industry, namely the chemical companies, who use the argument of aiding the nation's balance of payments to gain free access to foreign feedstocks; special allocations to a few refiners for the purpose of improving the economy of Puerto Rico or upgrading the quality of jobs in the Virgin Islands; and special historical protection for old, established importers and for a few northern-tier refiners. Lately, the import program has also been used as a device to help improve air quality. Each distortion of the import program has led it further from its fundamental purpose and has brought added confusion to our energy supply problems."

The economics of oil at this time were heavily weighted in favor of going into the international field rather than exploring at home. Despite the risks of overseas activities, here was an opportunity for money to work at a greater rate of return than in some of the other places in which the company was investing. The number of wells drilled in the United States, because of government attitudes toward the domestic industry, had dropped from 58,000 in 1956 to 46,700 in 1960 and to only 38,000 wells in 1966.

Sensitivity about national security and the increasing dependence on foreign oil led to the appointment in 1969 of a special Cabinet Task Force on Oil Import Controls, headed by George P. Shultz, then Secretary of Labor.

The subject was not a new one. A year earlier, the House Committee on Interior and Insular Affairs had made its own examination of the program and had come to this conclusion:

"Three presidents of the nation, beginning with President Eisenhower and continuing with President Kennedy and President Johnson, together with innumerable special task forces, commissions, and study groups, as well as several congressional committees, have all been of one mind on the objective of the mandatory oil import program. Its one and only reason for being is to insure the national security of this nation by reducing the country's dependence on foreign imports and assuring a strong and vigorous domestic petroleum industry."

The recommendation of the Cabinet Task Force headed by Shultz was unrealistic at best and so narrow in its focus as to be irrelevant. It centered its attention almost exclusively on crude oil, as if this were the only source of energy on the planet. The fact that natural gas, the second largest source of energy in the U.S., is produced largely by the same companies—employing the same equipment, technology, manpower, and capital which produce oil —was ignored.

As Swearingen pointed out at the time, "The U.S. energy market is a complex of different sources, including not only oil and gas, but coal, electricity, nuclear and hydro power, whose various usages, availabilities, and price levels interact directly on each other." He pointed out that any thorough economic analysis would have to take into account the interactions of these components before recommending far-reaching changes affecting the source of supply and price of one of the major components.

Historical hindsight permits comparisons in a few key areas which provide an index of how far off the mark the Task Force was. First, it confined its report to the decade up to 1980— focusing on only a ten-year forecast when it was already acknowledged that the United States had about a ten-year known supply of oil to cover that period.

In the area of prophecy, the Task Force's statements were an embarrassment. The report predicted that if no changes were made in the system, total U.S. imports of crude oil and products from the Eastern Hemisphere by 1980 would be no higher—or only some 500,000 barrels a day higher—than in 1970.

In place of the then-current quota system, the Task Force recommended adoption of a tariff program giving preference to oil from certain foreign countries, and designed to force an increase in the use of lower-cost imported oil—while bringing about an initial reduction of about 30 cents a barrel in the price of domestic crude, with further reduction envisioned later.

But even if enough low-cost foreign oil were brought in to drive down domestic prices by as much as 80 cents a barrel— which was the basis used in the report to test the risk to national security—U.S. dependence on the Eastern Hemisphere by 1980 would still be less than two million barrels a day, the report said.

For its part, Standard predicted that, at the sharply reduced price level used by the Task Force to test the security risk, Eastern Hemisphere imports probably would rise to over 10 million barrels a day—or more than 40 per cent of total U.S. demand—by 1980. Although import volumes were not at that level in 1980—having decreased to about 5.5 million barrels daily from 6.0 million in 1977 when production began from Alaska's giant Prudhoe Bay field—Standard's prediction as to the percentage of imports was right on target.

Testifying before the subcommittee on Mines and Mining of the House Committee on Interior and Insular Affairs in Washington on March 16, 1970, Swearingen submitted his own recommendations with respect to imports. They were:

1. The overall level of imports should be controlled through a quota system at approximately present (1970) levels.
2. Imports should increase at about the same rate that demand increases.
3. A reserve domestic producing capacity of about one million barrels per day should be maintained.
4. When reserve domestic producing capacity falls to the established minimum, imports should be increased, with preferential treatment being accorded Canadian production.
5. Imports should be allocated to prime users of crude in direct proportion to refinery runs.
6. The special exemptions included in the present (1970) program should be eliminated as quickly as practicable.

Recommendations 5 and 6 reflected the need for a policy to correct the distortions of the original program.

Two events in the Middle East had underscored the necessity of finding some way to be less dependent on oil from this highly volatile area. One warning signal came at the time of the first Suez crisis in 1956 when the British ended a 74-year military occupation of the canal area, and Egypt nationalized the canal.

The Six-Day War between Egypt and Israel in 1967 was a further cause for alarm, although Standard's facilities in the Gulf of Suez and other Middle East locations were undamaged and remained in operation. However, the closing of the Suez Canal to all shipping from June, 1967, to June, 1975, greatly lengthened normal tanker shipping routes, and added substantially to transportation costs.

In 1970, the company accompanied its annual report to

stockholders with a pessimistic view of America's energy policies. Standard called it a year which provided a "sobering foretaste of a period of energy scarcity which may lie ahead." During the year, there were shortages of natural gas and low-sulfur coal, which forced electric utilities and other industrial fuel users to turn to low-sulfur residual oil to meet new pollution control standards. Supplies of oil were stretched thin and shortages of electric power were widespread.

As the company looked at the year in review, it made these comments: "Once again, we had a demonstration of the unreliability of imported oil and the necessity for reserve domestic capacity. Actions by governments in the Eastern Hemisphere, restricting both production and transportation of crude, disrupted world oil markets.

"Tanker rates soared, as every available vessel was pressed into long-haul service from the Persian Gulf to meet Europe's needs. Suddenly, Middle East oil ceased to be low in cost. . . . Since then (remember, this was only 1970) the major Middle Eastern producing countries have successfully negotiated new agreements calling for sharp increases in crude prices over the next five years . . .

"The fact remains that (our) nation's proved reserves of oil and natural gas are declining as energy demand rises, while the cost of imported supplies escalates and deliverability becomes more and more uncertain. This trend must be reversed if the future needs of the United States for reliable energy supplies are to be met. The situation demands a clear national policy that our security requires increased domestic production of oil and gas and adequate economic incentives to find and develop the needed new reserves."

Perhaps the best commentary on what became an incoherent struggle to formulate a national energy policy on the need for self-reliance and access to supplies was written 20 years before the crunch of the Seventies became a reality. The commentary was the product of the President's Materials Policy Commission, popularly known as the Paley Commission, which Harry S. Truman constituted on January 22, 1951. Its task was to study the broader and longer range aspects of the nation's raw materials problem, Truman said, adding that "we cannot allow shortages of materials to jeopardize our national security nor to become a bottleneck to our economic expansion."

The Commission submitted its report in five volumes on

June 2, 1952. Entitled "Resources for Freedom," subjects of the report's first four volumes reflect the scope of the study: Foundations for Growth and Security, The Outlook for Key Commodities, The Outlook for Energy Sources, and The Promise of Technology. The fifth volume was made up of selected reports to the Commission.

Among the most serious of the report's findings was the dependence of the United States on other free world nations for critical materials the U.S. hadn't been able to find or produce in sufficient quantities within its own borders. Or, as Commission chairman William S. Paley phrased it, "the worsening relationship between our requirements and our means of satisfying them."

The premise which the Commission formulated as a base for its report also is revealing: "The overall objective of a national materials policy for the United States should be to insure an adequate and dependable flow of materials at the lowest cost consistent with national security and with the welfare of friendly nations."

The contents of the report drew little or no public attention until the late Edward R. Murrow, a noted pioneer radio and television news reporter and commentator, hosted an hour-long CBS documentary on January 10, 1954. Few, if any, government officials heeded the warnings.

John E. Swearingen reminded Washington news media representatives of the Commission's prophetic findings in an address at the National Press Club on July 24, 1973. Citing the report, Swearingen said:

"As a nation, we are threatened but not alert . . . In order to take advantage of its energy opportunities the nation must find new reserves; cut energy transportation costs; bring into practical use vast low-grade resources not presently economic; broaden and increase the efficiency of the conversion of primary fuels into more convenient secondary forms . . . (and finally) The federal government is not at present properly equipped to carry out its responsibilities for dealing singlemindedly with the many aspects of the problem. Dozens of government organizations—departments and agencies, bureaus and offices, and interdependent committees—have an active concern in one or more aspects of the problem . . . some necessary jobs are not being done well enough; others are not being done at all; and the whole effort lacks sufficient coordination."

Twenty-two years after the Paley Commission report was

issued and Standard's officers made their 1974 annual report to stockholders, the situation had not changed much. "It will take a decade of sacrifice, a change in lifestyle, and realistic measures to restore an adequate degree of energy self-sufficiency," they asserted. "The need for a coherent, long-range national energy policy and program is critical, if we are to remain in control of our own destiny."

Oil inevitably meshed with government because of its vital role in the functioning of an industrial society. But shortages induced by the Arab oil embargo of 1973-74 brought the federal government into the oil regulatory arena to a degree unprecedented in peacetime. Government's ultimate response was more controls, more regulation.

At the Senior Management Conference in 1977, Walter R. Peirson provided a succinct summary of the regulatory problems which Amoco Oil Company faced during the decade of the Seventies.

"We have been regulated and re-regulated to the point of distraction," the president of Amoco Oil said. "The purposes have not been without good intentions in some instances, but the methods and the execution have been generally bad.

"Controls have cost us money and profits, but more important, they have cost Amoco a considerable degree of flexibility. In the competitive world of refining-marketing, the inflexibility of allocations and channels of sale imposed by government controls has been one of our major challenges."

The oil and gas industry was no stranger to government regulation. Federal regulation of natural gas, for example, began in 1938 with passage of the Natural Gas Act, which empowered the Federal Power Commission (FPC) to regulate delivered prices for natural gas transported by pipeline companies across state lines. The United States Supreme Court ruling on June 7, 1954, in the case of *Phillips Petroleum Company vs. Wisconsin, et al.*, compounded regulation and threw the industry into chaos. The court's 1954 ruling expanded the FPC authority to include regulation of field (or wellhead) prices of natural gas sold by producers to interstate pipelines. This meant that instead of regulating delivered prices of natural gas sold by a comparatively small number of interstate pipelines, the FPC then had to attempt to regulate prices of natural gas sold by thousands of producers at the wellhead from thousands of wells having different technical and economic characteristics.

After six years of trying to set prices on what amounted to a conventional utility-type cost-of-service basis, the FPC concluded this system was not workable. "Producers of natural gas cannot by any stretch of the imagination be properly classified as traditional public utilities," the FPC intoned, after attempting to treat them in exactly that manner.

In 1960, as an alternative to the failed system, the FPC divided the principal gas producing regions into 23 separate areas and set guideline ceiling prices for each area (the so-called area-wide pricing system), believing that complexities would be reduced when it no longer attempted to regulate individual wells.

But there was one price for gas being sold under existing contracts, another price for gas to be sold under new contracts, and inherent regulatory problems that resulted in a backlog of thousands of cases begging for FPC decisions. Nevertheless, in 1963, the FPC reported to Congress that the new system "had become well-entrenched and was a major working tool in the regulation of independent natural gas producers."

The gas producers thought otherwise. The first pricing decision of the Commission had been challenged three years earlier and still wasn't settled. In this case, dealing with the Permian Basin area of West Texas, the hearings continued over a period of four years and the transcripts ran to more than 30,000 pages.

And costs were added to confusion. In October of 1963, the FPC sent a 10-pound questionnaire to 114 producing companies. It contained 500 pages and 35 pages of instructions. Standard's U.S. exploration and production subsidiary estimated that it would take 23,000 man-hours to complete the questionnaire.

Because the 1954 decision did not apply to gas sold intrastate, Standard benefited from a decision which had been made in 1941 to establish an affiliate called Amoco Gas Company with headquarters at Houston for the specific purpose of supplying the fuel needs of Amoco's Texas City refinery and to sell additional gas to industrial customers in the unregulated intrastate market. Later, Amoco Gas was transferred to Amoco Production Company. Its activities were considerably expanded to buy gas from other producers and to supply gas to affiliated companies and to the rapidly growing industrial belt along the Houston ship channel.

The artificially low price of interstate gas mandated by the FPC under the authority resulting from the 1954 Supreme Court decision made gas far cheaper than alternative fuels. This resulted in a soaring, unbridled demand for natural gas, the growth of which outstripped that of all other fuels.

Two events during the Seventies shocked the country into a recognition that a new natural gas policy was needed. The first was the Arab oil embargo of 1973-1974, when industrial and utility customers dependent on oil, found supplies cut off and discovered that gas as an alternate fuel was not available in adequate quantities to take up the slack. A second shock occurred during the winter of 1976-1977 when extreme cold triggered a widespread shortage of natural gas in the eastern two-thirds of the United States.

When the sudden surge in demand arose, there was no spare production capacity to meet it. The FPC itself had recognized the potential dangers created by its pricing policy and several years earlier had established a nine-level user priority system, which further distorted efforts to create a balanced energy program.

In one reaction to the situation, the U.S. Department of the Interior ordered an investigation of natural gas production in the Gulf of Mexico. A consultant, with the assistance of the Federal Power Commission, Senate Antitrust and Monopoly Subcommittee, and the United States Geological Survey, spent 11 days on the assignment, reported sharply falling gas production, and charged that some gas in four fields was shut-in. One of the fields was South Marsh Island Block 48 field, part of which was operated by Amoco Production Company. Some columnists and editorial writers accused oil companies of deliberately withholding gas to drive up prices. The secretary of the interior, Cecil Andrus, commented that complex geological and economic issues were involved, and initiated a second investigation. His responsibility, he said, was "to see that the maximum gas is produced from the Outer Continental Shelf consistent with safety and good conservation practices."

The second study was conducted by an impartial group under the direction of the National Research Council, an arm of the National Academy of Science (NAS). The commission included consumer group representatives and public officials as well as technical experts. They spent nearly a year reviewing data from the United States Geological Survey and operating information from the confidential files of the companies involved. Their ultimate finding was that the fields were mature, offered very little opportunity for increased production in the short-term, and such wells as were shut-in reflected sound operating and safety considerations at the time. Andrus confirmed that there had been no withholding of gas.

145

Commenting on the problems created by government pricing policies for natural gas, Swearingen pointed out in the company magazine *SpaN* in 1977 that even the highest price then permitted producers for new gas sold into interstate commerce was less than half the delivered price of liquefied natural gas imported from Algeria, about half the anticipated price of gas from Alaska's North Slope, and only about two-thirds the price of imported crude oil, based on equivalent energy value.

"As a result of such short-sighted policy," he wrote, "the United States for nearly a decade has been consuming gas faster than new gas supplies have been found and developed. Our supply in 1967 would have lasted nearly 16 years at the rate of consumption then being experienced. In 1975, we had only a 10-year supply at current consumption rates—11½ years if we count North Slope gas, which thus far remains inaccessible.

"Only in those states where natural gas is produced and where it can be sold in the competitive, unregulated intrastate market are supplies adequate," he continued. "From that fact alone, it should be obvious that the way to prevent further shortages is to free the interstate market from the controls which have bound it since 1954."

It was not only the spokesmen for the oil industry who surveyed the situation and assessed the damage caused by government policies. Stephen Chapman, writing in the liberally oriented *New Republic*, saw it the same way:

"What usually happens when the government imposes price controls on a commodity is that it becomes scarcer as producers who can't make money at the controlled price invest elsewhere, even as consumers are stimulated to consume more of the commodity than they would at a higher, uncontrolled price. By 1968, it was clear that the FPC controls had produced precisely this result.

"That was the first year that total annual consumption of gas exceeded the amount of new gas found in the United States. In 1971, recognizing the looming shortage, the FPC substantially raised the price producers could charge. But by then the damage had been done, and the next few years exposed it. The first shortage occurred in 1973, and severe ones struck in the winters of 1976-1977 and 1977-1978."

President Carter, rather than acting to deal with the problem, proposed a program with his energy czar, James Schlesinger, which actually expanded it. Specifically, he announced he was opposed to the growing sentiment in Congress for decontrol of interstate gas sales and instead proposed that controls be extended to gas sold intrastate as well. After 18 months of Congressional infighting, negotiating, and maneuvering, agreement was reached in October of 1978 for passage of the Natural Gas Policy Act of 1978 (NGPA).

Standard opposed the Act, contending that it was so complex a piece of legislation that it would create one more administrative morass. The law in fact was complex, with more than two dozen different price categories. It established even more vintages of gas with special price calculations required in each instance. In order to qualify for a new gas price, a well had to meet certain dimensional criteria, such as being so many miles away from the nearest well and so much deeper than the zone encountered in a marker well. To qualify for the "deep" gas price, the gas productive zone had to be one found below 15,000 feet. Gas produced from tight gas sands qualified for an "incentive" price but the definition of tight sand was stringent.

The administrative maze which Standard anticipated as materializing from the Act was not long in springing full-blown from the bureaucratic ground in which it had been planted. At the regional offices of Amoco Production in New Orleans, Houston, and Denver, it was necessary to double the gas marketing staff merely to accommodate the tremendous amount of paper work in filing requirements associated with provisions of the Act.

Still, the Natural Gas Policy Act of 1978 did have some positive effects in terms of planning capital commitments. Although it brought intrastate gas under federal price controls, it lifted some prices and, as Chapman pointed out, ended "the absurd dichotomy between interstate and intrastate gas." In 1979, the industry drilled 14,681 new successful exploratory and development gas wells in the U.S. compared to 9,085 in 1976, an increase of 5,596 wells, according to American Petroleum Institute statistics. Many experts were thinking that the long-range prospects for finding large new domestic reserves of gas were better than those for oil, although the number of successful oil wells increased 2,324 to 19,383 in 1979 from 17,059 in 1976.

For Standard, the effects of some price relief on natural gas production and the anticipation of relief from federal price controls on domestic crude oil were particularly beneficial. The impact of decontrol could be seen in the decision of Amoco Production to earmark almost a third of its 1980 exploration

147

budget for wells deeper than 15,000 feet. In Mississippi, the company budgeted $25 million to drill a single 26,500 foot well.

The government, however, continued to ignore the evidence. In 1977, James Schlesinger, the Secretary of Energy, had added his name to the list of doomsayers about the world's hydrocarbon reserves by announcing that the world's gas supplies should be regarded as "gone."

While new finds of substantial gas reserves continued to be reported, the government moved obstinately in the other direction, seeking to reduce the consumption of natural gas by federal fiat. The most deleterious of these efforts written into the 1978 Powerplant and Industrial Fuel Use Act forbade the construction of any new natural gas boilers by utilities or industrial firms and required existing ones to be converted to coal by 1990. The result was to force several utilities to switch from gas to oil, which, of course, was both in scarcer supply and more costly.

Even the promise of decontrol by 1985 was something of a myth. The legislation gave the president or the Congress the option of continuing price controls on "new" gas, "high cost" gas, and some intrastate gas for 18 months following the scheduled January 1, 1985, price control expiration date. As the Act stood, prices on all other categories of gas would be controlled indefinitely. The U.S. Department of Energy estimated that 28 to 34 per cent of the nation's domestically produced natural gas would still be under the Act's price controls in 1990.

Before the 1973-74 embargo galvanized officialdom to seek remedies of some kind, there were the painful experiences of 1972: Shortages of heating oil in the intense cold of the winter that year in the Midwest and Northeast; heavy summer demand for gasoline; and the mandated switch (for environmental reasons) of industrial companies and utilities from high-sulfur coal to natural gas or heating oil for boiler fuel, which worsened shortages and exacerbated confusion as to what course should be taken. The experiences of 1972 simply were the results of imbalance of supply and demand brought on by economically irrational production and market restraints, and of decades of social disregard for the environment.

Product shortages brought outcries from citizens and politicians for government to "do something." The federal government lashed out right and left. "Big Oil" was the villain. Bureaucracy was to be the Knight in Shining Armor.

Congressional and administrative reaction to the outcries

spawned a series of new agencies at the federal level. The tale of their formation begins with the Department of the Interior which had a long history of responsibilities in the governance of natural resources, and with the Office of Emergency Preparedness whose duties in times of national peril clearly involved energy supply.

The imposition of wage and price controls in August of 1971 gave rise to the Cost of Living Council (CLC) whose program was administered by the Internal Revenue Service (IRS) of the Treasury Department. The Energy Policy Office (EPO), an executive level organization, was created at the time of the Arab oil embargo. It was succeeded by the Federal Energy Office (FEO). Next came the Federal Energy Administration (FEA) which, in turn, was followed by the establishment in 1977 of the cabinet-level Department of Energy (DOE) with a payroll of some 20,000 employees and a 1979 budget of $10 billion.

Each of these various organizational units was headed during its day by a succession of officials whom media representatives and citizens at large delighted in referring to as "energy czars."

As government became more and more involved at every level, submitting to a flagrant, inbred tendency to build an ever larger bureaucracy, it also became more and more distant from the workings of the marketplace.

Management decisions were affected not only by the effects of bureaucracy but by the government's concurrent search for a coherent energy policy. The resulting, unrelenting confusion was to continue throughout the decade, creating severe restrictions upon the ability of Standard and other oil companies to manage their affairs and to make decisions. This was the environment in which Standard found itself.

While these ills plagued the nation, Swearingen and other Standard executives continued to sound the alarm about the peril to America of its increasing dependence on foreign oil. If not before, there now was ample justification for doing so: The Six-Day Israeli-Arab war in June, 1967, which closed the Suez Canal until June, 1975; the Israeli-Arab Yom Kippur war in October, 1973, followed that same month by the Arab embargo on oil exports to the U.S. which remained in force until March, 1974; and the quadrupling of oil prices by Arab oil producing nations in December, 1973. Meanwhile, federal price controls remained in effect on domestically produced crude oil.

On May 1, 1973, President Nixon had suspended volume restrictions on oil imports and installed a license-fee system in place of import duties. The objective of these and other provisions of the presidential proclamation was to relieve domestic short- and mid-term shortages while encouraging long-term domestic energy development. But war between Egypt and Israel broke out, followed by the embargo, before a long-range policy such as Swearingen and other industry leaders called for could be debated, much less adopted.

In the midst of worldwide energy shortages, Standard in 1973 produced more crude oil and natural gas than in any previous year. Pipelines were expanded and refinery production increased by 8 per cent. Domestically, in an effort to be sure supplies were spread fairly, the company established an allocation program limiting dealers, jobbers, and agents to no more than was provided them in 1972. In the fall, mandatory federal allocation rules for crude oil and products such as gasoline, propane, heating oil, diesel fuel, jet fuel, kerosene, and asphalt took effect. Standard declined to bid on new business and cancelled sales promotion advertising. It urged consumers to restrict their driving, dial down thermostats, and generally conserve energy. Shortages prevailed in Europe also; West Germans could not drive on Sundays; Great Britain instituted a three-day workweek.

The change in world prices for oil was to have a substantial impact on Standard Oil (Indiana). "Dramatic alterations in the environment in which our company operates took place in 1974," the management reported to stockholders in the 1974 annual report. "The embargo on shipments of oil to the United States from the Middle East during the first quarter resulted in product shortages, while the worldwide price of crude oil and refined products rose sharply by the unilateral decision of the major oil exporting nations.

"However, the higher costs of crude oil and refined products were allowed to be passed through to consumers, and the price of new domestic oil was permitted to rise to approximate world prices. The resulting higher cash flow made possible a significant increase in exploratory and development drilling for oil and natural gas within the United States."

Standard wasted no time in committing these funds to a search for new supplies, and the largest single portion of 1974 discretionary spending was devoted to efforts to find and develop oil and natural gas within the United States.

Another aspect of government reaction to the embargo was not so beneficial for Standard. In an effort to provide small

U.S. & World Crude Oil Prices

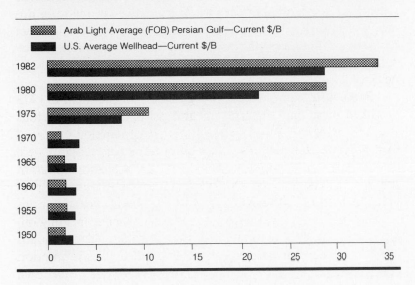

Arab Light Average (FOB) Persian Gulf—Current $/B
U.S. Average Wellhead—Current $/B

refiners with access to foreign oil, the government introduced a program called "entitlements." The effect of the entitlements program, designed ostensibly to "equalize" crude oil acquisition costs among refiners, actually penalized those who had worked to find oil in the United States and to reward those who had not made such an investment.

The stated purpose of the entitlements program was to force U.S. companies which refined a higher-than-average amount of domestic oil, which remained under federal price controls, to make cash payments each month to refiners who processed less price-controlled crude oil than the national average.

Part of the payments went to small refiners that government planners decided needed special assistance. The "small refiner bias" encouraged construction of inefficient, small "teakettle" refineries that would not have been built without subsidies mandated by the federal government program. This approach, of course, ignored the fact that smaller refineries tend to be less efficient and more costly; therefore, despite the intercompany subsidy payments, the overall cost to the consumer ended up as more rather than less.

John Swearingen was an outspoken critic of the program from its beginning. As the amount of the direct cash payments to

151

Standard's competitors passed $1 billion in April, 1979, Swearingen said: "Since its introduction in 1974, the program, coupled with crude oil price controls, has betrayed the nation's quest for energy independence and helped ensure the success of the OPEC cartel by discouraging domestic oil production and subsidizing crude oil imports."

Swearingen pointed out that "Standard's cash entitlements outlays (up to that time) of more than $1 billion are roughly equal to the cost of constructing a large new refinery or the drilling of more than 4,000 domestic oil and gas wells. Instead, the major portion of the money has gone directly to subsidize those companies which have high percentages of imported crude oil in their supplies."

Standard was penalized by this system more than most other oil companies. "Entitlements and crude oil price controls have punished those companies which have invested heavily in domestic oil exploration and production over the past several decades," Swearingen said.

"The entitlements program was a mistake from the beginning and has been made worse by the creation of additional unearned benefits for special interest groups," he said.

The cost of entitlements simultaneously raised Standard's refined product prices and lowered those of many of its competitors, Swearingen noted. "Our dealers and jobbers have been at a tremendous disadvantage when we are required by federal law to subsidize their competitors. Standard's entitlements costs during this period (1974-1979) represent more than two cents per gallon of gasoline sales."

The Standard chairman pointed out that companies receiving entitlements money "are not always small independents. Several large oil companies have received entitlements payments, as have some large companies from other industries which also own refineries. Several oil companies have received more money via entitlements than they earned in the marketplace in recent years."

By July, 1980, the amount of money Standard paid to its competitors under this program had passed $2 billion, "roughly equal to the investment needed to develop a 50,000 barrel per day capacity to produce oil from shale," Swearingen pointed out.

Following the end of the embargo in March, 1974, oil companies faced an entirely new marketing situation. For the first time in many years, the domestic and Free World oil industry processed and sold less volume than it had in previous years. Distribution of crude oil came under strict government regulation. As a result of directives from the Federal Energy Administration, Standard sold 23 million barrels of crude oil to other companies during 1974. The 1973 advertising campaign asking customers to "dial down" their thermostats and "slow down" on the highway was continued. The marketing emphasis was almost entirely on the sale of tires, batteries, and automotive accessories.

Modernization of Standard's distribution network continued. In 1975, Amoco Oil offered its 2,812 commission agents an opportunity to become Amoco Oil jobbers, in effect operating their own independent businesses.

The use of foreign crude oil continued to grow. Even so, Standard was less dependent on foreign crude supplies than the industry at large. In 1976, Standard was processing 28 per cent foreign crude versus 40 per cent for the industry, though Peirson warned that the failure of the federal government to provide adequate incentives for domestic exploration would probably bring Standard up to the industry average by 1981.

There were other disruptive effects. The unprecedented cold winter of 1976-1977 produced a record demand for fuel oil and natural gas. However, profits were down because of the need to take costly measures in transportation, labor, and maintenance to overcome the problems of frozen waterways and other operating difficulties created by the bitter cold.

The overthrow of the Shah of Iran in December of 1978 put additional pressure on supplies. The subsequent disruption of Iran's oil fields removed up to five million barrels of crude oil daily from the world market. Standard itself lost 180,000 barrels daily of proprietary oil production as a result of the Iranian revolution, a loss that seriously disrupted its supplies of crude and products.

The Department of Energy (DOE) attempted to allocate gasoline supplies to assure fair distribution but without success. In the summer of 1979, long lines of automobiles reappeared at service stations. The Department of Energy and the International Energy Agency estimated the worldwide shortage at 10 to 15 per cent of current demand. Standard reported to its customers through a newspaper advertisement that its supply of gasoline and distillates was only about four-fifths of what it had been at the same time the previous year.

The DOE issued regulations requiring the oil companies to

153

allocate gasoline to customers using the June, 1977, to June, 1978, period as a base; in general, allocations were 10 to 15 per cent less than during the same period the previous year, although demand continued to increase. Charges inevitably were made that the oil companies had contrived the shortage to increase profits; but Standard reported that its profit on each gallon of gasoline sold was only 3 cents; thus if all its profit on the sale of gasoline were wiped out, there would be little impact on the price at the pump.

Despite price increases and gasoline lines, oil imports and gasoline usage in the United States climbed steadily until 1979 when, for the first time since the Arab oil embargo, Americans actually reduced their consumption of gasoline, from 7.4 million barrels a day in 1978 to seven million in 1979. Still, the nation continued to import more than 40 per cent of its petroleum needs; its economy continued vulnerable to disruption of supplies, particularly from the Middle East.

Calls for a national energy policy echoed redundantly from every corner of the land. Congress seemed unable to develop a consensus which would reconcile the conflicting special interests of its various constituencies. In July of 1979, President Carter made an effort to prod Congress to approve his energy plan by taking the case to the American people in nationwide addresses in which he described the energy problem as "the moral equivalent of war."

In his speech, the President called for additional reliance on nuclear power and broader utilization of coal. He did not, however, propose accelerating the slow pace of decontrol of domestic oil prices which he had announced on April 5, 1979. In his April announcement, President Carter included a warning that "the most effective action we can take to encourage both conservation and production here at home is to stop rewarding those who import foreign oil and to stop encouraging waste by holding the price of American oil down far below its replacement cost or its true value." It was a strange contradiction of noxious anti-oil industry statements in the President's frequent comments to the public, and contrary to legislation his administration promoted.

As part of the energy plan which he advocated in his July speech, the President reiterated his call for a so-called "windfall profits" tax on the oil companies. Although the President's description of the tax made it appear the funds would come from oil company profits, it was in reality an excise tax on revenues which, as it was described in the administration's message to Congress, would be "imposed at the wellhead on the owners of property interests in domestic crude oil." The producers would not realize any of the "profit" the government proposed to tax away.

Congress wrangled with the issue of a national energy policy until March 1, 1980, when it passed legislation including the so-called windfall profits tax. Through a series of complicated procedures, part of the funds from this tax were to be distributed to develop synthetic fuels and other new forms of domestic energy. Other parts of the funds from the tax were committed to various welfare constituencies.

One of the panaceas advanced during the period of gasoline and energy shortages was that of gasohol, a mixture of gasoline with alcohol derived from grains. Special incentives were authorized by partial or complete waiver of federal and (in some states) state gasoline taxes to encourage oil companies to produce gasohol. These concessions made gasohol economically competitive, though from the standpoint of energy conservation it was clearly a negative.

Scientists were able to demonstrate that to raise corn and produce alcohol consumed 2.2 times as much energy as would be produced. It did not seem a logical approach to stretching energy supplies, but tax incentives and public pressure for alternatives led to a number of tests of its marketability. Standard initiated gasohol sales in Nebraska, Iowa, Wisconsin, and Illinois. Where tax subsidies were in place to make gasohol competitive in price, some of the motoring public bought the product; where there were no tax incentives, gasohol suffered a price disadvantage and was not successful in the marketplace.

Shortages of crude oil and refined products deriving from the Arab oil embargo of 1973-74 impelled the American government to freeze all petroleum prices as of May 15, 1973. Complex regulations issued by bureaucrats who did not understand the oil industry were confusing and sometimes contradictory. In many instances, they were issued retroactively, thus placing companies in a position of being in non-compliance when they had thought they were obeying the law.

One glaring example of retroactive changes involved the passthrough to retail prices of higher costs incurred by the companies. Such cost increases were segregated between "product costs" (such as higher raw material prices) and "nonproduct costs" (labor, utilities, rent, etc.). Separate cost "banks" for product costs and for nonproduct costs were established. Originally, the regulations did not stipulate any preference for the way product costs or nonproduct costs were to be used for passthrough purposes.

Some time later, the regulators decided that only product cost increases could be used to increase a retail price above the May 15, 1973, level, and that only a certain percentage of nonproduct costs could be used to sustain a price above that level. Still later— several years into the control program—the Department of Energy changed the rules again: It said that product costs could be banked for use in later months but that nonproduct costs could not be banked and must be used in the month following that in which they were incurred. This retroactive change in the regulations made Standard subject to allegations of having overcharged its customers by several hundred million dollars. As a consequence, Standard and several other companies filed suit against the DOE, and the court ultimately ruled in the companies' favor.

Another example of retroactive regulatory changes involved sales of natural gas liquids. The original rules clearly provided that Standard was entitled to a one cent per gallon markup on product sales from its Amoco Production subsidiary to its Amoco Oil subsidiary. But several years later, DOE "clarified" its regulations and decreed that it had never intended for such a markup to be allowed on product transfers between affiliated companies.

These were only two of the countless disputes Standard had with the DOE on questions of pricing, product transfers, costs of containers, interest expense, the cost of purchased products and numerous other topics. Virtually every transaction could be questioned if a regulation were changed or if a government auditor interpreted a rule differently from the company's own personnel.

Government auditors took up residence in Standard's Chicago offices. Early in 1974, two Internal Revenue Service auditors moved in to examine the company's records for compliance with price control regulations. But they were soon replaced by two energy agency auditors and the number quickly grew to 32. Standard provided office space, telephone service and copying machines so the government auditors could pursue their investigations on a full-time basis. Early in 1976, the government cut the number of auditors back to 20, but early in 1979 the total was raised to 50. By August of that year, 127 DOE auditors were working in Standard's offices.

The company was aware that specific but unfounded charges had been filed against Standard that aggregated several hundred million dollars. Because Standard personnel could observe the government people at work, they were also aware that the chaotic and changing DOE regulations could send the auditors charging off in different directions on any given day, again with the potential for new charges of violations. Extended and expensive litigation was also in prospect as Standard sought to defend itself against unwarranted allegations.

All of these considerations led Standard's management to conclude that the problems with DOE should be resolved by settlement if possible. As a consequence, M. J. Keating, associate general counsel, negotiated a comprehensive settlement that affected not only the cases already in dispute but all possible litigation that might arise from any petroleum price and allocation regulations issued from March 6, 1973, through the end of 1979.

On February 14, 1980, the government and Standard jointly announced the signing of a Consent Order with the Department of Energy. DOE expressly acknowledged that the consent order did not constitute a finding "that Standard has violated the federal price or allocation requirements." DOE also said that the company had "maintained procedures reasonably adapted to insure compliance with federal petroleum price and allocation requirements."

The comprehensive settlement included a payment by Standard of $100 million—$71 million to an escrow account to be administered by DOE and up to the remaining $29 million to be paid in refunds to direct purchasers of middle distillate products; commitment by Standard of $410 million for investments in new, expanded, or accelerated projects in its U.S. oil and gas exploration and development activities and in refinery improvements; reduction by $180 million in "banked" costs that otherwise could have been reflected in future gasoline and propane price increases; and a payment of $25,000 to DOE as a full settlement in lieu of penalties.

As the Department of Energy continued to exercise tight control over the pricing and allocation of crude oil and gasoline, Ronald Reagan, the Republican candidate for the presidency, campaigned vigorously against such controls and, in fact, called for the abolition of the Department of Energy. Following Reagan's substantial electoral vote victory and his inauguration on January 20, 1981, one of his first executive acts was to order the immediate decontrol of oil prices ahead of the Congressionally-mandated September, 1981, deadline. Prices of gasoline immediately increased as domestic crude oil prices rose to world levels, but later weakened as recession in the Western industrial nations coupled with price-induced conservation created a temporary worldwide oversupply of crude oil and products in 1981-82. Competition among marketers for the business of conservation-minded motorists was evident. Including taxes, the U.S. city average retail price per gallon of unleaded regular gasoline, reported by the Bureau of Labor Statistics at $1.298 for January, 1981, rose sharply to $1.417 in March following decontrol. The price ranged downward to a monthly average of $1.237 in May, 1982, then to a monthly average for January, 1983, of $1.228, or 7 cents less than it was prior to decontrol.

Research, Technology, and Innovation

14

The facilities of the new research center authorized at Whiting as World War II neared an end were equal to any industrial research center in the nation when they were completed in 1948. Whiting was one of Standard's two main centers of research, the other being at Tulsa where facilities were fast expanding and soon would be on a par, in its own field, with those at Whiting. Each had its own specialized role. Whiting's was in manufacturing, chemicals, and product development; Tulsa's was in exploration and production. Each had made notable contributions to the technology of the oil industry and to Standard's reputation and growth, and would continue to do so. But a time came for reappraisal of Standard's research direction and philosophy.

Almost a year to the day after Prior moved up to chairman and Swearingen to president, Swearingen posed the question "To what end should research be used?" in addressing a company Joint Technical meeting at French Lick, Indiana, on May 6, 1959.

The question was among many that managements of Standard and its principal subsidiaries would be seriously considering over the next few years as the company—largely because of the new top management's insights and objectives—entered two consecutive decades of impressive growth in size and profits.

The first question Swearingen asked at French Lick was "whether our company can continue to carry on research and development activities at the level of spending that we now have, or conversely, the question can be put—can we afford not to?"

Second, he asked for a reappraisal of the areas in which research scientists proposed to work. Specifically, he asked for an evaluation of whether it was cheaper to buy know-how from others or to develop it internally. The nature of the "know-how" was also a concern. "The only justification for a corporation spending money on research," he said, "is to be able to employ the results directly in its business. We cannot afford to pursue interesting ideas solely for the sake of increasing scientific knowledge, interesting though those activities may be."

Third, he proposed setting up programs and deadlines for specific projects, emphasizing that each project must take on a greater importance than individual projects had been assigned before. He emphasized the point by saying, "We must have the guts and judgment to discontinue projects that do not pan out."

Finally, turning to the fact that technical improvements historically have a relatively short life and are superseded by still more efficient developments, he reminded his audience that nothing grows to the sky . . . the importance of timing in the success of new developments should not be overlooked. "What is valuable today may be worthless five years hence," he told his audience of specialists.

As part of an evaluation of the research activities, Swearingen in 1961 asked Lawrence A. Kimpton, Standard's vice president of corporate planning, to undertake a study of all of Standard's research activities with the assistance of Arthur D. Little and Company. "I had been very critical of our research, particularly critical of American Oil's research conducted at Whiting," Kimpton said some years later in recalling the study. "I think research at Pan American Petroleum (at Tulsa) was considerably better." What the Arthur D. Little study found, in Kimpton's own words, was "not much more than we already knew."

The A. D. Little analysts said Standard's research at Whiting was organized far more like a university than industry research. Plaudits went to people who published papers, held membership in learned societies, or engaged in academically oriented research. Research was not pointed toward advancing the company's business interests. Kimpton described it as "more of a learned society than an industrial research enterprise." A. D. Little also found that the scientists themselves were unhappy and extremely critical of top management for not telling them what was expected.

As a result of these findings, management directed the research department to assume a leaner posture. Philip C. White, then director of research, had the responsibility for seeing that

American Oil's research organization was reduced in size and budget, while at the same time becoming more productive.

The rapid growth of Amoco Chemicals Corporation and establishment of its own research group at Whiting left little doubt that additional facilities would soon be needed. A compelling factor came with the agreement in 1967 for Standard's purchase of Avisun Corporation, a Sun Oil Company chemicals subsidiary. Standard had to decide where to relocate the Avisun research department and its 150-member staff that occupied facilities owned by and rented from American Viscose, a former part owner of Avisun, near Philadelphia. At the same time, in attempting to replace retiring scientists and add to the staff as chemical research expanded, Standard noted a reluctance among highly educated research candidates to work and live in the congested industrial atmosphere of the Whiting area.

These factors prompted a search for a suitable chemical research center location, and, finally, the selection of a 178-acre site near Naperville, Illinois, in 1967. The area was one of new suburban development where the lifestyle seemed appropriate to the kind of people Standard was trying to attract. It also was convenient to Chicago's O'Hare airport and to Standard's general office in Chicago.

Although the immediate need for a chemical research center had been a major incentive, Standard soon decided that the Naperville site also would be an attractive location for research which historically had been conducted at Whiting; by placing laboratories in separate buildings, the desired specialization could be maintained, and, when fully developed, the center would be one of the nation's largest and most versatile facilities for industrial research and development. Four principal laboratories and an administration wing had been completed when dedication ceremonies were held in May, 1971. Anticipating the center's growth, Robert C. Gunness, Standard's president, said at the ceremonies, "One of the major challenges will be the development of synthetic substitutes for scarce natural materials; chemicals and plastics research will take on a new urgency."

The wide range of problems to be solved included development of new and improved refined petroleum products as well as chemicals and plastics, and further progress in ways to control air and water pollution, Gunness said. In addition to Amoco Chemicals' research activities and Amoco Oil's manufacturing and refining specialties, Standard itself would have separate laboratories for research into subjects whose potential practicality would be far in the future and which were outside the interests of the current business units.

Only exploration and production-related research, which was conducted at Amoco Production's facility at Tulsa, would not be consolidated into the new Naperville complex.

One of the problems in the past in some areas of Standard's research had been that a line of research might be continued although there appeared to be little prospect that a commercial application would result. To prevent this happening in the future, the company adopted a project system for research. And, as a corollary of the organization, each operational unit was required to fund the research which was relevant to its operations.

For example, if Amoco Oil Company wanted some research done in developing an improved motor oil, the subsidiary had the authority to fund it—and the authority to withdraw funding if there were no satisfactory results. Swearingen termed it "user-driven research."

Following the general policies Swearingen outlined in the research conference at French Lick, Indiana, in 1959, each project at the laboratories was aimed ultimately at developing or improving some product, process, or technique.

Scientists working for Amoco Oil sought better fuels and lubricants to meet the increasingly severe requirements of new automotive and heavy duty engines, improved quality for fertilizers, pesticides, mineral oils, waxes, and other products derived from petroleum.

Much of Amoco Oil's research activities at Naperville centered on improving methods for refining crude oil. Scientists worked with pilot plants—miniature replicas of full-scale refineries controlled by similar computerized processes. These pilot facilities enabled Standard's research teams to test various methods of processing low-quality crude oil at a cost substantially less than would have been required in a full-scale operation.

Amoco Chemicals' research was directed at finding new techniques to improve the physical properties of plastics, and to develop or improve methods of processing plastics into new product applications. Much of this research centered around the polymers or chemical building blocks which could be shaped into many forms; the beverage bottle in the refrigerator and the polyester shirt on one's back, for example, might be totally different in form, but chemically they were identical.

In addition to research for operating subsidiaries, it was possible to explore ideas in areas where the company was not active through corporate research at the Naperville Center, which was closely allied with the Corporate Development Department at Standard's general office where original analyses and recommendations on many possibilities took place. If, as an example, corporate directors thought a new means might be devised for recovering metal from an ore, which had nothing to do with the lines of business in which the company was then engaged, or if they thought there might be some commercial application of the findings of microbiology, or whether hydrocarbons could be used as a base in food production, then recommendations for this speculative research, if adopted, would move from corporate development to the research center and would be funded by the parent company.

The chronology of the growth of Standard's exploration and production research at Tulsa is similar to that of the Naperville Research Center whose history traces from the primitive Burton laboratory of the 1890s at the Whiting refinery to the "campus of laboratories," as one phrase maker described it, at Naperville.

It begins in 1931 when a laboratory was established in a single room on the tenth floor of the Stanolind Building, now the Amoco North Building, in downtown Tulsa. Laboratory work consisted of simple tests of well cores to determine susceptibility of oil-bearing formations to acid treatment to increase flow into the bore of an existing producing well. This work was moved later that year to a corrugated sheet metal building on Tulsa's north outskirts which is remembered as the first research center of Stanolind Oil and Gas Company. Full-time laboratory work began in 1934 when a permanent brick and stucco building was completed on the site.

Exploration research began that same year when Stanolind Oil and Gas acquired a major stock interest in Western Geophysical Company, Inc. Ltd., a California corporaton based in Los Angeles and headed by founder Henry Salvatori, a pioneer in oil field seismology. In 1938, Stanolind built a new laboratory adjoining its Tulsa production research facility, and exploration research functions were transferred there from Western's Los Angeles laboratory. In the late 1950s, after Stanolind's exploration research was well established, Salvatori bought back Stanolind's stock interest. A number of early day Western Geophysical employees stayed on at Stanolind. Salvatori merged Western Geophysical into Litton Industries in 1960.

Until 1943, Stanolind had no department of research as such. Employees doing research were members of the exploration and production departments. But in July of that year a research department was established and facilities were expanded at the north Tulsa location. In 1953, a new research center was completed on a 60-acre tract on the southeast edge of the city. Over the years, the original research and administration buildings were enlarged and new buildings and parking lots added, all sited on landscaped grounds back from streets and the residential sections which border on two sides.

Geophysics as a companion to geology in the search for oil and natural gas was new when research in this field first began at Stanolind's Tulsa Research Center in the 1930s. But already there had been centuries of evolution of theories and of instruments that came to be used as a matter of course.

The long period of development is well illustrated by dates from George Elliott Sweet's "The History of Geophysical Prospecting," published in two volumes in 1966 and 1969 by Science Press:

A John Michell (1724–1793), known as the grandfather of both geology and geophysics, founded the science of seismology, a field of geophysics, and in 1777 invented a torsion balance, a tool of the geophysicist used to measure gravitational attraction of subsurface rock; J. D. Forbes in 1841 built a primitive seismograph, a device which records vibrations of the earth and is used by modern oil geophysicists to record artificially generated shock waves; Robert Mallet (1810–1881) pioneered the use of artificial shock waves in 1845 by burying and detonating a dynamite charge and measuring time lapses of acoustic waves the blast created at varying distances; the first magnetometer, a device that measures the relative intensity of earth's magnetic effect, was built in 1870; John Milne and an associate named Gray in 1885 first used a falling weight—a precursor of the oil geophysicist's mechanical thumper—to generate seismic waves which they recorded simultaneously with two seismographs.

Such scattered and primitive developments had not been brought together in the first two decades of the 1900s. So it is hardly surprising that World War I Allied army artillery officers pooh-poohed the use of sound ranging to locate the positions of the German Big Bertha cannon. This weapon in 1918 intermittently shelled Paris at a range of 76 miles, a distance never before attained. Tradition-minded officers were forced to admit they were wrong when they chose targets that proved to be camouflaged dummies while the real gun continued firing from locations which more innovative-minded officers pinpointed by sound ranging.

Sound ranging developed during World War I was another in the chain of developments that would coalesce into an effective petroleum-finding tool. In the 1920s, the torsion balance and the seismograph were used to locate salt domes along the Gulf of Mexico coast, known by experience to be prime oil prospects. In 1924, oil was discovered in Fort Bend County, Texas, on a salt dome whose discovery was credited to use of the seismic method, and from that year through 1929, 44 salt domes were reported found by refraction seismograph and 11 by torsion balance. In the 1930s, many oil companies considered the use of the reflection seismograph as essential.

The oil industry made great strides in earth sciences and many patented innovations sprang from the work of scientists and technicians at the Tulsa Research Center. But despite phenomenal strides in the use of earth sciences such as geology and geophysics and industry's many efforts to explain its knowledge of the subsurface, one of the greatest modern misconceptions about oil involves the conditions under which commercial oil deposits are found. Most people who see an oil well pump or a derrick in a field envisage it as drawing liquid gold from a pool of oil, with waves of the black liquid lapping against the sides of some underground cavern. The facts are that oil is not found in pools, but in rock, or rather the pores of certain kinds of rocks. Often these rocks are about the consistency of a concrete sidewalk. (The word petroleum comes from the Latin *petra*—rock—and *oleum* —oil; in Chinese, the language characters for oil translate literally as "liquid from a rock.")

But there are distinctions among rocks as there are among people. The oil geologist knows that the igneous rocks of granite, basalt, or lava are not good prospects for oil. What the geologist looks for are the formations of sandstone or limestone deposited in the sedimentary basins of an ancient sea, faulted and folded by

165

elemental forces of eons past and now buried below the surface of land or beneath the watery floors of seas as disparate as the Gulf of Mexico, the Persian Gulf, or the North Sea.

Whether onshore or offshore, a sedimentary formation is essential to the finding of oil. Once a geologist finds a sedimentary source bed, he hunts for reservoir rock into which oil may have migrated and there been trapped by a nonporous rock barrier. From his geological observations of surface outcrops and study of logs from wells that may have been drilled in the area, he is able to draw a map portraying the way the subsurface might appear in cross section and augments his findings with those of the exploration geophysicist.

Improved technology to measure gravity and magnetism, and to propagate and record elastic and electromagnetic waves in the earth have established oil geophysics as a remarkably useful tool. While the geologist's map of subsurface geology provides indications of where oil and gas may be trapped, the geophysicist seeks more accurate information with which to pinpoint areas where accumulations of oil and gas may occur.

The seismograph provides the only direct way to acquire subsurface structural information without drilling wells. To acquire the information and record it in a form from which he draws conclusions that may be used to decide where to drill, the geophysicist creates artificial shock (seismic) waves—the offspring of Big Bertha in World War I and earlier discoveries.

In the search for petroleum deposits, the geophysicist first used dynamite detonated in shallow well bores to create shock waves. Today, he may use a charge no larger than à shotgun shell, a compressed air gun, or a mechanical earth vibrator—a "thumper" reminiscent of the falling weight which Milne and Gray used in 1885 to generate seismic waves.

Whatever the means the exploration geophysicist may use, the principle is the same. The artificially created shock waves travel downward, and the time is measured for rock layers to reflect these waves back to the surface. Because of variations in the density of the layers of rock, the waves travel at different speeds, and part of the energy is reflected back to the surface while the balance penetrates to lower depths.

The reflected signals can be recorded, and the geophysicist receives a printed seismogram from which he can determine the depths of various strata. By repeating the process at a number of locations, the geophysicist is able to identify patterns in the buried rock strata. While he doesn't "find" oil, determining the configuration of underground rocks is the contribution of the petroleum geophysicist to the search, and it is an important one. If seen in cross-section, these patterns might appear as a series of subterranean hills which are by no means regular in their contours nor conformable at depth. By putting all his data together, the map-maker is able to construct a subsurface structural map which tells him whether or not there are closed features which the geologist calls "anticlines" or "faults" or "pinchouts" into which oil might have migrated and been trapped.

By the use of computers, improved geophysical tools, well logs, paleontology, and palynology, map-making and the means of searching for oil have grown more sophisticated through the years. But unfortunately, except for the drill, all of the exploration tools indicate only whether a trap may exist; only the drill can determine whether oil or gas is actually present.

Natural underground forces are not notably efficient in pushing oil to the surface, even after a well is drilled. When natural inflow of water provides the driving mechanism, the ultimate recovery is usually only about 40 to 50 per cent of the oil originally present in the rock. Where the expansion of natural gas serves as the force to push oil to the surface, the rate of recovery may be only 20 to 30 per cent. This, of course, can vary greatly between fields and depends upon how permeable the rock is— that is, how easily it will permit the passage of fluid. "Tight" rock —or rock in which the pore spaces are not well connected— makes it difficult or sometimes impossible for oil or gas to flow.

Such tight rock formations can often be made to produce more oil or gas by a process of "fracturing"—that is, cracking open splits or fractures in the rock layer through which oil or gas can flow.

In this process, special sand selected for its toughness, or some other crush-resistant propping material such as sintered bauxite, is mixed with a gel-like material and pumped into a well under high pressure. The force fractures the tight rock and, after pumping pressure is released, the propping material keeps the fractures open, allowing oil and gas to flow more easily into the bore of the well. The process was developed by scientists at the Tulsa Research Center of Standard's subsidiary, Stanolind Oil and Gas Company, and was first licensed to others in 1949 under the name "Hydrafrac," derived from "hydraulic fracturing." In 1977, it was estimated that this process alone had added another 10 to 12 billion barrels of recoverable oil to North American reserves; it had made 25 to 30 per cent of proven domestic oil and natural gas reserves economically recoverable. Through licensing the process, Standard had received approximately $30 million in revenues.

Nature's energy may be supplemented by injecting additional fluids into a reservoir to force oil into a production well bore. The most common method is called "waterflooding." Simply stated, and widely demonstrated in television commercials in the 1970s, this involves injecting large amounts of water from the surface into the reservoir through one set of wells, thus flushing oil out of the rock to another group of wells where it can be raised to the surface. This procedure is known as "secondary recovery." In a field where no natural water influx is present, waterflooding can recover an additional 20 to 25 per cent of the original oil in place, depending on the nature of the rock, the efficiency with which water can move through it, and other factors which the reservoir engineer must take into account.

Even more sophisticated means of getting additional oil from an aging or a stubborn reservoir emerged in the 1970s through Tulsa Research Center laboratory work and field tests. These methods of enhancing the recovery of oil are called "tertiary recovery."

Tertiary recovery programs are of several kinds, defined as thermal, miscible, and micellar. Thermal recovery uses steam or fire in the reservoir and is generally used to recover heavier oils. Miscible recovery floods the reservoir with a fluid that mixes with the oil and lightens it, permitting it to flow more easily. Micellar recovery uses a chemical which acts much like a dry-cleaning fluid. When pumped into a formation, it alters surface-tension effects which bind oil to rock, and allows oil to be swept into the well bore where it can be pumped to the surface.

When Swearingen addressed a meeting of research and development employees at Red Crown Lodge on September 20, 1976, he repeated, in summary, the points he had emphasized at French Lick. Calling their attention to Standard's record of contributions to oil research and technology over the more than 70 years since it stepped into the unknown in developing the revolutionary high-pressure, high-temperature cracking process, Swearingen admonished the assembled scientists that "research is a high risk business." But he both encouraged and challenged them to pursue long-range projects which might benefit one or more subsidiaries or, more ambitiously, lead to the creation of entirely new commercial ventures.

Basically, Swearingen enunciated four precepts at Red Crown which he said should govern Standard's research activities in the last quarter of the century. They were:

1. "Our corporate assets are such that we could diversify into almost any area, but we strongly prefer that such areas be ones where our own technology is strong.

2. "Diversification through 'grass roots' exploratory research is preferred, but whether this way or through acquisition, R&D is responsible for making opportunities possible through new technology and innovation.

3. "Any major redeployment of assets will be an enormous and lengthy process, as witness our Amoco Chemicals operation where, after 20 years, capital investment just passed the $1 billion level last year. Thus, new enterprises must start early and grow steadily.

4. "The biggest single problem confronting our company is the question of what our business will be at the end of the century. We can be sure it will be different from today."

John E. Kasch, vice president of supply and technology for Standard, whose portfolio of general responsibilities included research and development, reemphasized the points Swearingen had made:

"Historically, it has taken the United States about 50 years to convert from one dominant energy source to another," he said. "We must begin now to make a substantial shift into other energy forms. These will include coal, synthetic fuels, nuclear power, and solar. This time, we must complete much of that shift in only 20 to 25 years. It will require an effort unprecedented in our country's history."

The broad horizons of new frontiers challenging oil company scientists were reflected in the appointment in 1976 of Edward A. Mason as vice-president of research, reporting to Kasch. Just prior to his appointment, Mason had been a member of the United States Nuclear Regulatory Commission and was previously head of the nuclear engineering department and professor of nuclear and chemical engineering at Massachusetts Institute of

Technology. He was given responsibility for overall coordination of research activities as well as Standard's corporate exploratory research program.

Mason found himself directing a staff trained and experienced in a wide variety of scientific disciplines. Among them he identified chemistry, biology, microbiology, process metallurgy, physics, and others. The staff not only had authority to do exploratory research on its own but also provided technical evaluations for investments in small firms with a leading edge in high technology which might hold major commercial promise. The scientists also sought new ideas wherever they might be found, whether in a university laboratory or the home workshop of an imaginative inventor.

"Ultimately," Mason said, carrying out the theme expressed by Swearingen at the Red Crown Lodge meeting, "the base of our company's existence—conventional petroleum—will require substantial bolstering with new and viable areas of technology, especially in the energy field."

Noting America's tremendous coal resources, which in 1980 had been estimated by the U.S. Geological Survey at 1.7 trillion tons—enough to supply the nation's needs beyond the middle of the 21st century—Standard's scientists persisted in seeking more efficient ways not only to produce oil and gas from this source but also to improve the economics of conversion processes.

The technology for coal conversion had advanced considerably since the Germans used it in World War II. But the efficiency level left much to be desired as did high capital costs. "We're taking a completely new look at coal conversion," Mason told Standard's shareholders through the pages of *SpaN* magazine in 1979. "The idea is to produce synthetics at efficiencies and costs that compare favorably with conventional oil and natural gas operations. One approach requires us to understand thoroughly how nature put typical coals together, both physically and chemically. Although nearly a century of research has been devoted to studies of coals, only recently has their true structure begun to emerge. We may soon be able to take coals apart 'gently,' selectively breaking their very big carbon-based molecules into smaller pieces at low temperatures and pressures. We are a very long way from doing that commercially, but the potential rewards are enormous."

170

In addition to coal, oil sands (often called tar sands) and oil shale—both found in North America—were to emerge as sources of raw material for synthetic fuels of commercial potential. In the late 1970s, Standard acquired interests in oil sands deposits in Utah, in the vicinity of Sunnyside, and assigned responsibility for managing a study of commercial feasibility to its Alternative Energy Development department.

Standard was no stranger to research on oil sands development. It had sought ways to recover oil from Athabasca oil sands too deep for economic surface mining, beginning in the post-World War II years at the Tulsa Research Center. The Athabasca oil sands had initially been discovered by Peter Pond, a fur trapper and explorer in Canada, in the 18th century. Pond found a black substance oozing from the banks of the Athabasca River in Northern Alberta. Camping with local Cree Indians, he watched them boil the sticky grit to get a heavy oil they used both as a campfire fuel and as material to waterproof their canoes. He had come upon an outcrop of a mixture of bitumen, or heavy oil, and water locked in a deposit of quartzitic sand. This sandy gumbo was only one tip of four major deposits which cover 19,000 square miles in the provinces of Alberta and Saskatchewan.

More than a trillion barrels of bitumen and heavy oil are estimated to exist in this area—an amount exceeding the entire petroleum resources of the Middle East. Standard's Canadian subsidiary, Amoco Canada Petroleum Company Ltd., held mineral rights to 208,000 net acres of this territory with bitumen and heavy oil deposits of an estimated 62.2 billion barrels, more than double the size of all conventional recoverable oil reserves in the continental United States. The unanswered question: How much of it would be economically recoverable over the years?

Standard's Stanolind Oil and Gas Company had begun initial field tests on recovery of oil from deep oil sands in Canada in the late 1950s using an underground combustion process developed at Tulsa.

In this process, injection and production wells are drilled in a pattern throughout a small plot. The underlying oil sand formation is ignited, and air is pumped in through the injection wells. The air sustains combustion. As the combustion front moves forward in the oil zone, hot gases thin the oil, partially refine it, and force it to producing wells. A major phase of production testing was completed in 1981.

It was the opinion of George H. Galloway, then president of

Amoco Production (formerly Stanolind) and chairman of Amoco
Canada, that given sufficient price incentive and capital availability, Amoco's Gregoire Lake lease area on which *in situ* testing
took place, could theoretically support a production volume of
more than a million barrels a day for 25 years.

In other parts of the oil sands area, where the formation was
close enough to the surface to permit the economical removal of
the overburden, open-pit mining was being used by other companies. Amoco Canada held 10 per cent interest in the proposed
140,000 barrels-per-day Alsands surface mining synfuels project,
also in Alberta. When Canada's National Energy Plan did not
permit an adequate return on investment, Amoco Canada and the
other private companies involved in the Alsands project withdrew from participation early in 1982.

Another alternative energy source vigorously pursued by
Standard was oil shale. Deposits were known to exist in a number
of locations in the United States, the richest believed to be the
Green River formation ranging across parts of Colorado, Wyoming, and Utah, much of it on public lands administered by the
federal government. Estimates in 1978 were that the formation
contained 1.8 trillion barrels of shale oil, perhaps one-third of it
potentially recoverable. About 80 per cent of it was believed to be
in the 1,380-square-mile Piceance Creek Basin in Garfield and
Rio Blanco counties in Colorado. That oil could be produced
from oil shale by mining, crushing, and heating it had been known
for more than 100 years. Because of the high costs involved,
efforts to produce oil from shale had not been pursued in earnest
because less expensive supplies of fossil fuels were available.

As the 1960s ended, however, increased U.S. dependence on
imported oil, greater control by foreign producing countries over
production rates and prices, and, finally, the 1973–74 Arab oil
embargo with its subsequent rapid escalations in crude prices,
reinforced the belief in the United States that alternatives to
conventional crude oil soon would be necessary. The U.S. government adopted a Federal Prototype Oil Shale Leasing Program,
with stipulations calling for testing new technologies and developing environmental programs. Private owners retained their land
patent rights.

Six shale tracts in the area were selected for the program by
the Interior Department in 1972. Standard and Gulf Oil Corporation, in a 50-50 partnership the two companies named the Rio

Blanco Oil Shale Project (Company, later), submitted the winning bonus bid of $210 million for 5,100-acre Colorado Tract C-a, the first lease issued under the program.

Bonus payments were to be made in five installments with a little over one-third going into Colorado's Oil Shale Trust Fund for use in aiding state areas and communities impacted by oil shale development. The government provided a progress incentive under which the lessee could credit against the fourth and fifth bonus payments any expenditures it made in development operations on the tract, provided the expenditures were made before the anniversary dates of the lease. Subsequently, the federal government leased another Colorado tract and two Utah tracts to other operators. Several projects also were underway on sites in the Colorado-Utah portion of the oil shale area on privately owned lands.

The Rio Blanco leased-tract was situated in Rio Blanco county, Colorado, on the western flank of the Piceance Creek Basin. Estimates in 1981 of the amounts of oil that the shale on the tract would yield ranged from two billion barrels, by using modified *in situ* burning technology, to five billion barrels by open-pit mining and retorting. The government in 1976 approved Rio Blanco's Detailed Development Plan to use open-pit mining, but, later in the year, Rio Blanco petitioned and was granted a 24-month suspension of operations on its lease, postponing payment of the final two installments.

Major problems dictating the request for suspension included the fact that during the course of base line environmental studies it was conducting, Rio Blanco discovered that natural levels of ozone, particulates, and nonmethane hydrocarbons exceeded existing federal ambient air quality standards. These were "natural" and had nothing to do with the presence of man on the tract. Therefore, nothing could be done toward development until provisions of the Clean Air Act and the "no significant deterioration" regulations of the Environmental Protection Agency were resolved.

A second major problem arose because the Interior Department's Final Environmental Impact Statement for the oil shale lease program required that the lessee avoid waste of the oil shale resource and recognized that the Rio Blanco tract was amenable to open-pit mining, the most efficient method known to fulfill that requirement. As a result, an off-tract site was needed for disposal of the processed shale rock. But the Interior Department believed it didn't have authority to lease off-tract acreage for this purpose and needed to seek legislative approval by Congress.

In 1977, the Interior Department approved Rio Blanco's revised plan calling for an underground method (referred to as modified *in situ*) of extracting oil from the shale. The term "modified *in situ*" meant that recovery of shale oil would take place both on the surface and below ground. Underground rubblized shale retorts would be created by blasting. One-fourth to one-third of the shale would be removed to the surface through a vertical shaft. The shale remaining in the underground retort would be ignited to form a combustion front that would burn downward through the rock at rates controlled by the volumes of air and steam injected. Shale oil vaporized by the burning process would flow downward and liquefy as it cooled. The liquid then would be collected at the bottom of the retort and pumped to surface tankage. The spent shale would remain in the burned-out retort. The shale mined to create the chamber and processed in an above-ground retort would be disposed of off-tract in an environmentally acceptable manner.

Rio Blanco ignited its first burn in 1980 and its second in 1981. Both were completed successfully, recovering approximately 25,000 barrels of shale oil which was used primarily for research. The two burns convinced Rio Blanco and Standard that shale oil in fact could be recovered by the modified *in situ* method, but it was noted again that only an estimated two billion barrels could be recovered in this way as opposed to perhaps five billion by open-pit mining. No additional below-ground retorts were planned.

Prospects brightened for open-pit mining with the introduction of federal legislation which would make off-tract land available for processing facilities and for disposal of spent shale and overburden. With proper market conditions, Standard estimated that by 1987, shale oil could be produced commercially, perhaps in volumes of as much as 50,000 barrels a day. In 1981, however, the company calculated that facilities on this scale would require an investment of about $2 billion. Given the unknowns of supply, demand, and oil prices in the years ahead, the question remained whether an investment of that magnitude would be practicable.

In addition to coal gasification, tar sands, and shale oil projects, each with future potential, tertiary recovery projects to produce additional oil from aging fields were vital if the nation were to reduce its dependence on foreign oil. In 1980, Amoco production considered a project to pipe carbon dioxide (CO_2) from the Bravo Dome in northeast New Mexico into Permian Basin oil fields in West Texas. The estimated total cost of the project was $1.5 billion. Studies had shown that carbon dioxide acts as a solvent to overcome the forces trapping oil in rock pores, and field test results were favorable. Standard was hoping that injecting this simple gas might help recover a significant share of oil still beyond the reach of conventional production, if economics would support the tremendous cost. On September 28, 1982, a net investment of $556,900,000 during 1983 through 1986 was approved for the installation of carbon dioxide flooding in four of the company's West Texas properties, to develop the Bravo Dome carbon dioxide unit to provide the gas for the four properties, and for construction of a pipeline from Bravo Dome to West Texas.

As Standard sought to extract more oil from existing fields, improved seismic techniques and computer processing of seismic data developed by the company's Tulsa Research Center scientists advanced its ability to locate new and promising hydrocarbon prospects. Other new technologies permit geochemists to measure the thermal maturity, or age, of organic matter in the earth's crust to determine whether natural forces have heated source beds to levels necessary for the creation of deposits of oil and natural gas.

The number of scientists needed by Standard continued to increase. Research goals included being more definitive and more quantitative in geology and in developing new geophysical methods of mapping underground rock characteristics from the surface. Experiments continued toward achieving increasingly effective "fracturing" of rocks around the well bore. The laboratory also worked on the design of structures for offshore drilling which were environmentally safer and more economical to operate. Another project was to develop a platform capable of handling oil and gas produced from wells drilled in very deep waters of 1,000 feet and more.

At Naperville, microbiology was a field of research not traditionally associated with such massive capital-intensive industries as petroleum. But microbiology held the potential to revolutionize numerous industries, including chemicals, health

175

care (human and animal), food, energy, and agriculture. To Mason, it was reminiscent of the information and electronics revolution which emerged from the semiconductor technology of the 1950s.

Kasch shared Mason's enthusiasm for the potential of research in microbiology, particularly the techniques of recombinant DNA. DNA knowledge permits one to make chemicals as well as pharmaceuticals, Kasch said, and it continues the natural evolution of the chemical knowledge on which oil industry refining processes were based.

Although bacterial processes were costly in the experimental stage because of the low productivity of the procedure, Kasch was confident that this problem could be overcome. Standard scientists believed techniques of recombinant DNA would initially offer alternative, less costly means of producing many useful pharmaceutical compounds such as insulin, endorphins (brain hormones that act as pain-killers), interferons (natural antiviral agents used in cancer treatment), and in toxic waste treatment, where bacteria have traditionally been used in water purification. In a more distant time frame, they envisioned application in chemicals, petroleum processing, and mining. The accuracy of their vision was borne out by the market introduction in November, 1982, of human insulin, the first consumer product developed from recombinant DNA technology.

Standard's own research efforts in the field of microbiology had opened up other opportunities. In 1972, Standard formed a subsidiary called Amoco Foods Company to develop manufacturing processes utilizing the company's proprietary knowledge in the production of commercial food-grade yeasts, and a plant utilizing the process was constructed at Hutchinson, Minnesota.

The name of the subsidiary was changed to Pure Culture Products, Inc., in 1980, reflecting the fact that the company was the world's only producer of pure-cultured primary food yeast grown in a closed, pressurized fermenter. This patented fermentation process and proprietary technology enabled Pure Culture to produce a variety of yeast food ingredients with outstanding purity and uniform flavor, marketed under the trademark names of Pur-Cultur and Zyest.

Taken together, these research activities, involving a variety of disciplines, provided a technological compass pointing Standard in new directions for the 21st century. The effort was a significant one, supported by the resources of a company which had moved to a prominent position among America's largest industrial corporations.

The growing dimensions of the company's research efforts continued through the years. Between 1950 and 1960, more than 900 patents were issued to the company; in the following decade there were 1,135, and from 1970 through 1979, the figure was more than 900. At the end of 1980, the company held more than 3,000 active patents.

Standard's patent licensing income in 1980 in the U.S. and elsewhere exceeded $20 million. But income derived by licensing technology developed by its scientists was far less important than the growth and profits resulting from Standard's own utilization of technology the company invented, purchased, or purchased and improved.

Research, other professional work, and the technological explosion in general, generate enormous amounts of information, opening the way to major opportunities. The problem has been how to gain access to the information quickly and, as quickly, to use it.

The problem of communications is corollary. Just as Standard focused its research efforts, it also developed plans for profitable use of computer technology. In 1950, there were no more than 15 computers in use in the entire United States. Twenty years later, there were some 40,000, and the number was forecast to double in the next 15 years.

Standard, as did other companies, saw the potential early but recognized that small, stand-alone computers at scattered locations with little interrelationship fell short of providing an adequate information system. Timely and complete information had a large economic value to the company.

A planning group was formed in the early 1960s under Frank G. Pearce, general manager of information services and management sciences, to develop a system-wide approach. By the end of the decade the group had supervised the design of a sophisticated two-center company-wide system. The computer centers, one at Chicago and one at Tulsa, were connected by leased line and satellite to terminals at other locations which had their own small computers. Data on every important aspect of Standard's worldwide operations could be channeled to the centers. These centers created a vast library of information that could be accessed for use by professionals and managers on a need-to-know basis, yet was protected from unauthorized use by a tight security system. Capabilities ranged from accounting and check writing to storing data on wells, analyzing drilling programs, and processing seismic data.

To serve one of the heaviest users—seismic recording interpretation and display—special computers were required at field locations to preprocess data which are transmitted via high-capacity systems to the centers, processed, and returned. The benefits in this one function alone are substantial: Raw data acquired by seismograph crews can be analyzed and printouts produced in a fraction of the time previously required. Improvement in the signal-to-noise ratio produced clearer printouts leading to identification of "bright spots"—good prospects for the drill that otherwise would remain hidden.

Early in the process of bringing the computer system on line, Amoco Production Company's Tulsa Research Center was chosen to develop Standard's electronic office system (EOS). The project was under the general direction of Amoco Production's vice president for research, M. R. Waller, and the manager of computing research at the center, J. G. Steward. With the cooperation of an electronic office equipment supplier, cathode ray tube (CRT) units with typewriter-like keyboards at office locations were connected into computer centers enabling administrative and scientific employees not only to exchange messages "on the tube" but to file and retrieve data stored in computers for display on CRT units at their individual work locations. A similar system was installed at the general office of Amoco Canada at Calgary, Alberta. Connecting it successfully with the Tulsa Research Center and Standard's Tulsa Data Center soon was followed by a system providing computer access by field locations, other subsidiary offices, and the establishment of the electronic office system in Standard's general office in Chicago.

Computers operate refining processes, a number of Standard's producing fields, and measure produced oil and gas. Timely information is provided for crude oil purchasing, transportation, refining, distribution, and sale of products. A customer service system for chemicals coordinates delivery of the right products in the right packaging at the right place at the right time.

As essential as these capabilities have become in the advancing frontiers of a technology-dependent society, the computer system's assistance in planning may override them all in importance. Relevant data on trends that affect the company, drawn from information stored in computers, can be fed into computer models that simulate the company in terms of its petroleum reserves, production capacity, transportation systems, refineries, chemical plants, marketing systems, financial policies, and similar matters. Foresight based on computer analysis is by no means perfect. But the computer has made available more and better information upon which decisions can be made, and faster than ever before.

Chemicals: A New Frontier

15

Prior to World War II, Standard's interest in producing and marketing chemicals was little more than desultory. The domestic chemical industry had become large and diversified by the 1930s after overseas supplies were shut off during the first world war, and petroleum was one of its important raw materials. But chemicals was not a line of business generally of interest to the oil industry. Like most others in the oil industry, Standard saw crude oil as a very complex mixture of hydrocarbons which could not easily be separated into individual components where purity specifications were important.

The first application of petroleum to the manufacture of chemicals was during the first world war. There was a great demand for acetone to be used for airplane dope (a thick lacquer used to increase tautness and strength of the fabric covering of wings and fuselage of early-day aircraft). Another company built a small plant in New Jersey to make this product and isopropyl alcohol from cracking unit gases supplied by a nearby oil refinery. Typical petroleum-based chemical products of the immediate post World War I period were solvents for paint and lacquer where purity specifications weren't critical.

During the 1920s, however, the new technology of continuous flow began replacing the batch method of refinery operations. Chemical engineering principles were introduced and applied. Improvements in distillation, heat transfer, and other refining steps made it practical to build larger and more efficient units. Conversion of hydrocarbons into chemicals of great purity now could be actively considered.

The revolutionary catalytic cracking technology introduced by the Houdry process was soon followed—with Standard scientists as significant contributors—by the development of a fluid catalytic cracking process which had advantages in capacity and yield and in the production of chemical raw materials.

As the industry began using this new technology, Standard's associate director of research at Whiting, W. H. (Herbert) Balke, prepared studies in 1941 and 1943 in which he recommended that Standard increase its research and development in chemicals toward establishing a position in the chemicals field.

Making volumes of new and more sophisticated war materials for World War II presented a host of new problems related to the field of chemicals. Standard's first effort to make anything approaching a pure hydrocarbon took place just before the war when the company built a plant at Whiting to make isooctane for use as an octane improver in aviation gasoline. With urgent military needs dominating oil industry activities, Standard concerned itself with the manufacture of aromatic hydrocarbons— benzene, toluene, and xylene—by hydroforming, and built the first commercial hydroforming unit at its Texas City refinery and the first commercial fluid bed catalytic cracking unit at its Wood River refinery. The hydroforming process was adapted to the production of toluene for TNT, which went into bombs and artillery shells. The output of both the hydroforming and catalytic cracking units was used to make high-octane aviation gasoline, necessary for fueling the engines of fighters, bombers, and other military aircraft.

When the U.S. was shut off from established Malaysia and East Indies sources of rubber, development of a synthetic substitute became critical for use in the manufacture of aircraft and over-the-road vehicle tires, and in hoses and many other parts for war machines.

Butylene, a hydrocarbon produced in the cracking process, was dehydrogenated to make butadiene. Benzene, produced by hydroforming and separated in the recovery of toluene and xylene, was reacted with ethylene to produce styrene. Butadiene and styrene were reacted to produce synthetic rubber. This was the process, but Standard wasn't one of the companies that got into the synthetic rubber business as such; the government cancelled a production plant at Gary, Indiana, which Standard was about ready to build. However, the various individual chemicals —isobutane, normal butane, isopentane, butadiene, benzene, toluene, xylene, styrene, and others, which had been successfully produced under the stress of war—opened up possibilities of many new products for the oil industry generally.

The research and refining practices in which Standard and

the petroleum industry were compelled to engage during the war made it clear that it was not only possible but necessary to make high-purity, individual chemicals out of petroleum streams. After the war, Standard had a much broader view of these urgencies than it had only a few years earlier, and it was then that the company decided to make a major, clear-cut effort to get into the chemical business.

The versatility of oil was epitomized in its conversion to chemicals. As oil, it was valuable, but when upgraded into chemicals, it was even more valuable. It made sense to divert a portion of the crude oil raw material and convert it into products for which demand was developing in the economy, and which could be sold at higher prices.

An early postwar project was an attempt to produce detergents as a substitute for soap. To make detergents it was necessary to produce long molecules of straight chain olefins. Some isomerization technology had been developed during the war. The chemistry was right, but mechanical and corrosion problems were severe, and the market wasn't receptive. After several years of frustrating experience, the company abandoned the effort.

Another postwar project which seemed to have potential was the conversion of natural gas into gasoline. The company had large quantities of natural gas which could be sold, if at all, for only two to five cents a thousand cubic feet—in effect, giving it away. Pursuing the same logic which was leading it into the chemical business, management reasoned that if natural gas could be converted to gasoline for which public demand was growing by leaps and bounds, a higher price could be obtained for it.

The method Standard proposed to employ in the conversion of natural gas to gasoline began with the burning of methane gas with oxygen to produce carbon monoxide and hydrogen. These two components were then made to react with each other over an iron catalyst to produce gasoline and water. It was the Fischer-Tropsch hydrocarbon synthesis process developed by Ruhrchemie, A. G., which the Germans, with limited petroleum supplies but an abundance of coal, utilized to make gasoline during World War II.

Before the war, Standard and The Texas Company, through their jointly owned Process Management Company in New York, investigated the possibility of using the process in the United States when Ruhrchemie transferred patents for the process outside Germany to Hydrocarbon Synthesis Corporation in which

Standard (New Jersey) had 680 shares, Shell and Kellogg 425 each, and I. G. Farben 170. Jay H. Forrester, a chemical engineer who joined Standard at its Whiting research laboratory in 1929, was one of a team of four engineers—two from Standard and two from The Texas Company—that was dispatched to Germany to appraise the process.

The team was there in 1938 when Hitler moved into Austria and took Vienna, the capital city. After completing their appraisal of the process, the team submitted a negative report, and the idea of using it was shelved. Following the war, Standard revived the idea of utilizing the technology, and extensive research was conducted in pilot plants at Stanolind's laboratories in Tulsa under the direction of George Roberts, Jr., manager of research, and Scott W. Walker, director of process research. The results showed promise and Stanolind was considering whether to build a commercial scale plant when Paul R. Schultz suggested that Swearingen be invited to Chicago from the Whiting research center to discuss crude oil and product price relationships which Swearingen and his group had been studying.

The plant was to be built at Garden City, Kansas, in the huge Hugoton natural gas field in which Stanolind owned reserves. Forrester, who had taken a leave of absence before the Germany trip to get a chemical engineering Master's degree at Massachusetts Institute of Technology, transferred to Stanolind Oil and Gas Company in Tulsa to work for John Rouse, who had transferred from the general office in Chicago at the end of 1945 to head what was called the manufacturing department.

It was to this department that Swearingen transferred from Whiting research and where he worked on the Garden City proposal and other projects with Schultz, an engineer and economic analyst, both reporting to Forrester. The manufacturing department had been assigned an aggressive program of building natural gasoline and cycling plants in the company's U.S. oil and gas producing fields. These plants were designed to extract propane and butane (liquefied petroleum gas), as well as natural gasoline from the natural gas produced with oil and from high-pressure natural gas fields rich in condensate. The department also built plants to produce elemental sulfur in fields where gas production was high in hydrogen sulfide content. Thus, it was to be expected that construction of the proposed plant to utilize the basic Fischer-Tropsch technology in processing Hugoton field natural gas would be assigned to the Stanolind Oil and Gas manufacturing department. Construction began early in 1948.

While the main purpose of the plant was to upgrade give-away-priced natural gas into more profitable gasoline at a time when petroleum economists were forecasting an imminent shortage of crude oil, a valuable by-product was the variety of oxygenated chemicals in the water stream produced in the process—aldehydes, ketones, methyl, ethyl, and higher alcohols.

Stanolind Oil and Gas conducted a great deal of research on separation and recovery of the chemicals and on bringing them to market, and a chemicals plant was planned in conjunction with the gasoline plant. Construction was barely underway, however, when it became apparent that the economics of the project had changed. Capital costs were increasing, the crude supply situation had improved, and natural gas prices had more than doubled from the two to five cents per thousand cubic feet that had earlier prevailed. Observing these developments, economic analysts at Stanolind recommended against proceeding with construction, and the Garden City plant was cancelled in August of 1948.

Almost concurrently with Standard's planning for the Garden City plant, The Texas Company and Hydrocarbon Research, Incorporated, a design engineering company, were studying the Fischer-Tropsch process, and Hydrocarbon Research designed a plant to be built in Texas to make synthetic gasoline and chemicals from natural gas.

The plant was first planned to be situated in the Carthage gas producing field in East Texas. The economics became adverse at Carthage, however. A new site at Brownsville, in the Rio Grande valley, was chosen, and Carthage Hydrocol, Inc. built the plant in 1951. Stanolind Oil and Gas contracted to buy the raw chemical stream from the gasoline plant, and built facilities adjacent to the Carthage Hydrocol plant to recover water-soluble chemicals from the stream.

Carthage Hydrocol had problems in keeping the plant on stream, however, and shut the project down. In 1954, Stanolind Oil and Gas acquired the plant, along with its natural gas feedstock supply, and was able to put the plant into operation. The plant provided a mixture of oxygenated hydrocarbons which were recovered and purified in the adjacent Stanolind facility. But Stanolind closed the project in 1957 as a result of increasing natural gas prices and inability to keep the Carthage plant functioning without massive investment to redesign and rebuild it. It was a technical success but an economic failure.

Given the concentration of the company's scientific minds at the highly advanced research center adjacent to the Whiting refinery, it was reasonable to expect that chemical research as a separate function would have its beginnings at the Whiting research laboratory.

So it was that pioneering work, characterized as a departure from lines of research that oil companies traditionally conducted, occurred at the Whiting research center in the early 1950s. At that time, actually beginning in the late 1940s and extending into the 1950s, Standard was conducting exploratory research along two lines at Whiting. One, by the oil group, was on conversion of olefins, basically ethylene and propylene, to liquid products. In this search, the oil group hit upon catalysts that resulted in high-density polyethylene, the first ever made. The other line was by the chemicals group, which was experimenting on ways to improve processes patented by other companies for making polyethylene by using improved catalysts at lower pressures than the pressures being utilized commercially.

In the midst of these two lines of research, a 31-year-old research scientist, Alex Zletz, who had just received his Ph.D. degree in physical chemistry at Purdue University, came to work in the exploratory research group. He was assigned to the polyethylene project as an assistant project chemist, working with Donald R. Carmody, Edwin F. Peters, Allan K. Roebuck, and Bernard Evering, group leader.

In experimenting with a new group of catalysts, Zletz found that molybdenum oxide on alumina was better than catalysts earlier researchers had used in producing polyethylene. Zletz recognized that his catalyst might be used to produce a solid polymer from propylene, something that had never been done. He tried out his idea in August of 1950, and it worked; he thus could claim that he had invented the first solid polypropylene.

Soon afterwards, Zletz was assigned to a high-priority government research project Standard had undertaken, and other members of the exploratory research group continued small-scale polypropylene research, based on Zletz's work. In early 1953, research chemist Edwin F. Peters, using the Zletz catalyst under modified conditions, produced higher yields of the product now characterized as crystalline polypropylene, completing his basic work in March, 1954.

Standard filed its first significant patent application on crystalline polypropylene (as a composition of matter invention based on first production—not on the process of production) in early October, 1954. But research doesn't take place in a vacuum. By 1957, at least five companies in the U.S. and abroad had applied for patents, and, as a result, in 1958 the U.S. Patent Office initiated what are called interference proceedings to determine which applicant was entitled to the U.S. patent rights for inventing crystalline polypropylene.

On November 29, 1971, the Board of Patent Interferences awarded priority to Montedison S.p.A. The legal marathon resumed when this decision was appealed early in 1972 by Standard, E. I. duPont de Nemours and Company, and Phillips Petroleum Company. The three cases were consolidated in the U.S. District Court in Delaware on May 15, 1975, and hearings resumed before Senior Judge Caleb Wright.

The District Court's opinion, delivered in January, 1980, affirmed the claim of Montedison that it was entitled to a June 8, 1954, priority date. But much to the surprise of all, the court held that Phillips was entitled to a priority date no later than January 27, 1953, instead of the January 11, 1956, date assigned to it by the Patent Office. Since the priority date awarded to Phillips predated the others, the remaining litigants promptly appealed.

The U.S. Supreme Court refused to review the case on April 5, 1982, with the result that Phillips was awarded the patent in the composition of matter interference, based on the lower court's determination for Phillips of the January 27, 1953, invention priority date.

A composition-of-matter patent provides rights to claim royalty on a covered product regardless of the process used in its manufacture. Similar patent interference proceedings had been pending in Canada. Canada recognized Zletz as the first to invent crystalline polypropylene, and awarded the basic patent in Canada to Standard.

Under a cross-licensing agreement entered into by Standard and Phillips, Standard's Amoco Chemicals subsidiary received a royalty-free license under any Phillips patent right arising from the U.S. interference, and Phillips gained similar privileges under Standard's Canadian patent. Thus Standard was freed of any U.S. royalty obligation to Phillips while most of the others in the polypropylene industry would be subject to a Phillips patent for 17 years from date of issue.

Another early venture of Standard in the chemical field was an effort to get into the fertilizer business. Several factors combined to propel the company in this direction. In the late 1940s and early 1950s, when Stanolind Oil and Gas built a number of plants to recover propane and butane from natural gas, large volumes of these materials were generated which could not be used in Standard's refinery system and had to be sold to others.

To avoid selling them on a low-return brokerage basis, the company decided to enter into the direct marketing business and formed, on June 1, 1954, a subsidiary, Tuloma Gas Products Company, to wholesale these liquefied petroleum gases. This eventually led to the establishment of bulk plants throughout the intensive farming areas of the midwest, southeast, and southwest.

Once the bulk plants were in place and the tank trucks necessary to transport LPGs were traveling rural routes, it seemed only logical that these same trucks be used to haul ammonia, to be used in fertilizing the land. After all, the demand for ammonia was in the spring and summer during the planting season, while the demand for propane and butane—LP gas—was chiefly in the winter. So the theory was that going into the ammonia business would permit the company to make full year-round use of its equipment.

To produce anhydrous ammonia and ammonium nitrate solutions, Standard organized Calumet Nitrogen Products Company as a joint venture with Sinclair Refining Company to build and operate a plant to combine nitrogen from the air with hydrogen produced as a by-product from catalytic reforming operations at Standard's refinery at Whiting and Sinclair's at nearby East Chicago. The plant, in full operation by 1957, was small relative to the plants that would be built in the industry, and was equipped with high-cost, high-maintenance reciprocating compressors. It never was truly successful, and it was closed in 1968.

The first rotary compressor ammonia plant Standard built at Texas City worked well enough, and in 1965 the company decided that it would build another. The second plant, however, was designed to produce 1,500 tons daily while competitors were building smaller 1,000- to 1,200-ton-a-day plants. Problems with compressors, heat exchangers, and furnaces forced major downtime and changes. It was a number of years before the plant operated satisfactorily from a mechanical standpoint.

When the farmer bought ammonia from his distributor, he also wanted to buy the other components of fertilizer—phosphorous and potassium—as well. Since phosphorous and potassium were in ample supply, the company decided to buy these products from others for resale rather than attempt to develop its own supplies. At first, the fertilizer business was profitable; but so many people came chasing after these profits—not only oil companies, but chemical companies and rural co-operatives—that the bottom fell out of the market and Standard retrenched. The growth of rural co-ops was a major factor in this change of direction. They paid dividends to their members but no income taxes. This gave them a cost advantage in the market no other entrepreneur could match. But in addition, the price of natural gas used as a raw material in the manufacture of ammonia increased greatly. In 1980, Amoco Chemicals discontinued the manufacture of anhydrous ammonia at Texas City and began supplying the 365 retail fertilizer facilities it had at the time through outside purchases.

These and other postwar developments signaled Standard's growing interest in the production of chemicals, although a major commitment was a few years down the road. Unlike an old-line chemical company, a major oil and gas producer has large quantities of the basic building blocks for chemicals and fertilizers, and plants which routinely produce primary chemical feedstocks in great enough volume to make separation and recovery economically feasible.

Enormous quantities of aromatics, such as toluene and xylene, are needed to make premium gasoline. In Standard's case, making unleaded Amoco Super Premium in particular made toluene separation commercially attractive. Large volumes of aromatics, such as benzene and xylenes, also are needed in chemical operations. Thus, the dual need permitted the design of major refinery units to meet growing demand in petroleum as well as in chemicals.

But Standard did not enter into the chemical field heavily until it had built a solid commercial and technological base for long-term growth. Most significant was the recommendation of Dr. Herman Francis Mark, an Austrian chemist with a worldwide reputation and a consultant to Standard, who targeted terephthalic acid—the intermediate product in the manufacture of polyester fibers—as an area of great potential growth for the chemicals industry.

William E. Kennel, then director of research and development for Amoco Chemicals, heard at a scientific meeting that Scientific Design Company held a patent on a procedure for direct oxidation of paraxylene (a hydrocarbon that could be produced in refineries) into terephthalic acid. He immediately reported the information to Joseph K. Roberts, then a director and general manager of research and development for Standard, and an advocate of expanding Standard's chemical activities.

Although this particular technology was in the early stages of development and had not been tested commercially, Standard acquired rights to it through the purchase on August 25, 1955, of Mid-Century Corporation, a spin-off of Scientific Design; and, believing there eventually would be a substantial market for the new polyester fibers, immediately began work to develop the newly acquired technology into a commercial process. Standard began building its first terephthalic acid plant, at Joliet, Illinois, in 1957, the same year all chemical activity was consolidated in Amoco Chemicals Corporation.

The Joliet plant symbolized the company's commitment to chemicals. But it had its problems. The plant originally was designed to utilize a mixed xylene feedstock which came directly from the Whiting refinery. The mixed feed was then oxidized simultaneously to phthalic acid, terephthalic acid, isophthalic acid and other isomers. These mixed acids were then separated and purified.

But this procedure didn't work satisfactorily. One problem was corrosion, others were mechanical. The acids attacked titanium and stainless steel liners in separators, and the material solidified in piping. It was like "trying to move a hundred tons an hour of toothpaste a hundred feet when the toothpaste would set up like plaster if we didn't move it fast enough," Swearingen was to recall some years later.

Starting with an impure feedstock with the idea of separating pure products turned out to be all wrong; the first step should have been to purify the feedstock as much as possible, and then to make a single product. As Robert C. Gunness once remarked, "There's a whale of a difference between a valuable mixture of chemicals and a mixture of valuable chemicals." So the procedure was changed. Whiting research scientists had worked out the technology to separate paraxylene from its isomers. Paraxylene would be separated from the mixture of xylenes at the Whiting refinery; paraxylene then would be oxidized to terephthalic acid. A major breakthrough came when Standard scientists perfected a unique process to produce purified terephthalic acid without going through an esterification step—the basis of Standard's polyester fiber intermediate business.

Chemicals, little more than a faint ray on the horizon as a

possible future line of business before World War II, was still the new boy on the block by the beginning of the 1960s in Standard's basic upstream-downstream oil and natural gas business. But it had become important, and it was growing. Sales of chemical products were $73 million in 1963, up from $24 million in 1957.

Standard developed a strong patent position in methods of producing thermoplastics and organic intermediates, and its research scientists engaged in a wide range of petrochemical studies. The manufacture of viscous polypropylene, a new chemical intermediate, began in 1961 at Standard's El Dorado, Arkansas, refinery. Marketing of trimellitic anhydride, a component in plasticizers and in protective coating resins, began in 1962 from a semicommercial unit at the Joliet chemical facility. A unit at the Texas City refinery began production in 1962 of a new, light-colored hydrocarbon resin for floor tile and a variety of other uses.

At Haverhill, Ohio, the company began operating a new plant as a joint venture with a subsidiary of Pittsburgh Coke and Chemical Company to produce oxo-alcohols. In 1963, Amoco Chemicals introduced additional products including styrene monomer, a component in the manufacture of plastics and synthetic rubber. The capacity of the Joliet facility was expanded. At Texas City, plans were underway to build a new 250 million pounds per year styrene monomer plant.

Expansion continued outside the United States also. In the Netherlands, a Standard half-interest company neared completion of a new plant at Delfzijl which would use Standard's oxidation process to make dimethyl terephthalate for the partner's use and for European market sales.

Because of such developments as these and, perhaps more directly, the differences in marketing practices in the chemical business as contrasted with gasoline marketing, it became clear that someone with knowledge of the field was needed in the organization if the company's efforts were to measure up to the apparent potential. Frank Prior once admonished Swearingen, then president, "Don't put another penny into chemicals until you find the right man to run it."

That man proved to be Herschel H. Cudd, who joined Standard in 1963. He had been president of Avisun Corporation, formed by American Viscose Corporation and Sun Oil Company to manufacture polypropylene. Cudd was a versatile and resourceful Texan who, in addition to acquiring a Ph.D. in chemistry from the University of Texas, had earned part of his education by serving as chief chemist for the Texas Liquor Control Board immediately after the repeal of Prohibition. With an associate, Cudd had written all the standards for alcoholic beverages in Texas.

After he received his degree his career followed a more conventional course; he served first with DuPont in Buffalo (from which he was driven by the depth of winter snows) and with International Minerals and Chemicals Corporation in Atlanta. Prior to joining Avisun, he had been in the research division of a Georgia textile company and head of the Engineering and Experimental station at Georgia Institute of Technology.

Cudd came to Standard as a vice president, but it soon became apparent that it would be necessary to name him president of Amoco Chemicals with direct operating control. In his own words, "When I came to Standard, the people here had the impression that if they had raw materials and technology and money that they could make money; but nothing could be further from the truth. Without marketing integrity and skill, no money was to be made."

As Cudd was to explain later, individuals whose only background had been in the oil industry sometimes confused sales with marketing. In an effort to make sales of new and unfamiliar products they made promises on which they could not deliver or followed pricing practices that disrupted the market they were attempting to serve.

In Cudd's view, industrial marketing required developing contacts, confidence, and rapport with customers, and the establishment of a long-range plan for developing the market. Then, as he was to demonstrate, sales would follow. It was equally important in his view that the long-range plan have the trust and backing of management. With that assurance he committed himself and the company to three goals:

1. A ten-year plan for success in the terephthalic acid business.
2. A program for diversification among chemical products.
3. A plan to move heavily into plastics.

Cudd believed two elements were crucial in making a success of the chemicals business. One was timing, for the growth-demand curve changed so rapidly that once a market opportunity was identified, it was essential to announce and execute expansion plans quickly before competitors could preempt the field. As he was often to remind his colleagues, "Either do it at the right

191

time or don't do it at all." The other element on which he placed
great emphasis was a sales technical service group which could
work closely with customers in the chemical business to first
determine their needs and then how these needs might be met by
Standard.

Conscious of the importance of timing, Cudd worked with
the management team of Amoco Chemicals to develop a program
which would achieve his goals. Included in the Amoco Chemicals
planning group were Kennel, John G. (Jack) Lambertsen, general
marketing manager, and L. L. (Larry) Smith, vice president for
manufacturing.

When they were finished, they presented Standard management with a plan calling for a principal emphasis on the production of the starting materials for polyester fibers. If the plan were
properly executed, they predicted that Amoco Chemicals would
increase sales from $40 million a year in 1963 to $740 million in
1974.

The strategy outlined in the ten-year plan began to take
shape. One of the early projects was a plant at Decatur, Alabama,
to manufacture 200 million pounds per year of dimethyl terephthalate (DMT) and purified terephthalic acid (PTA). It was
completed in 1966 and its capacity was doubled in 1967. PTA
capacity was increased to 1.8 million pounds per year by 1976 and
manufacture of DMT was phased out. Cudd then turned to other
projects, one of which was the desire to license from Avisun the
technology to produce polypropylene, a versatile polymer used in
making a wide variety of products including carpet backing,
bagging for baling wool and cotton, film for packaging food and
clothing items, and household appliance and automotive parts.
Cudd believed Standard had a reasonably good patent position in
polypropylene, but it did not have manufacturing technology.

Kennel was assigned the task of negotiating the agreement.
When he approached Avisun, its officers surprised him with an
offer to sell Standard the entire company. Cudd was at first
unenthusiastic. When he was with Avisun, Avisun had no affiliated company to which it could market part of its product. It was
Cudd's strategy for Standard that there be an assured "in-house"
market for 35 per cent of the company's basic output.

Since Cudd had left, however, Avisun had acquired a half-
interest in Patchogue-Plymouth Company, a manufacturer of
carpet-backing made of woven polypropylene. This provided an
assured customer, which, in Cudd's opinion, greatly strengthened

the attractiveness of the Avisun purchase. On Cudd's recommendation, Swearingen went to Robert G. Dunlop, president of Sun Oil Company, in 1967, and negotiated a purchase agreement which was signed on January 29, 1968.

Patchogue-Plymouth took polypropylene manufactured by Avisun, extruded it into a thin sheet, slit it into tape, and then wove the tape into a mat which was used for carpet backing. Shag carpet was becoming increasingly popular, and it required a backing into which the face yarn could be punched. Historically, this backing had been made with jute, but several things were happening almost simultaneously which created a market for synthetic materials in this application.

Troubles in India and Bangladesh, the traditional sources for jute, made the supply uncertain both as to availability and price. As a natural material, jute had knots and nodules in it which would break needles and shut down the carpet-making operation until the needles were replaced. Moreover, jute absorbed moisture, and carpets which had this backing would become taut in the winter when the heat was on and humidity was low, and develop a roll in the summer when the humidity was high and the material loosened up. The material produced by Patchogue-Plymouth did not absorb moisture; once it was put down, it stayed flat. With polypropylene, Standard was in a position to deliver both a uniform material and a guaranteed supply at competitive prices.

The half of Patchogue-Plymouth not owned by Avisun belonged to Bernard Schwartz, president of Patchogue-Plymouth. Sensing the great potential of this new product, Cudd undertook to negotiate the purchase of the other half of the company rather than be subject to interminable negotiations over the transfer price of polypropylene and what its impact might be on profits of the minority interest in the subsidiary. This also was accomplished. Subsequently, the company built a series of plants in Georgia, Canada, Germany, Australia, Brazil, and the United Kingdom.

In 1968, about half of the Free World capacity to produce the polyester intermediate, terephthalic acid, and some 40 per cent of the Free World capacity for paraxylene, the chemical feed stock used in making terephthalic acid, were based on Standard's processes, being used by its own plants or by its licensees. The company's own investment in plants to manufacture the new products accelerated rapidly—visible evidence of where Standard stood in its long-range program to diversify into chemicals.

Construction of additional chemical and refining facilities at Standard's Texas City refinery had about used up ground space for expansion, and on July 9, 1968, Amoco Chemicals laid plans before Standard's board of directors to build a $200 million chemical manufacturing complex on a 2,400-acre tract near Alvin, Texas, on the banks of Chocolate Bayou, from which the complex got its name.

The first plant to be built on the tract would produce 100 million pounds per year of high-density polyethylene. Construction began in 1969. Also in 1969, construction began on a 150 million pounds per year polypropylene plant. Each was put on stream in 1971. In 1972, construction began on a one billion pounds per year ethylene plant. It was completed in 1976, and its twin was completed in 1977. A second high-density polyethylene plant was completed in 1976 with a capacity of 300 million pounds per year, and a second polypropylene plant, with a capacity of 240 million pounds per year, went on stream on 1979.

Purified terephthalic acid (PTA) continued to increase its dominance in the marketplace, with demand increasing at an 11 per cent annual rate during the '70s. Polyester continued to displace other fibers and in 1980 accounted for one-third of all United States fiber consumption. To help meet the demand, Standard in 1978 opened the world's largest PTA plant on the Cooper River near Charleston, South Carolina, capable of producing a billion pounds of PTA per year. Soon after its dedication, it was operating above its design capacity.

In constructing the Cooper River plant on 3,500 acres of South Carolina land, Standard sought to produce a model for future industrial development in the United States by demonstrating that a facility could be constructed with due respect for the environment and ecology of the area. For example, when it was necessary to dredge two miles of the Cooper River to accommodate sea-going vessels, it was done only after consultation with the State Archeological Commission about ways of finding and preserving items of scientific interest. Prior to the dredging, Amoco Chemicals supported a six-week diving expedition in the river that yielded more than 5,000 pounds of fossils and historical artifacts. These were later stored at the South Carolina museum to be cleaned, filed and catalogued. Archeological finds from early Indian tribes and plantations were also recovered, preserved, and donated to the South Carolina Institute of Archeology and Anthropology.

To replace the wildlife feeding ground lost to the actual plant site, Amoco environmental specialists planted open areas with wild grains. A Charleston forester was consulted on routes into the plant that would least disturb nesting areas. Space cleared for construction was replanted with shrubs and flowers common to the area. Along the main road leading into the plant, more than 5,000 individual plantings were made.

Despite the company's success in supplying PTA to the apparel field for making polyester fibers, the cyclical and seasonal nature of the clothing industry made it desirable to find a market to help iron out peaks and valleys of demand. Under William Kennel, who had played a key role in Standard's original entry into terephthalic acid and plastics, Amoco Chemicals research scientists at Naperville began the search for a means of producing a plastic bottle that would meet the exacting requirements of the carbonated soft-drink companies.

In 1971, Amoco produced its first clear bottle from polyester resin and the commercial development group began making contacts with major soft-drink bottlers to see if its properties were acceptable. Standard at the time was also reassessing its investments in plastic products and in the middle of the decade was beginning to divest itself of some of its interests in consumer plastic products such as housewares and plastic cups.

The opportunity to manufacture and market plastic bottles, for which the company had the advanced technology necessary, provided a double opportunity. The first was to make a profit on the plastic product manufacturing operation; the second was to expand the market for the terephthalic acid.

At the time, Coca-Cola had been working with Monsanto to develop a plastic bottle and Pepsico was working with DuPont on a similar project. By 1975, Coca-Cola was in the market with a test bottle when DuPont suddenly announced it had decided not to market a beverage bottle but instead to license its bottle technology. The move left Pepsi without a bottle supplier. Pepsi quickly sought other manufacturers, including Amoco Chemicals, to inquire if any of them could make a polyester bottle in commercial quantities able to meet Coke's competitive challenge.

In 1976, a letter of intent and later a contract were signed with Pepsico, and Amoco Chemicals began a crash program to convert its Seymour, Indiana, plant to the manufacture of beverage bottles, the latest in a series of chameleon-like changes in the character of this southern Indiana facility.

195

The commitment to new ventures based on chemicals and plastics reflected a corporate conviction that chemicals in the future would be a major growth area for Standard. There were several reasons for this. First, the chemical business is one that requires raw materials of which an integrated oil company has a supply that an old-line chemical company ordinarily couldn't match.

At one time, Union Carbide decided it was going to get into the oil business, invested a lot of money, and then decided it didn't have the resources necessary to support the effort. Celanese had a similar experience. German chemical companies had never even attempted it, nor had DuPont until it acquired Continental Oil Company in 1981.

Throughout the 1970s, Standard's strategy in Amoco Chemicals was one of developing new markets for products which in turn would create a demand for the basic and intermediate chemicals it produced. Despite cyclical variations in the demand for some products, sales grew at an accelerated pace, from $73 million in 1963 to more than $3 billion in 1980.

Recognizing the need for specialized marketing skills in various product areas, Amoco Chemicals aligned its manufacturing and marketing functions in four subsidiaries:

Amoco Engineered Plastics Company, incorporated on December 19, 1966—molded structural foam thermoplastics;

Amoco Fabrics Company, incorporated on May 7, 1970—produced and marketed carpet backing and synthetic fabrics and fibers for the tufted carpet industry;

Amoco Foam Products Company, incorporated on May 21, 1974—manufactured and marketed disposable foam plastic dinnerware, food service products, automobile headliners, and other industrial foam products;

Amoco Container Company, incorporated on August 23, 1978—manufactured and marketed plastic bottles and containers.

The importance of Herschel Cudd's emphasis on rapport with the customer was illustrated by an incident growing out of the 1973–1974 Arab oil embargo. Amoco Chemicals had won Standard's approval for construction of a cracking unit for the production of ethylene on the condition that contracts were signed in advance for the sale of a major portion of its output. At the time, ethylene was selling at a low price because the cost of the crude oil from which the feedstocks were drawn was low.

Before the plant was finished, the oil embargo and the OPEC price increases which followed radically changed the cost factors and market price of ethylene. An executive vice president of an important customer which had contracted for the output called Cudd to say that he was sure Standard could not afford to sell ethylene at the contract price and suggested a renegotiation might be in everyone's best interest. After the market settled down, this was done; to Cudd this was the kind of reward which could be expected from building a reputation for integrity.

As the company entered new markets, each was carefully evaluated as to whether potential volume and rate of return were appropriate for Standard. Two of the new marketing efforts had been in molded home furnishings, called "cubicals," and in plastic consumer products for outdoor living. Because the market acceptance of these products was below the performance levels Standard had established as desirable, the company announced in 1974 that it was withdrawing from their manufacture and sale.

Other market areas were more promising. Amoco Chemicals improved its position in the polystyrene packaging market with its acquisition in 1980 of Western Foam Pak, Inc., a manufacturer of food packing trays of formed polystyrene, and merged it into Amoco Foam Products Company. Amoco Fabrics Company designed a new family of woven and nonwoven synthetic fabrics called ProPex Geotextiles. Engineered for specific applications, they protect construction and prolong the life of projects where they are used. ProPex Geotextiles are used to stabilize the soil under railway roadbeds, temporary roads such as those built by drilling crews or loggers, and in highway construction.

Standard's involvement with civil engineering fabrics—their generic name—began in the early 1970s when the Amoco Fabrics Division of Amoco Deutschland GmbH, West Germany, developed a heavy, woven, polypropylene fabric for use in Dutch land reclamation projects. Called Sea Carpet, the fabric was used to reinforce earthen dikes, canal banks, and piers against the eroding effects of changing tide levels, currents, and wave wash.

Civil engineering fabrics have the economic advantage of lowering the cost of construction. For example, a layer of fabric placed over subsoil allows roadbuilders to reduce sharply the amount of aggregate they must install beneath pavements. In some cases, aggregate use can be cut 40 per cent, providing substantial cost savings with excellent long-term performance.

By 1981, Standard's chemical business was well established, with identifiable assets of nearly $2.8 billion and annual revenues

197

in excess of $3.2 billion. Amoco Chemicals ranked among the top 10 U.S. chemical companies and was poised to capitalize on future growth in demand for its major product lines.

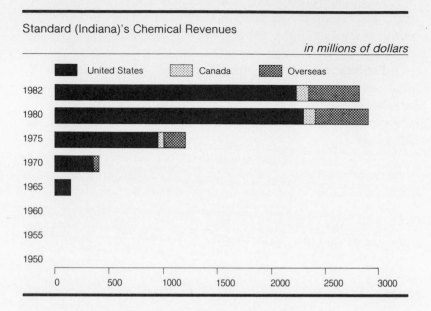

Standard (Indiana)'s Chemical Revenues

in millions of dollars

With products of its chemical plants, using for the most part proprietary technology, the company was producing synthetic materials based upon petrochemicals for the manufacture of four human needs: food, clothing, shelter, and transportation.

Diversification within the field of chemicals—another of the ten-year plan goals—was accomplished by acquisition of a factory at Fullerton, California, to produce plastic housewares and out-door living items. Plants for making plastic food packaging materials, acquired in Wisconsin and California, were expanded.

Manufacture of plastic pipe was another of the diversification measures. At one time during the 1960s, Standard had five plants manufacturing lightweight pipe from polystyrene produced from its chemical plants. However, within a brief period polyvinyl chloride proved to be a superior material for the pipe. Because Standard did not produce polyvinyl chloride in its own plants, it later sold the pipe operation and returned to its fundamental business philosophy of maintaining a direct supply relationship between its fabricating activities and its basic output of chemicals.

Out of all of these experiences, Swearingen recalls that the company learned several things about doing business in chemicals. The first was that the company had the ability to make materials of chemical purity out of hydrocarbon raw materials. Second, that the proper way to proceed was to separate and purify the hydrocarbon feedstock going into the system rather than purify the end products. Third, that it was necessary to put strong emphasis on marketing.

The basic goal, as defined by Swearingen, was to manufacture products in which the company had a unique technological advantage over its competition. But in the chemical field, as in any other, there is no such thing as a permanent technological advantage.

Exploration in Foreign Lands

16

To a reader living in the last two decades of the Twentieth Century, the state of Oklahoma may seem to be an unlikely choice of localities in which to begin a story about Standard's reentry into the international oil arena. Yet, it was in the board room of Standard's subsidiary, Stanolind Oil and Gas Company, at Tulsa, Oklahoma—then called (with some accuracy) "The Oil Capital of the World"—that a decision was made in November, 1947, to investigate the advisability of Stanolind's expanding its operations to Canada and other Western Hemisphere countries.

Inauspicious though it was, this action led to the company's first operations outside the United States since 1932. Because the 1947 decision involved exploration and production only and was limited to the Western Hemisphere, some considered it a mere extension of domestic operations. A decision by Standard to broaden activity outside the United States and the Western Hemisphere was yet to come and would then be based on plans that would encompass the functions of an integrated operation: refining, marketing, and transportation, as well as exploration and production.

Colonel Stewart's drive to make Standard an international enterprise had resulted in an integrated overseas operation. But his goal went by default when his successor as chief executive officer, Edward G. Seubert, sold the Pan American Petroleum and Transport foreign properties in 1932.

Seubert's successor, Robert E. Wilson, also was reluctant to invest outside the United States. The exceptions to Wilson's philosophy, though limited to the Western Hemisphere, largely resulted from the advocacy of three men.

Alonzo W. Peake, then president of Standard, was oriented

toward expansion of Standard's oil exploration and production activities.

Abetting Peake's philosophy were two oil and gas field veteran experts who had been Peake associates since Dixie Oil days in the 1920s: Frank O. Prior, now a Standard director and vice president for production, and Edgar F. Bullard, a geologist and president of Stanolind Oil and Gas. Under the leadership of these men, Stanolind Oil and Gas had been almost from 1931, the year in which it began operations, a major growth and profit contributor to the Standard corporation.

With this enviable record, and because Stanolind Oil and Gas was Standard's principal oil and gas explorer, it became the explorer's role to step out into new territory.

Stanolind Oil and Gas formed a foreign exploration department in 1948. That same year the department established a Canadian division with an office in Calgary, Alberta, Canada. It was about a year after the spectacular oil field discovery by another company at Leduc, 13 miles southwest of Edmonton in February, 1947. Charles F. Schock, division landman, was in charge. He was named division manager on January 1, 1950.

Results were slow in coming. In 1951, Prior asked Swearingen to have a study made to see if Standard should remain in Canada. At this time, Prior had moved up to executive vice president and had brought Swearingen in from Stanolind Oil and Gas to be Standard's general manager for production. The exploration experts at Stanolind made a convincing case that there was real undiscovered potential in Canada, and Prior gave them another year to prove their case.

Almost simultaneously with the completion of an update of that study and near the end of the reprieve, another operator struck oil in a wildcat well in the Pembina area of west central Alberta, which became one of the great oil fields of North America. Stanolind held extensive acreage in the area and its successful wildcat and development drilling helped extend the field substantially. The company became one of the field's largest operators.

Heading the Canadian organization have been a number of executives whose accomplishments in Canada were followed by experience in other parts of the world and advancement to higher positions in Standard. George H. Galloway was named division manager in 1952. He subsequently became a director of Standard and president of Amoco Production Company where he guided that subsidiary in major lease acquisitions, exploration, and field development during the 1970s. Frank C. Osment, who followed Galloway in 1959, later became an executive vice president and a director of Standard and has been recognized by his peers for his leadership in developing the international organization which returned Standard to the ranks of successful overseas oil exploration and production companies and later for the development of Amoco Minerals Company.

John C. Meeker, who served first in Canada as division geologist beginning in 1957, was elected in 1969 to be the first president of Amoco Canada Petroleum Company Ltd., the Canadian corporation formed that year as a wholly-owned Standard subsidiary to qualify as a lessee of Crown lands. When Standard combined worldwide oil and natural gas exploration and production into Amoco Production Company in 1981, Meeker followed Galloway as president of Amoco Production Company (USA).

Kenneth J. Barr was named division production manager of the Calgary (Canada) division of what was then Pan American Petroleum Corporation in 1965, and was elected vice president for production when Amoco Canada was formed. He later became executive vice president of Amoco Production Company, then president of Amoco Minerals Company, another worldwide Standard subsidiary. Henry O. Boswell replaced Barr as Canadian vice president for production in 1970, and followed Meeker as president of Amoco Canada in 1973. He became president of Amoco Production Company (International) in 1981 and president of the consolidated Amoco Production Company and a director of Standard in 1983. Fraser H. Allen followed Boswell as president of Amoco Canada in 1976. He retired in 1981 and was succeeded by Norman J. Rubash.

In the same year in which it became active in Canada (1948), Stanolind Oil and Gas incorporated Santa Marta Oil Company and Colombian West Coast Oil Company to conduct exploration in Colombia. Standard exploration operations in Colombia did not actually get underway until 1960. Because of political disturbances no drilling was conducted in Colombia, however.

In the mid-1950s, the seeming political stability of the West Indies offered an opportunity to expand Western Hemisphere exploration. Both Cuba and Jamaica appeared potentially productive. As a result, in October, 1955, Stanolind Oil and Gas organized a wholly-owned subsidiary, Cuban Stanolind Oil and Gas Company, and signed contracts with two Cuban firms to explore concessions in Cuba. The two Cuban firms, Cuban Venezuelan Oil Voting Trust and Trans-Cuba Oil Company, held over 17 million acres in Cuban onshore and offshore concessions.

Shortly after Stanolind executive vice president Albert L. Solliday, the former Dixie Oil land man and a leasing specialist, negotiated the Cuba concessions, Fidel Castro established his guerrilla headquarters in the mountains out of Santiago. The rebels soon learned that on Thursdays a truck bearing fresh vegetables and meat would appear on the road leading to the drilling area. Just as regularly, they would hijack the food, an act made easy because the government troops were so afraid of the guerrillas they refused to escort the truck. The result was that hijackings became regular events.

However, the company found that permitting Castro's men to hijack the food supplies meant they would not interfere with drilling, so for a time matters were allowed to take their course. But Castro soon began appropriating the trucks and equipment as well as the food; and, since the drilling had only produced dry holes, it was decided in 1958 to shut the operation down—just before Castro took over the government in 1959. Results in nearby Jamaica, though without the hazards in Cuba, were equally disappointing.

In July, 1956, Stanolind Oil and Gas incorporated Venezuelan Pan American Petroleum Corporation, marking an exploration thrust into an area Standard gave up in the 1932 sale of foreign properties. Soon, under the new name Stanolind acquired in Standard's functional reorganization on February 1, 1957—Pan American Petroleum Corporation—the company expanded its activities to Europe, the Middle East, and Africa.

On January 21, 1958, it consolidated foreign operations under a new subsidiary, Pan American International Oil Company, with two groups—one for the Western and one for the Eastern Hemisphere. Headquarters were established in New York City. Canadian exploration and production continued to be operated as a division out of the Tulsa headquarters. Another leg supporting Standard's return to international operations was the 1958 organization of Amoco Trading Company to handle the purchase and sale of foreign crude oil and products outside North America.

With Prior firmly in control as chairman after Wilson retired on March 19, 1958, and Swearingen as president, stockholders were told that "behind these activities is a simply stated policy:

203

we are interested in opportunities for profitable operation wherever they may exist." At the same time, stockholders were assured that these new ventures did not "represent an abrupt departure from past policies, but rather a vigorous expansion of activities designed to establish Standard as an important factor in the international oil picture."

Since Standard had been out of the international field for a quarter of a century when its Pan American Petroleum subsidiary formed Pan American International Oil Company in 1958, Edgar F. Bullard, then president of Pan American Petroleum, looked outside the ranks of Standard for someone with international experience to head the operation.

The man he chose on February 1, 1958, to be president was C. F. Dohm, an experienced oil geologist who had worked for Standard (New Jersey) and later for Conorada Petroleum Corporation, a company formed for exploration outside North America by Continental Oil Company, Ohio Oil Company, and Amerada Petroleum Corporation. William E. Humphrey, who earned a Ph.D. in geology from the University of Michigan and who had worked overseas for a number of companies, was hired by Dohm as vice president for exploration.

In joining the company, Dohm expressed a strong desire that he be permitted to negotiate an agreement to explore for oil in Iran. Dohm told Prior, Bullard, and Swearingen that he once had an offshore concession in Iran tied up but that the Conorada group had refused to approve it. It was clear he was highly motivated to complete the deal for Standard in order to vindicate his judgment. Only two weeks after he was hired, Dohm came to Standard's board with a request for a $25 million cash bonus to acquire an Iranian concession in the Persian Gulf, plus an exploration commitment to spend $8.5 million annually in the first four years, and $6 million per year more during the next eight years.

If commercial production were found, Pan American International and Iran's state oil company, National Iranian Oil Company, would each be entitled to 50 per cent of proceeds from the sale of produced oil. Standard's 50 per cent share would be subject to a 50 per cent Iranian government tax. The result amounted to an effective 75–25 split. The proposal was approved.

The agreement with Iran was controversial within the industry, although it wasn't the first time the historic 50–50 profit split formula, typical of oil operations around the world, had been broken. Italy's Ente Nazionale Idrocaburi had signed an effective 75–25 split in favor of Iran. What was different, according to Dohm, was the amount of the bonus.

An interesting sidelight of these negotiations and a discouraging aspect of the operations of the U.S. government's representatives overseas was recounted by Prior. He had gone to Iran for the signing of the agreement because the Shah thought it important that the chief executive of Standard be present even though the company was represented by Dohm, the president, and Solliday, the executive vice president, respectively of the international subsidiary and its parent company.

At a dinner at the house of the leader of the Iranian opposition party (who also happened to be well-connected to the Shah), the American ambassador took Prior aside and said, "Now you are going to have an audience with the Shah again. You have met the Shah, and you might have some influence. Will you please interest the Shah in giving other concessions to other U.S. oil companies and not charge as much money as you have paid?"

Having just committed more than $25 million of his company's money and taken considerable risk, Prior was stunned to be asked by his own country's ambassador to help negotiate a cheaper contract for his competitors. As he recalled later, "I just looked at him. I didn't want to use words, so I just stared at him, and I got out of the room as quickly as I could. I never was so upset. I never met a man who had that much brass. Incredible— for a U.S. ambassador to try to get me to help a competitor get into Iran at a cheaper price than we got in."

Another experience of Prior's on that trip is also illuminating because it is a reminder that in dealing with persons of different cultural backgrounds, there are often issues which are of more importance than dollars and cents. When Prior initially met the Shah, the first thing the ruler said was, "You know—we are not Arabs. We are Aryans, and we are the same race as you are, and we have a great history. We have great pride." Prior replied, "Oh yes, we know, your Majesty." After that, the audience with the Shah went very easily. Expectations for Iran were confirmed with the 1961 discovery of a major oil field (Darius) south of Kharg Island in the Persian Gulf. By 1970, three more offshore fields (Cyrus, Fereidoon and Ardeshir) had been discovered in the Gulf.

Other overseas agreements made during 1958 included contracts for oil exploration rights in Libya, Algeria, and Mozambique in Africa, offshore rights along the coast of Italy, and an agreement with the state oil agency of Argentina to begin exploration there with a commitment to drill 50 wells in the first year. A successful oil well was completed in Venezuela early in the year. Trinidad, Colombia, and Indonesia were soon added to the list.

The international subsidiary's growing operations merited parallel status with its Tulsa-based parent in the Standard organization. Consequently, on July 1, 1962, the parent, Pan American Petroleum Corporation, reverted to a strictly North American operation and all overseas operations including Pan American International Oil Company and Amoco Trading Corporation were consolidated into a new Standard subsidiary named American International Oil Company with headquarters in New York City.

L. Chase Ritts, who had been the parent company's coordinator of crude oil production, purchasing, and transportation, and was better attuned than Dohm to Standard's internal systems of conducting business, was elected president of the new international subsidiary. He was expected to provide what Standard regarded as needed discipline for Chris Dohm's freewheeling methods. Dohm was named executive vice president reporting to Ritts.

Overseas expansion in the late 1950s and early 1960s came at a time when the United States was trying to deal with surplus producing capacity internally by the use of both voluntary and mandatory import controls. It therefore became imperative that Standard not only find and produce crude oil overseas for future U.S. needs but develop refining and marketing overseas until the oil would be needed in the United States. No matter how much oil was found in some of these out of the way places, it wasn't going to be profitable until it could be "monetized" by being converted into gasoline, fuel oil, and other products and sold in overseas markets. Accomplishing that objective wouldn't be easy. Frank Prior once commented that "if you went around Europe with a bucket of oil, it would be easier to sell the bucket than the oil."

The search for markets was the reason for the establishment in 1958 of the so-called Paris group (Societe Civile Amoco) headed by Joseph K. Roberts whose career up to the time of his Paris appointment had been in research as both a practicing chemical engineer and as an executive. Both Roberts and Paris were curious choices. Roberts was a director of the company and had considered himself a competitor of Frank Prior's for the position of chairman. Personal relations between the two men were not the best. Roberts had enough independent authority, however, to choose Paris as his headquarters because, according to later interviews, of its technical libraries and central location. Others would argue that London was the financial and commercial gateway for the Eastern Hemisphere, and would have been a better choice.

The method of operating the Paris group was improvised to make use of existing skills in the company. As soon as the group initiated a project, a group of domestic refining and marketing specialists would be sent from Standard's foreign market planning group in Chicago to analyze the proposal and evaluate it as a possible recommendation to management in Chicago.

Again, there was an organizational problem. Chris Dohm knew a lot about foreign exploration operations but very little about refining and marketing and how Standard did business. In Paris, there was a group of people from the domestic side, who knew the company, as well as the technology of marketing and refining, but almost nothing about international business characteristics applicable to oil. Friction was a natural byproduct of the association of these disparate groups, and it was not lessened when Frank Prior, accompanied by George Myers, arrived in Paris to deal with the situation.

History will not confirm whether it was Prior who said, "Joe, you're fired," or whether it was Roberts who said, "I quit," but the outcome was the same. Donald A. Monro, manager of Standard's purchasing department and former chief engineer in its manufacturing department, was dispatched to Paris to take over from Roberts in late 1959. Roberts took early retirement on January 13, 1960. The Paris staff of Societe Civile Amoco was strengthened by assignments from Standard's Chicago headquarters, but in 1962, when American International Oil Company was formed, the Paris office was closed. Several members of the staff were returned to Chicago and others were assigned to the office of Amoco International, S.A., which had been set up at Geneva, Switzerland, in 1960.

In any event, a refinery at Cremona, Italy, and 700 service stations in northern and central Italy had been acquired in 1961. Amoco petroleum products were being sold also in Germany, the British Isles, and Switzerland. A subsidiary was established in Australia to develop refining and marketing activities there.

In 1959, Dohm had sought a concession in the Western

207

Desert of Egypt but had been outbid. In 1963, he was able to sign an agreement with the United Arab Republic and the Egyptian General Petroleum Corporation for petroleum rights on 18 million acres in another section of the desert, and, in the course of these negotiations, developed a close relationship with Egyptian government and oil industry representatives. As a result of this good will, Standard was able to enter into a 50-50 joint partnership agreement with the government-owned Egyptian General Petroleum Corporation, and in February of 1964, this joint venture was granted petroleum rights covering 1.6 million acres in the Gulf of Suez.

There were obvious risks in going into Egypt. In 1956, the Egyptian government under President Gamal Abdel Nasser had nationalized the properties of foreign companies doing business there, including the oil companies, and in 1961 had extended nationalization to many other industries and businesses.

Some of Standard's directors had reservations about investing there; Jacob Blaustein, Standard's largest individual stockholder and a member of the board, was particularly vehement in opposing the Egyptian operations. However, as a result of Dohm's persuasion and the support of other directors, Standard approved the agreements with Egypt. Exploration in the Western Desert began in 1963, and in the Gulf of Suez in 1964. Within a year, El Morgan, a major oil field, was discovered in the Gulf.

The Egyptians proved to be knowledgeable and sophisticated partners. Because commercial oil production in Egypt was more than half a century old, many of the people working for the government oil company were trained technicians, some of whom had at one time been employed by foreign oil companies. Another positive factor for Standard was that for economic reasons, Egypt, unlike some of its Middle East neighbors, was interested in producing as much oil as rapidly as possible and selling it for the best possible price—objectives which coincided with those of Standard. The drilling of nine wells confirmed the major proportions of the El Morgan field, and development drilling began. Five permanent platforms and flow lines to onshore storage facilities were completed, and the field was brought on stream in April, 1967.

Despite this auspicious beginning, there were perils ahead. On June 2, 1967, a group of Standard executives arrived in Egypt to visit the El Morgan field, and on June 5, accompanied by company officials assigned to Egypt, embarked on a work boat to visit one of the drilling and production platforms. Aboard, in addition to the Egyptian crew, were Frank C. Osment, vice president of Standard for worldwide exploration coordination who would be elected president of American International Oil Company a few weeks later; F. Randolph Yost, president of Pan American Petroleum Corporation; Richard M. Morrow, executive vice president of American International Oil Company; James W. Vanderbeek, in charge of American International's Egyptian operations; C. Clark Fuller, Egyptian operations manager; and an executive of the Egyptian General Petroleum Corporation.

The trip started out as a routine undertaking. The executives were experienced in offshore as well as onshore oil field operations, and had ridden in many work boats during the course of their careers. But as the boat approached the platform, they suddenly noticed a change in the attitude of crew members. Some gathered around a small portable radio; others held transistors to their ears. As Yost was to describe it, the friendly atmosphere of a few minutes before was replaced by a sense of tension. From the Egyptian executive, the visitors learned that Israel had launched an attack on Egypt and that the workers' homeland was being bombed—with American planes and equipment. It was the beginning of what came to be known as the "Six-Day War."

The Egyptian advised a quick return to Cairo. Onshore, Fuller stayed behind at Ras Shukheir to bring out company and contractor expatriates who were working on the drilling rigs and other assignments. As the remainder of the group proceeded toward Cairo over the road along the west bank of the Gulf of Suez, they were faced with a series of military roadblocks. Because they were Americans, the questioning was intense; they were glad to have the support and assistance of the Egyptian executive. The only other traffic on the highway consisted of gun carriers and tanks; soldiers in foxholes lined the road with machine guns pointed menacingly down the highway.

After passing columns of soldiers, the group arrived in Cairo and went immediately to Vanderbeek's home in an area of Cairo where many foreign nationals lived. There were few people around since foreign dependents had been evacuated a week earlier. A call to the United States embassy elicited the information that the heads of foreign companies in Egypt were to be at the embassy for a briefing the next day (June 6). A vehicle with police guards would be available to deliver them.

Yost and Vanderbeek were designated to attend the briefing. As they arrived, a crowd of white-shirted Egyptian youths was demonstrating outside the embassy and at one point began breaking down the gate and climbing the walls, much as students were to do in Iran some years later. A handful of Marines stood guard with pistols and tear gas grenades. But before the situation got out of hand, a group of Egyptian police astride white horses and swinging long bamboo rods dispersed the crowd. Yost and Vanderbeek were told to return home and await instructions. Fuller completed evacuating company and contractor expatriates to the Nile Hilton Hotel in Cairo by Wednesday.

On Friday, June 9, word came that Osment, Morrow, and Yost should go as quickly as possible to the Nile Hilton to join other U.S., British, Canadian, German, and Lebanese citizens seeking a way out of the country. Many years later, as vice president, production, for Amoco Production Company (International), Fuller recalled that an Israeli air raid over Cairo and a blackout added to the tension and confusion.

The official word was that foreigners would be moved out of the hotel at about three or four o'clock in the morning. But that night, Nasser announced he was resigning and within half an hour, the people at the hotel could hear a roar in the distance as crowds estimated later at 50,000 to 100,000 poured into the streets shouting "Nasser, Nasser." Some demonstrators tried to force their way into the hotel but were repulsed by police.

The demonstrations continued through the night but were diverted away from the area of the hotel. Shortly before dawn, a convoy of buses arrived at the Nile Hilton to take the evacuees to the railroad station for transfer to Alexandria where they were told a ship would be waiting for them. Egyptian security regulations kept the windows blacked out during the train trip.

Arriving at dockside, more than 500 people were jammed into a small terminal; the ship had not yet arrived. Finally, a Greek ship designed to hold no more than 350 people pulled into port and on June 11 they were taken aboard (with the caution that they should not all go to the same side of the ship). Once in international waters, the ship was escorted by vessels from the United States Sixth Fleet until it made port at Piraeus, Greece. Families of Amoco employees were among those who left Egypt for safer countries. But Vanderbeek, Fuller, and other Standard employees assigned to Cairo stayed behind, the only expatriate oil company people to do so. It was a decision much appreciated by the Egyptian government and the Egyptian General Petroleum Corporation, further cementing relationships. Oil from the El Morgan field was extremely important to them, and production was maintained through the military disruption. At the end of the year, El Morgan was producing 100,000 gross barrels daily.

Production from the El Morgan field was growing steadily in 1968, but that year was a significant one in other ways. For the first time, overseas operations had become a contributor to profits, albeit in a modest way. Overseas production of crude oil and natural gas liquids increased by 51 per cent to an average 117,268 barrels daily, and product sales were up 59 per cent to an average 79,525 barrels daily. Following a contract dispute with Argentina which had dragged on for almost four years, drilling had been resumed in that country. Exploration was under way or concessions had been obtained in Norwegian, United Kingdom, Netherlands, and West German waters, and elsewhere.

An agreement with the Government of Trinidad and Tobago granting Standard's Pan American International Oil Corporation and two other companies oil rights on two million acres off the east coast of Trinidad had been entered into in early 1961 on the basis of recommendations made to Pan American International by a one-time English mining engineer with the rather impressive name of Daniel George Fallon Bailey. Dohm felt that Bailey had done a persuasive job of reconstructing the geologic history of the area and that oil might be there. Humphrey, who signed the contracts for Pan American International, disagreed with Bailey's geological reconstruction but still believed there was a high probability of oil's being found. Osment agreed with Humphrey and pushed for carrying through with the exploration play.

Pan American International was operator for the group. Following seismic surveys, approximately one million acres of the concession were released back to the government, other members of the group dropped out, and by October, 1965, Standard's international subsidiary held 100 per cent interest in the remaining concession area. Additional acreage was acquired, bringing the total to about 1.5 million acres. Drilling of the first exploratory well in the concession area began in 1967, and by the end of 1968 three of five wells drilled found natural gas. Significant quantities of both oil and natural gas were confirmed during the following year.

The offshore Trinidad concession became one of the company's valuable oil and gas properties. Discoveries included

Samaan, Teak, Poui, and Cassia fields through 1980 when daily production averaged 105,000 barrels of oil and 193 million cubic feet of natural gas for the year. Tankers brought the produced oil to U.S. ports, and natural gas was delivered to the National Gas Company for use in the Trinidad and Tobago industrial sector where demand was increasing.

Deliveries of natural gas to the Trinidad and Tobago Electricity Commission began in 1974 after a 1972 plan to build a gas liquefaction plant to process gas for U.S. markets was shelved. In 1977, the Government of Trinidad and Tobago and Standard's subsidiary formed a company called Fertilizers of Trinidad and Tobago Limited (Fertrin) to build and operate a $250 million (U.S.) anhydrous ammonia plant at Point Lisas, Trinidad. Natural gas from the offshore concession would be used as the plant's energy source and as feedstock. The plant was funded 51 per cent by the Government of Trinidad and Tobago and 49 per cent by Standard. The output of the plant, projected at approximately 635,000 tons per year, was for export primarily to the United States, Brazil, and Western Europe.

The agreement signed with Indonesia in 1962, which represented Standard's first entry into oil exploration in the Far East, granted the company petroleum rights to 8,650,000 acres in central Sumatra and adjacent territorial waters. Early results were disappointing; there were operating and financial problems and the first nine wells were dry. When exploration efforts continued to be unsuccessful and political interference became severe, Standard relinquished its holdings in Sumatra in 1966.

Elsewhere, important acreage in other countries was acquired for exploration, a second oil field was discovered in the Persian Gulf off Iran, and crude oil production in Argentina, Colombia, and Venezuela increased. Preparations had begun for a refinery in Australia, an agreement had been entered into to acquire a substantial interest with crude supply rights in a small refinery to be built in Antigua, British West Indies. The refinery at Cremona, Italy, had been owned for a little more than a year. Foreign marketing broadened.

The aggressiveness with which Chris Dohm pursued his objective of making Standard a leader in the world search for oil was not without price. Dohm was a pioneer, an explorer, a good trader with the ability and enthusiasm to make a deal with a government, an oil man, or a trader anywhere in the world. But he was little interested in the administrative structure that was necessary to follow up on these arrangements. As George Myers was to find when he was given responsibility for overseeing international operations, the details could be as important as the "big deal." These included such factors as the price settlement terms to be negotiated, the tax structure, the provision for credit against U.S. taxes, the company's management rights vis-a-vis the host government, and commitments which might have to be made for future expenditures.

Annoyed, if not contemptuous of the new direction from Chicago established when Ritts took over as president of American International, Dohm nonetheless pushed Standard into new overseas ventures. With a team consisting of William E. Humphrey as vice president for exploration, and Walter Mac-Donald as his chief negotiator, he continued a tendency to ignore administrative matters and pressed on in his individual style.

Bailey, the Englishman whose theories contributed to Dohm's interest in exploring off Trinidad, also had theories about possibilities in the North Sea, and Humphrey assigned Myron T. Kozary, a Hungarian geologist who served as a consultant to Standard, to make a study of areas bordering those waters. Prolific gas discoveries by others in the Netherlands had spurred widespread interest in neighboring offshore areas. Humphrey said he believed Kozary probably had more to do with delineation of North Sea possibilities than Bailey.

Following Kozary's work, American International participated with a group exploring German waters and, as operator for itself and partners in the North Sea, conducted extensive marine seismic studies in English waters. In 1964, the British Gas Council-Amoco (U.K.) Group, for which Amoco (U.K.) was operator, was awarded 36 blocks totaling 2.1 million acres in the offshore concession area. Standard had 31 per cent interest in the acreage.

As Standard's commitment to overseas petroleum operations increased, Frank C. Osment, who had been serving as executive vice president of Pan American Petroleum Corporation in Tulsa, was elected a Standard vice president on September 1, 1965, with coordinating responsibilities for worldwide exploration and production. Osment was an experienced oil geologist and was thoroughly versed in Standard's internal systems of responsibilities and reporting. Moreover, after he joined Standard's domestic exploration and production subsidiary in 1945 as a geologist at Shreveport, he had advanced through a number of exploration positions. Bullard, relying on him to assist in early foreign efforts in the Western Hemisphere, had named him manager of exploration planning on September 15, 1956, as exploration began on the Cuban concessions. Osment's experience as vice president in charge of the Canadian division was also valuable background.

In 1965, the British government opened new areas for bidding in its portion of the North Sea. The British Gas Council-Amoco (U.K.) Group was awarded 15 blocks totaling 739,000 acres. Standard had 22 per cent interest in these blocks. As operator, Standard's subsidiary by the end of 1966 had drilled three successful wells in its first three attempts, and drilled a successful step-out five miles south of one of the wells.

Deliveries of natural gas to an onshore terminal at Bacton, England, began from the Leman field in 1969, and from the Indefatigable field in 1971. Discovery and development of additional fields followed. Standard's production licenses in the United Kingdom increased to one million acres, most of it offshore, by 1971.

Negotiating the gas sales contracts required frequent travel from American International's stateside headquarters by its executive vice president for upstream operations, Richard M. Morrow. He was to recall later that during his first two years with the international subsidiary, beginning in 1966, he made 25 trips to London in 24 months (interspersed by trips to other locations outside North America where the company had operations).

Farther north in the British portion of the North Sea off Scotland, Standard discovered oil in 1969 on a 154,539-acre block in which it held 30.77 per cent interest, and the company and its three partners were awarded two additional production licenses in 1970 covering 385,000 North Sea acres.

In the Norwegian portion of the North Sea, the Standard company, as operator for a group of companies, discovered offshore oil in the Torfelt area, 183 miles southwest of Stavanger. The company had interests in approximately 1.4 million concession acres in Norwegian waters at the end of 1970.

Its activities outside North America were growing. Reports on exploration and production, refinery operations, and product marketing in 20 countries around the world were included in Standard's 1967 report to stockholders.

In 1967 Standard decided to move the headquarters of American International Oil Company from New York to Chicago effective February 1, 1968. Dohm had resigned January 31, 1967, and worked as a consultant. Ritts, who had strong ties in the East, resisted the move to Chicago, resigned, and worked for other companies. Osment was elected to replace Ritts as president on July 1, 1967.

Risk and Reward

17

For almost 20 years before 1967, developing an overseas position again had been an important part of Standard's long-range strategy. Foreign operations were a drain on consolidated income prior to 1967, but that year they contributed a modest four million dollars to profits, and within five years the profit figure had grown to $82 million, making international operations the largest contributor to profits growth during the 1967-1972 period. Domestic profit contributions, although proportionally large, were essentially flat.

Standard continued to increase production in 1971 in Iran's Persian Gulf area from the Darius field, where production was restricted during price negotiations, and from the Cyrus field where production was shut down for two months to permit installation of a one-million-barrel storage barge with desalting equipment. Development drilling began in the Fereidoon field in 1973 and in the Ardeshir field in 1974.

In 1977, a negotiating team led by Henry O. Boswell, at that time regional vice president in charge of activities in the Middle East; C. Clark Fuller, then vice president, planning and economics; and Thomas S. James, associate general counsel, renegotiated Standard's Iranian concession agreement. Though substantially increasing the Iranian tax and royalty rates, the new terms provided a reasonable return on Standard's investment and favorably resolved outstanding pricing and other issues.

In Egypt, production in the Gulf of Suez, in which Standard held 50 per cent interest with the Egyptian General Petroleum Corporation, continued to grow steadily as new fields were discovered and brought on production.

16. Crude oil and natural gas from producing fields discovered by Amoco off Trinidad's east coast are processed at Amoco Trinidad Oil Company's Galeota Point facilities, shown here.

17. Production began in 1983 at the Cyprus Thompson Creek molybdenum mine near Challis, Idaho.

18. High density polyethylene, polypropylene, and ethylene are manufactured here at the Amoco Chemicals Corporation Chocolate Bayou chemicals complex on 2,400 acres near Houston, Texas.

19. Sulfur extracted from natural gas produced from Canadian fields is shown stockpiled for shipment at the Whitecourt processing plant in Alberta of Amoco Canada Petroleum Company Ltd.

20. The Amoco Chemicals Corporation plant completed in 1978 on the east bank of the Cooper River 16 miles up river from Charleston, South Carolina, has capacity to produce one billion pounds per year of purified terephthalic acid (PTA). PTA, a pure, white crystalline powder, is the basic chemical raw material for production of polyester fiber, film, and molding resins.

21. Much of Standard Oil Company (Indiana)'s history stems from its refinery at Whiting, Indiana. The first units—long since replaced—were completed shortly after the company was organized in 1889. The refinery has been expanded and modernized over the years, incorporating new technology as crude oil supplies and markets for petroleum products changed. Its operable capacity in 1982 was 376,000 barrels of crude oil daily, second among Amoco Oil Company's refineries after the refinery at Texas City, Texas.

22. Amoco Oil Company's refinery at Texas City, Texas, ranks as the company's largest with operable refining capacity in 1982 of 415,000 barrels of crude oil a day. Major upgrading in the early 1980s equipped the refinery to process larger quantities of high sulfur crude oils and to eliminate production of heavy residual oil.

23. A modern-day rig drills ahead for Amoco Production Company in this scene of West Texas where the company first became active in 1931. The vast plains area became a great oil and natural gas producing region with Amoco among industry leaders in its development.

24. Service station design changes as market conditions change. This 1982 station contrasts dramatically with a 1920s station shown on page 121.

25. Frontier Pipeline Company began accepting tenders of crude petroleum in the fall of 1983 for shipment through its 290-mile-long 16-inch pipeline in Utah and Wyoming, shown here under construction. Amoco Pipeline Company is a partner in the line. The line's route is from the Anschutz Ranch area of the Overthrust Belt in Northeastern Utah to Casper, Wyoming, where it connects to existing pipelines serving Rocky Mountain and Midwestern refineries.

26. The tanker Amoco Savannah moored to a loading facility off Sharjah to take on a cargo of condensate from the Sajaa field.

In the North Sea, the Amoco-British Gas Council group became the largest supplier of natural gas to the United Kingdom. The British government approved Standard's plans to build an 80,000 barrel-a-day oil refinery at Milford Haven, South Wales. Retail outlets in Italy increased to a total of more than 1,200.

In the Western Hemisphere, exploratory wells offshore Trinidad continued to produce favorable results. Production in Argentina stabilized as Standard increased its drilling activities in accordance with an agreement reached in 1967 to settle a contract dispute with the government. In Venezuela, production in the Lake Maracaibo region was expanded, and production of heavy asphaltic oil began from Standard's Jobo field in the eastern Orinoco basin.

Southeast Asia once again engaged the company's interest, despite the earlier disappointments in Indonesia. Seismic surveys and wildcat drilling were conducted off Japan, Taiwan, Papua New Guinea, and in Pakistan. Standard was awarded exploration rights off both Australia and Thailand. In Singapore, a refining and marketing company in which Standard had one-third interest, in 1971 began building a 65,000 barrel-a-day refinery on Merlimau Island in Singapore harbor to process Iranian crude oil. Standard had an option to supply 90 per cent of the refinery's crude oil for 10 years and 66 per cent for the succeeding decade. In 1979, Standard sold a portion of its equity in the refinery to two other oil companies, reducing its own interest to about 10 per cent. The capacity of the refinery was expanded to 165,000 barrels a day in 1980-81, and facilities were added to upgrade the product stream.

By 1973, the net undeveloped leaseholds outside North America totaled 24.4 million acres, slightly exceeding the 24.1 million acres in the United States at that time. Leaseholds in Canada totaled 6.2 million acres. In addition substantial acreage was held under reservations, options, or permits.

Canadian operations, despite the friendly relations between the U.S. and Canadian governments, presented special problems. In 1974, the provinces of Alberta, Saskatchewan, and British Columbia drastically increased royalty rates while the federal government in Canada was proposing an income tax that did not provide credit for taxes or royalties paid to the provinces. As a result of this double taxation, Standard curtailed its exploration program in Canada.

Standard again reappraised its commitments in Canada in 1980 after the Canadian federal administration of Prime Minister

Pierre Trudeau implemented a national energy policy aimed at forcing American oil companies to sell majority interests in their operations to Canadian owners.

The impact was substantial. Standard's subsidiary Amoco Canada Petroleum Company Ltd. reduced its 1981 expenditures for crude oil and natural gas exploration and production by 56 per cent. Because of the petroleum revenue tax imposed by Canada, the cash flow from the Canadian subsidiary was cut by 25 per cent.

The expansion of Standard into new overseas areas predated the oil price explosion commencing in 1973 and the time when heavy government intervention in the oil-producing business became the norm. By the 1970s, although by comparison not one of the largest oil companies internationally, Standard was operating in some 45 countries overseas. But there was a steady trend on the part of all host governments to increase their share of revenues generated by the petroleum industry, in some cases leaving United States companies with little incentive or no opportunity to continue operations. When Venezuela expropriated the properties of private oil companies in 1975, for example, the government in Standard's case provided compensation at a small fraction of fair market value and at a level below net book value.

By 1980, oil operations had been nationalized in Mexico, Venezuela, Algeria, Iraq, and Iran. They were partially nationalized in Libya, Saudi Arabia, and Nigeria. In none of these countries did the private oil companies set prices on oil or gas or even the rates of production. But the oil companies were equally powerless to make these decisions in such Free World countries as the United Kingdom, Canada, Norway, and the United States itself.

The trend could be measured in the percentage of overseas crude oil production controlled by private companies and the various host governments. In 1971, about three-fourths of the 29 million barrels a day of free-world overseas crude oil production was managed by the seven largest international oil companies, and the remaining one-fourth about equally by other private oil companies and foreign government entities. By 1980, the relationship had been altered substantially. The foreign governments' share had increased to slightly over 50 per cent; the seven who had once managed three-fourths of this overseas oil found themselves with only about 40 per cent of overseas oil production.

For every foreign venture, Standard required a thorough

inventory and assessment of the political risks. Identifying a risk did not, of course, mean that the company would not undertake an operation. Risk is relative and there are risks even in operating in the United States. But it was essential that management be able to identify and evaluate the risk and reach a decision after taking that information into account.

In general, the foreign affairs function within the company was seen as one of providing advance intelligence so that, in most instances, whatever occurred would be a manageable event for the company. If the situation in a country got out of control or changed radically, there was very little the company could do about the course of history; but by being alerted, it could plan for an emergency and deal with it from a broader perspective.

In Argentina, Standard continued to do business through 18 changes of government involving at least four distinct major political upheavals, although at times the company's operations in that country were shut down. Doing business involved continuous and delicate negotiations in which an accurate appraisal of the domestic situation was of critical importance. In 1976, Standard was able to settle a long contract dispute by agreeing to continue drilling and to initiate additional secondary recovery projects in return for improvements in price which had been seriously eroded by inflation and devaluation of Argentina's peso.

Not all risk evaluations involve political risk; the economic policies of a particular government also play a role. For example, before committing to exploration off Norway, the company's foreign affairs group was asked to make an evaluation of whether the strongly Socialist (but stable) government of that country would permit a fair rate of return. Norway seemed promising. Standard entered into a partnership with the government and offshore exploration rights were obtained in 1965. The Tor field oil discovery in 1970 by the group of companies for which Standard was operator was followed by the Southeast Tor field discovery in 1972, Valhall in 1975, and Hod in 1976. Standard also had a minor interest in the giant Statfjord oil field.

Norway was an example of the increasing need to find new opportunities in countries that hadn't been explored and developed and to discover the hard-to-find gas and oil that either was overlooked in the past or had been too expensive to seek out. That meant exploring in deeper water, going into countries where there might be only short-term possibilities that were yet profitable, and carrying out a number of programs that would not have been economically feasible when oil was selling at three dollars a barrel.

In Iran, when the reign of the Shah was in jeopardy and tension mounted in the fall of 1978, Amoco expatriate employees began receiving death threats from individuals who identified themselves with various radical groups. As most of these were written in semi-literate notes or delivered over the telephone in broken English, they were not at first taken seriously.

However, as the weeks passed, the quality of the English language in the threats improved dramatically; furthermore, the threats were addressed to each individual by his full name and sent through the company mail services, using Iran Pan American Oil Company envelopes. Concern increased as it was evident the threats were coming from Iranian employees within the company.

Standard's foreign affairs group had forecast that the most serious crisis facing the Shah in his quarter century of rule was likely to reach its climax in the month of Muharram (December). In Iran, staff members watched developments with apprehension and prepared contingency plans in the event the Shah were overthrown or civil war erupted.

Those events transpired. The Shah was compelled to flee the country in mid-month, and the revolutionary forces led by the Ayatollah Ruhollah Khomeini began taking over the country amid a wave of anti-American demonstrations.

In late December, Paul Grimm (acting manager of OSCO, the multinational consortium of companies operating oil properties in Iran) was assassinated on the way between his home and his office in Ahwaz. Standard's subsidiary in Iran was not a member of the consortium, but the following day, each U.S. employee of Standard in Iran received a letter which said, "If you do not want to join Paul Grimm, leave Iran before January 8, 1979." The specific nature of the individual threats left no alternative but to begin the evacuation of non-Iranian nationals and their families.

Plans had already been made to bring employees from the Kharg Island and offshore operations in the Persian Gulf to Tehran for the Christmas holidays. This move was to expedite and simplify the later evacuation.

On Christmas Eve, all Amoco expatriate employees had been invited to the home of V. M. (Vern) Temple, an administrative executive of Amoco International, for a reception. A number of employees left the Amoco office at 2 p.m., and, working their way through and around demonstrations and military checkpoints, arrived at the Temple home about 6 p.m. At the reception, Temple notified each of the families that plans had been made to evacuate them via commercial airlines from December 26 through December 29. All those scheduled to leave during the first three days departed according to plan, but by December 29 no more commercial aircraft were landing in Iran.

A. E. (Art) Piper, president and general manager of Standard's Amoco Iran Oil Company, promptly began seeking alternative ways of getting Temple, who was in the last group, and the remaining employees out of the country. Fortunately, Piper learned of an airplane scheduled to come into Iran to pick up some newsreel film for the television networks and fly it to Amman, Jordan. Arrangements were quickly made for the remaining employees and their families to board this plane and continue on to Dubai after the film had been delivered to Jordan.

For the Temples and others it was a difficult leave-taking. Temple called his wife, Mickey, and told her she had one hour to be ready to leave. She could bring just one suitcase. Other families were given the same instructions. Finally, after four hours at the airport, the charter pilot located them, and after clearing customs they flew out of Iran, leaving behind all the family possessions acquired during the years.

Later, there was to be a bright note to this dismal leave-taking. Through the efforts of Amoco's manager, an Iranian, who was left in charge, and with the support and assistance of the company, the Temples and others were to recover most of the household goods and personal effects they had been forced to leave behind.

In Dubai, a headquarters in exile was set up, with the hope that the situation would ease and make it possible for Amoco to resume operations in Iran. Unfortunately, this was not to be, and in June of 1979, the Dubai operation was closed down.

In 1980, the Iranians notified the company that Amoco's agreement with Iran had been declared null and void. The company's claims against Iran for expropriation of its properties were submitted to an international arbitration tribunal but the matter was unresolved as this book went to press.

The shutdown in Iran came at the end of a year (1978) in which new production records had been set by Amoco in that country. The loss of this production resulted in a decrease of more than 35 per cent in Standard's total overseas production of crude oil and natural gas liquids.

The most serious aspect of the Iranian take-over was the loss of 180,000 barrels per day of proprietary crude oil from Standard's total supply. To make up the deficiency, Standard had to buy crude where it could, chiefly on the spot market at premium prices. That placed the company at a disadvantage compared to its competitors in terms of the prices it was forced to charge for refined products. Nonetheless, Standard's overseas net income actually increased following the loss of Iran, primarily because of the dramatic crude oil price increases initiated by the OPEC nations.

Despite the revolution and subsequent political instability in Iran, the company continued efforts to improve its position in the Middle East, which remained clearly the world's largest known source of hydrocarbons. "One fact stands out," Osment had told the 1973 Senior Management Conference. "The Middle East dominates the supply picture. It is so big and so important that it overshadows every other foreign area, not only individually, but collectively as well. What's more, its dominance tends to grow rather than to shrink."

In 1973, Robert C. Gunness was predicting that the Eastern Hemisphere, which supplied the United States in 1970 with less than a million barrels a day, might be called upon to deliver up to seven million barrels a day by 1980. The U.S. imports figure in 1978 was 5,662,000 barrels a day of crude oil and refined products. In 1980, three years after Alaska's Prudhoe Bay field had begun production and United States consumption had started its decline, imports totaled 4,396,000 barrels per day.

In the early years of overseas exploration, the emphasis among oil companies had been on finding giant oil fields such as those in the Middle East. But as prices rose and host countries became more aggressive in nationalizing oil operations or pressing for a larger share of the revenue, contract terms and taxation became just as much a determining factor in the decision to go into a country as geology, the size of the fields, and the quality of production. In instances where a country might previously have been considered to have only marginal production, that production might become economically attractive if the proper terms for its development could be worked out.

Geologists estimated that there remained many possibilities for exploration. One estimate published in *The Wall Street Journal* identified approximately 600 petroleum basins around the world. Of these, 160 were commercially productive in 1980,

240 were partially or moderately explored, and the remaining 200 were essentially unexplored. The necessity of working out satisfactory agreements with host countries could be deduced from the fact that although the United States, Canada, and Russia had drilled 93 per cent of the world's oil and gas wells, only 37 per cent of the prospective basins were under their control.

For Standard, Egypt was the shining example of successful exploration, production, and cooperation with the host government. Following the loss of Iranian production, Egypt continued to be Standard's largest source of proprietary foreign crude oil. Some small fields were located in the Western Desert but most of the production was from the Gulf of Suez, where new fields were being explored and developed.

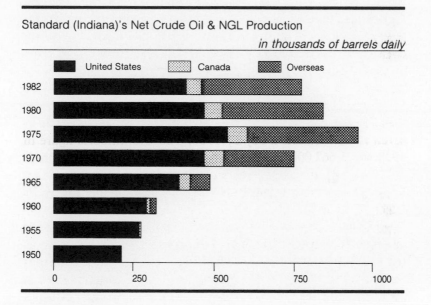

Standard (Indiana)'s Net Crude Oil & NGL Production

in thousands of barrels daily

Altogether, about 75 per cent of Egypt's oil was produced by Standard. More than 90 per cent of the staff was Egyptian, many of them trained by Standard's expatriate professionals. Standard provides 100 per cent of the capital through the joint-venture company. The partnership has been a stable and profitable one, providing probably the largest single source of foreign exchange for Egypt.

Elsewhere in the Middle East, Standard's acreage position in the Eastern Arabian peninsula was increased during 1980 with the

231

acquisition of an onshore permit for more than 617,000 acres in Abu Dhabi and 50 per cent interest in 270,000 acres onshore in Fujairah. The new acreage was added to an existing 100 per cent interest in 600,000 acres onshore Sharjah, 50 per cent interest in 720,000 acres onshore and offshore Ras al Khaimah, and 85 per cent interest in 5,250,000 acres offshore Oman.

In late 1981, Standard announced that a new field in the United Arab Emirate of Sharjah ranked among the largest natural gas and condensate discoveries ever made by the company. Extensive tests from three wells in the Sajaa field indicated potential natural gas reserves of several trillion cubic feet and recoverable condensate reserves in the hundreds of millions of barrels, Leland C. Adams, president of Amoco Production Company, reported. He emphasized that more accurate estimates of recoverable reserves would be made after further field delineation. Other overseas discoveries included three wells drilled during 1980 and 1981 and a fourth in 1982 in the ocean waters of Gabon, off the west coast of Africa.

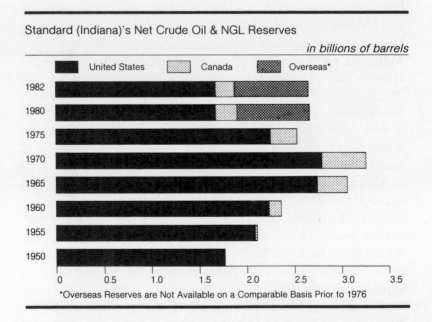

Standard (Indiana)'s Net Crude Oil & NGL Reserves

in billions of barrels

United States   Canada   Overseas*

*Overseas Reserves are Not Available on a Comparable Basis Prior to 1976

In the Far East, following a 1979 trip to the People's Republic of China by a delegation of Standard officials headed by Swearingen, Standard received permits to participate in seven offshore geophysical survey projects. Standard operated one of the survey areas for a group of 30 participating companies, and participated in the first round of competitive bidding. Standard hoped to continue negotiations for exploration and production rights on portions of the survey areas as the writing of this book neared completion.

In the Philippines, sea-floor wellheads and a floating production system were installed in the small Cadlao field off Palawan Island in which Standard had 50 per cent interest. A license agreement was signed with the government of Papua New Guinea covering an onshore exploration area of about two million acres, and Australia granted the company a prospecting permit for a 929,000-acre onshore tract in the continent's Northern Territory.

Further organizational changes accompanied this steadily increasing thrust into diverse and widely separated areas of the world. Since 1968, Amoco International had maintained its headquarters executives and staff in Chicago. But the company found it increasingly difficult to get geologists, geophysicists, engineers, and landmen to come to Chicago for assignment at a time when there were many opportunities in the oil industry in the southwest and west for these professions. There also was a need for a home base for U.S. employees assigned overseas from time to time. Moreover, earth science professional societies, well established in Houston, New Orleans, Denver, and in California, did not exist in Chicago. Although recognized as one of the world's premier financial, manufacturing, marketing, transportation, and cultural centers, the city of Chicago "isn't oil country," as Henry O. Boswell, president of Amoco Production Company (International), once remarked.

Faced with these problems, as well as increasing pressure for space in Standard's general office building in Chicago, Frank C. Osment, Standard's executive vice president for worldwide oil, natural gas, and minerals operations, directed a survey to determine a better location for operating units which could logically be moved from Chicago. A committee was formed to recommend an appropriate location. Tulsa, Oklahoma, once known as "the oil capital of the world," was first considered, but the final choice was Houston, generally considered to be the operating headquarters of the oil industry in the United States.

Two regional headquarters, one for operations in South America, Central America, and the Far East, and one for Africa and the Middle East, were moved to Houston. Regional head-

233

quarters for operations in Europe remained in London, England. In a subsequent move, much of the Chicago general office engineering staff of Amoco Production Company was moved to Houston.

Amoco International Oil Company was merged into Amoco Production Company in April 1981, and Leland C. Adams, former president of Amoco International, became president of the combined company upon the retirement of George H. Galloway as president of the domestic exploration and production subsidiary.

With the reorganization, Amoco International's refining and marketing operations in Australia, Italy, and Great Britain were assigned to Amoco Oil Company. (Amoco Oil Company sold its petroleum refining, transportation, and marketing facilities in Italy to Arabian Seaoil Corporation in 1983.)

Standard formed a new subsidiary, Amoco Marine Transportation Company, to manage the marine transportation function of the discontinued Amoco International subsidiary. At year-end 1981, the company had 15 ocean-going tankers totaling 2.2 million deadweight tons. It also had under charter five vessels totaling 313,000 deadweight tons, five less than the preceding year as a result of lower petroleum demand.

A tragedy at sea in March, 1978, claimed a tanker owned by one of Standard's subsidiaries. Bound from the Persian Gulf to English channel ports with a charter cargo of light crude oil, the 233,000-deadweight-ton Amoco Cadiz stranded on rocks off Brittany, France, after its steering mechanism failed in heavy seas and towing efforts were unsuccessful. The tanker broke up and sank. Its cargo was lost. Cleanup crews and the forces of nature cleared away oil that washed from the tanker onto the beach east of Portsall. The incident resulted in numerous claims against Standard and its subsidiaries. Litigation hadn't ended as this book was brought to a close.

Amoco Chemicals discontinued its international division in 1972, and worldwide marketing authority and responsibility were given to each of its product-line managers. This proved particularly useful during the 1973-1974 oil embargo and shortages when the manager of a particular product could look across national borders and say to all customers, both domestic and international, that they would be treated alike. At the time, the chemical company, for example, was involved not only in trade between the United States and other countries but in an entire range of multilateral arrangements among various overseas nations.

Swearingen said he believed the removal of geographic limitations by making each of the four major subsidiaries—Amoco Oil, Amoco Chemicals, Amoco Production, and Amoco Minerals —a worldwide operating unit would help assure that the company's capital and manpower resources were most efficiently utilized.

A Winning Strategy

18

"We like to drill a lot of wells," George H. Galloway, president of Amoco Production Company, told a *Fortune* magazine reporter in 1980.

"Most of the favorable results we've had were completely unforeseen—by us or anybody else.

"That happens if you drill a lot of wells," he said.

Taken out of the context of Galloway's full remarks, the quotation ignores the company's long history of research into scientific ways to search for oil and natural gas, its successes achieved by applying the results of innovative research of its own and that which it licensed from others, and its assiduous attention to the findings of earth scientists.

However, the few words of Galloway to the *Fortune* magazine reporter made the point beyond question: The drill is the only tool so far devised that *finds* oil or natural gas.

"By generating a lot of activity—and allowing the important element of the unexpected to come into full play—our explorers can expect to find and develop oil and gas reserves that otherwise might have been overlooked had we concentrated exploratory efforts on only a few isolated prospects," Galloway said.

Drilling a lot of wells and generating a lot of activity involved leasing acreage—lots of it—where the company itself could drill or where it could secure assistance by farming out prospective acreage to other exploration companies. It also meant contributing money to wells to be drilled by others where those wells would help evaluate Amoco acreage, also a common practice in the oil industry.

It was a strategy that was a tradition in Standard's domestic exploration and production subsidiary. As early as 1959 the strategy was noted in company records: "In the last 15 or 20 years, because of competition, the tendency has been to lease land first and do the exploration afterwards." Even so, it was not as simple as it might sound. The advance surveys of geologists, oil scouts, and seismograph crews were essential guides to informed leasing.

Alonzo W. Peake and Frank O. Prior established the practice of aggressive leasing at Dixie Oil Company after Standard acquired that small, Shreveport, Louisiana, company in 1919. Prior reinforced it as the first president of Stanolind Oil and Gas Company after it was organized in 1931. And it continued through succeeding administrations.

Acquisition of exploration rights ranged throughout most of the active and prospective onshore oil and gas provinces of the United States and Canada, and expanded during the 1950s and 1960s into offshore state and federal waters.

Standard's offshore history began in 1947 when its domestic exploration and production subsidiary—with two other companies, Kerr-McGee Corporation, the operator of the drilling venture, and Phillips Petroleum Company—participated in the first commercial oil well drilled out of sight of land. The well was the wildcat No. 1, Block 32, State Lease 754, ten miles off Point au Fer, Terrebonne parish, Louisiana, in the Gulf of Mexico. From that day forward Standard's marine operations extended farther from shore into federal waters around the nation's perimeter and became a prime domestic source of both oil and natural gas.

The Gulf of Mexico burgeoned into a favored and highly productive oil and gas area. Other North American offshore exploration areas included Alaska's Cook Inlet, Canada's Arctic Islands, and the Grand Banks off Canada's east coast.

Large-acreage holdings brought the company notable discoveries of its own and important participation in reserves discovered by others including fields whose names became famous in the oil industry. The early ones included ten that Pan American Petroleum ranked in 1957 as its largest producing fields: Hastings, Midland Farms, East Texas, and High Island, all in Texas; Elk Basin, Cottonwood Creek, and Winkleman Dome, in Wyoming; Hackberry, in Louisiana; Sloss, in Nebraska; and Pembina, in Canada where operations then were administered as a division of the U.S. subsidiary.

These were not the only ones. A selection of other famous-name fields of the pre-1970s included: Spindletop, Slaughter, South Cowden, Wasson, Old Ocean, Levelland, and South Fullerton, in Texas; South Black Bayou, West Hackberry, South

Pecan Lake, Red Fish Point, and Bastian Bay, onshore Louisiana; Eugene Island, South Timbalier, West Delta, South Marsh Island, Ship Shoal, East Cameron, and Bayou Carlin, offshore Louisiana; Salt Creek, and Beaver Creek, in Wyoming; Hobbs, and Basin Dakota, in New Mexico; Eola, Velma, West Edmond, and Red Oak, in Oklahoma; and Hugoton, in Kansas.

Standard's exploration efforts had always had a heavy American flavor. While the company had also moved into foreign exploration in the 1950s and 1960s, its American strategy took on new meaning in the 1970s. The Arab oil embargo against the United States in 1973–74 demonstrated the folly of heavy reliance on unstable overseas sources of oil. The volume of oil coming into the U.S. was cut by 1.3 million barrels daily, or 7 per cent of demand. In addition, prices of foreign oil were quadrupled in a matter of months. The U.S. economy suffered the double-barreled shock of reduced supply and soaring prices.

Reliability of imports from Middle East producing countries became more than ever endangered. Domestic reserves forecasts bristled with ill-founded warnings that America was running out of oil. And, perversely, exploration in the frontier areas of federal waters off the east and west coasts and on tracts onshore that were candidates for wilderness classification was restricted by lobbying efforts of environmentalists.

Nonetheless, it was apparent to Standard and to Amoco Production that the times called for a resurgence of activity in North America and particularly in the United States. Price controls were still in effect on natural gas, and had been invoked on crude oil and petroleum products in 1971, along with controls on the entire American economy. Controls were lifted on all other commodities in 1973, but they were continued on natural gas, crude oil, and products. The Emergency Petroleum Allocation Act of 1975 assured that controls would be in place for at least another 40 months beyond December, 1975.

Even under controls, prices for oil and gas improved somewhat, and there was at least the hope that the end of controls was in sight. Renewed investment in American resources seemed not only promising but necessary.

In 1977, Amoco Production Company saw itself confronting four basic questions:

1. Adequacy of the resource base. Did the U.S. contain enough undiscovered oil and gas to provide an adequate target for Amoco's efforts?

2. Declining inventory of reserves. Would the current downward trend continue into the future?
3. Declining production trends. Would they continue?
4. Profits and cash generation. Could they be maintained or increased in the future?

In dealing with these issues, Amoco Production took a close look at bidding on leases offered in the Baltimore Canyon, the first of the areas opened for leasing by the federal government off the Atlantic coast. The sale area covered acreage in 130–600 feet of water 47 to 92 miles off New Jersey and Delaware.

Opening Atlantic federal water to exploration leasing faced strong resistance by coastal state governments and their constituencies, especially those in tourist-oriented sea coast locations, and by environmentalists generally. Amoco Production joined with the American Petroleum Institute in an educational program to try to allay fears of onshore damage to beaches and wetlands that many thought would be bound to result if any oil and gas were found.

When the first Baltimore Canyon lease sale was held in August, 1976, however, Amoco Production bidding was noticeably restrained as other major oil companies offered very high bonuses for a chance to explore this untried area. The company didn't place a single winning bid, a result about which it wasn't at all unhappy.

The U.S. Atlantic offshore was one of the most extensively studied regions of the world. Structural and depositional features of the continental shelf indicated a history of continental drifting during the Triassic period of the Mesozoic era, sea-floor spreading beginning in the early Jurassic period of the Mesozoic, and large scale subsidence in the later Mesozoic and the Cenozoic eras. By plotting from a tectonic map of the United States and by interpretation of seismograph printouts, geologists traced the trough known as the Baltimore Canyon.

Scientists at the company's Tulsa Research Center analyzed pulverized shale rock samples from a stratigraphic test well and took a small portion from the sample that looked like coal dust. This was kerogen, the "mother" substance of petroleum and coal. Laboratory tests indicated these kerogens were the type of sources principally for natural gas, with small potential for oil. The geochemists believed the kerogens from the test well "need another 20 million years of cooking." After that time period they could move from the source beds into reservoir rocks of the area.

239

There were other considerations as well, including the fact that if production of either oil or gas—but especially gas—were found, the reserves would have to be extremely large to justify building production facilities and pipelines in the hostile natural environment of the Atlantic ocean. Siting of terminals onshore where the human environment was hostile also would have to be dealt with. In Standard's opinion, the risks were clearly out of line with the price paid by others in bidding for leases.

Amoco Production's comparatively weak bidding in the 1976 Baltimore Canyon sale was contemporary with a number of public statements by oil industry officials, including Standard's, that onshore there remained great potential for increasing the nation's oil and gas reserves.

So, instead of risking high bonus bids and tying up large exploration, drilling, and production investments for a period likely to extend over several years, Amoco Production decided to limit its offshore bidding to what might be described as semi-frontier areas, such as some in the Gulf of Mexico, or elsewhere where prospects might be better or leases cheaper.

Perceptions of another Atlantic offshore area overlain by up to 7,300 feet of water several miles farther offshore than the Baltimore Canyon tracts were more optimistic on December 8, 1981, when another federal lease sale was held. Here the general geological situation provided a basis for inferences that source beds were probably older and buried deeper than those sampled in 1976. Standard and its Tulsa Research Center scientists hoped that would prove to be the case; the kerogens, cooked longer and at higher temperatures, hopefully would have generated mature hydrocarbons that migrated into overlying reservoir rocks. Standard's Amoco Production Company (USA) subsidiary teamed up with Sun Exploration Company and Shell Offshore, Inc., in successfully bidding on 20 tracts in the 1981 lease sale. Shell, as operator for the group, planned test drilling on two of the tracts during the last half of 1983.

Amoco also decided to reemphasize and expand its already substantial ongoing domestic leasing program in the continental United States. Although some of the potential acreage lay under wilderness areas, proposed wilderness areas, and areas adjacent to them where petroleum operations were prohibited or at best restricted, Amoco Production saw many opportunities. Its goal was to obtain exploration and production rights on large areas to afford it maximum flexibility in its prospecting decisions.

240

When, in January of 1981, the *Wall Street Transcript* selected John E. Swearingen as the outstanding chief executive officer in the oil industry, it delineated the reasoning which lay behind Standard's strategy. "Over the course of the last decade," the paper reported, "Swearingen developed a clear-cut view of how the economics of the industry were changing and how to position his company. He came to the view that the industry was going to compete too aggressively with itself. So he purposely steered away from many of the offshore competitive lease sales and built up a far larger position in onshore exploration."

Two examples of the success of this approach were the experiences of Standard in Louisiana's Tuscaloosa Trend and in the Western Overthrust Belt.

In the Tuscaloosa Trend, Amoco Production moved quickly to acquire large leaseholds after an initial discovery by another operator. By making extensive commitments, Standard emerged as the major participant in developing natural gas and condensate reserves in the area.

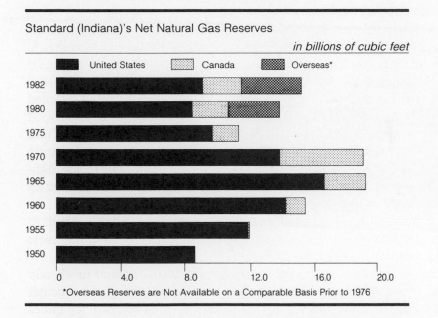

Standard (Indiana)'s Net Natural Gas Reserves

in billions of cubic feet

United States   Canada   Overseas*

1982
1980
1975
1970
1965
1960
1955
1950

0   4.0   8.0   12.0   16.0   20.0

*Overseas Reserves are Not Available on a Comparable Basis Prior to 1976

The Tuscaloosa Trend is approximately 20 miles wide and more than 200 miles long across southern Louisiana. Wells must be drilled to below 15,000 feet to penetrate the productive deep Cretaceous sand. Amoco Production's first field discovery in the trend was the Port Hudson field near Baton Rouge in 1977. Following were Moore Sams in 1979, and Lockhart Crossing and Morganza fields in 1980. A fifth field discovery well was drilled in 1981, and a sixth in 1982. The fields are situated within about a 100-mile stretch on the Gulf of Mexico side of the Lower Cretaceous shelf edge. Amoco Production expected its net production from these fields to peak by the mid-1980s at about 12,000 barrels of liquids and 165 million cubic feet of gas daily. Early discovery wells in the Tuscaloosa Trend led to forecasts that some 6 to 10 trillion cubic feet of condensate-rich natural gas ultimately may be found by the industry in this area.

Standard's successes in the Western Overthrust Belt in the late 1970s and early 1980s represented the culmination of many years' interest in the Rocky Mountain west.

A major share of Standard's domestic exploratory activity—reaching back into the 1920s—had been directed toward the mountain country, despite failures mixed with successes in that vast area. The acquisition of Midwest Refining Company properties had been of great importance to the company. Other acquisitions and developments had occurred over the years.

An important acquisition, including oil properties in the Rocky Mountain area, occurred on October 18, 1961, when Standard purchased from Honolulu Oil Corporation 1,114 net producing wells, interest in 70 producing fields in the United States and 19 in Canada, 3.7 million undeveloped acres in the U.S. and Canada, and half interest in about 100,000 undeveloped acres in Alaska. The price was approximately $73 million in cash and future production payments amounting to more than $200 million. With interest, the total amount when payments were completed in 1973 was over $380 million. On its face and its potential for growth, it was Pan American Petroleum's most significant acquisition of producing and non-producing properties since the purchase of Yount-Lee Oil Company properties in 1935.

Antitrust litigation pressed by the Department of Justice in the U.S. District Court at San Francisco sought first to prevent the acquisition, then, when that failed, to compel the company to divest itself of the purchase. But the court ruled in favor of Standard's subsidiary in 1964, and the purchase was sustained when the Justice Department decided not to appeal the decision.

In 1963, Standard added large blocks of acreage to its leases in the Williston Basin of North Dakota and Montana, and increased its holdings in the Rangely field in northwestern Colorado. The Rangely field had an interesting background. The Rangely anticline had been mapped in 1875 by the first geologist to pass through the area. Oil seeps prompted drilling after the turn of the century, and oil was discovered in 1902. By 1930, over 100 wells were producing from the Mancos shale formation. Deeper production from the Weber sand was discovered in 1931 by The California Company (Standard Oil Company of California) No. A-1 Raven well, which was shut in early in 1933 for lack of pipelines and markets. World War II petroleum requirements revived interest in the field, and by the end of the war, Rangely was recognized as a giant-class field.

In 1945, Standard, through its Stanolind Oil and Gas Company subsidiary, increased its already substantial leaseholdings in the field by 2,400 acres, and followed up with additional acquisitions. By 1952, Standard had 115 of the 475 wells in the field. The field produced approximately 23 million barrels in 1955, making Rangely one of the nation's top producing fields.

Standard, The California Company, Union Pacific Railroad Company, and other Rangely operators in 1957 entered into a unit agreement covering the principal producing formation underlying the field, the Weber sand. About six years later, in 1963, Union Pacific sold its 12.97 per cent interest to Standard for $9,245,625 and a $53,000,000 production payment, increasing Standard's interest in the Rangely unit to 23.89 per cent.

A chance conversation between representatives of Pan American Petroleum and Union Pacific, who happened to be assigned adjacent seats on a commercial flight between Los Angeles and Denver in 1969, sparked an interest in the offices of Union Pacific that led to one of the biggest oil and gas exploration programs in the history of the Rocky Mountain region.

William T. Smith, vice president and manager of Pan American's Denver region, was sitting next to a Union Pacific executive who introduced him to two UP attorneys riding in the seats behind them. The conversation came around to Union Pacific's vast land grant holdings and Union Pacific's conservative approach to minerals development as reflected by its farming or optioning out one 160- or 640-acre parcel at a time to oil operators who would then drill on that limited prospect.

Smith told the Union Pacific men he felt that was the wrong approach if Union Pacific wanted to realize the full value of its acreage. When asked what he thought Union Pacific should do,

243

Smith suggested selling the land grant or turning it over to a competent oil operator who could develop and coordinate a comprehensive exploration and development plan; this then could involve other oil operators by way of farmouts.

A few days later, Smith got a telephone call from Union Pacific asking whether Smith would be interested in discussing the matter further. Smith and members of the Denver division exploration department met with Union Pacific representatives who expressed interest in an exploration program covering one or two million acres. Smith, however, proposed that a much larger portion of the land grant acreage be made a part of any agreement.

As a result, Union Pacific awarded Pan American Petroleum an option in 1969 to explore approximately 7.5 million acres of Union Pacific land grant holdings, a checkerboard strip roughly 20 miles wide along the railroad line through Colorado, Wyoming, and Utah. It was the largest single U.S. land-holding ever optioned for exploration to a single oil company. Because of divided ownerships many portions of the area were virtually unexplored by the drill although it encompassed parts of six major and three lesser geologic provinces where substantial oil production had existed for more than 50 years.

Under the Standard-Union Pacific agreement, Standard obtained the opportunity to explore for oil and gas on the 7.5 million acres. The terms of the contract provided options for Standard to acquire leasehold interests in up to 75 per cent of the acreage. Standard agreed to pay Union Pacific an annual cash bonus for the first three years, totaling $9 million, and to spend or cause to be spent $15 million in exploration funds over a three-year period. Rights under the contract could be extended five years. Standard planned to conduct its own exploration and production programs, and, through contributions of acreage and money, to encourage exploration of some of the potentially productive acreage by farmouts to other companies.

As a footnote to the successful negotiations and subsequent exploration and development of the acreage, Union Pacific acquired Champlin Petroleum Company in January, 1970, and hired Smith to head that company as president in 1975 just after Smith had advanced to executive vice president of Standard's Amoco Production subsidiary.

By the end of the extended contract term in 1977, Standard had caused the drilling of approximately 2,900 wells. As a result, it controlled 2.5 million of the acres held by production or by five-year leases. Parts of the acreage are within the currently defined productive portion of the now famous Western Overthrust Belt.

The term "Overthrust" refers to sheets of rock that have been pushed or "thrust" over the top of other sheets of rock. Generally, this structural trend is believed to extend in an irregular pattern approximately 50 miles wide from Mexico on the south, through the Western States and Canada to Alaska—or as James W. Vanderbeek, who succeeded Smith as Denver vice president and regional manager, puts it—from Acapulco to Anchorage.

Standard's and the industry's early exploration efforts in the U.S. portion of the belt were unsuccessful because crude oil prices weren't high enough to offset exploration costs and seismic technology hadn't advanced enough to be of much help toward solving the complex geology. Improved computer-assisted seismic techniques, incentives of higher crude oil prices, and more experience increased the success ratio. Still, there were surprises. In some locations the drill may go first through older, then younger, and finally back to older formations. "It's mind-boggling" said one geologist with worldwide experience. "In Libya," he said, "you could put down two wells 20 miles apart and encounter basically the same formation. In the Overthrust Belt, two wells a mile apart may be in two entirely different geologic worlds."

Standard became the leader in developing the Overthrust Belt. Five years after the first discovery in the Union Pacific portion was announced in 1975, Standard owned one-third of the oil and gas reserves found and had interests in 15 of the 16 fields discovered up to that time. It operated almost half of all the drilling rigs active in the area. Standard's wildcat success rate in the Wyoming-Utah belt area was 50 per cent in 1979. By 1982, Standard's Amoco Production owned interests in 24 of the 26 fields that had been discovered, and it predicted that active exploration would continue for many years to come.

In 1978, Amoco Production, as the operator of record, completed 1,030 wells in the United States, over 300 more than the next most active company, according to statistics of an independent agency. The agency said Amoco Production that year ranked as the nation's leading wildcatter, completing 128 wildcat wells. Spending on exploration and production rose from 62 per cent of total company capital spending in the late 1960s to 78 per cent in 1979. Standard's lease holdings in North America totaled 34.5 million acres at the end of 1979. Of that, about 80 per cent was in the U.S., representing more than double the leased acreage of any other company.

By 1980, Standard's North American strategy was paying off. The company was a predominant participant in most of the active and important exploration and production areas in North America. These included the Deep Basin gas play and West Pembina D-2 reef trend in Canada, the Tuscaloosa gas play in southern Louisiana, the Western Overthrust Belt in Utah and Wyoming, and the Michigan Basin, as well as in more traditional oil country in Texas, Oklahoma, New Mexico, and the Gulf Coast. It had production in Alaska's Cook Inlet and was participating in exploration on the North Slope, but not to the extent of some other companies. Exploration was initiated in the Appalachian mountain area in what became identified as the Eastern Overthrust Belt.

Natural gas discoveries became an increasingly important aspect of the search for new reserves. In 1980, Galloway said that approximately 75 per cent of the money spent in the United States in the exploration-production part of the business was directed toward gas rather than oil targets.

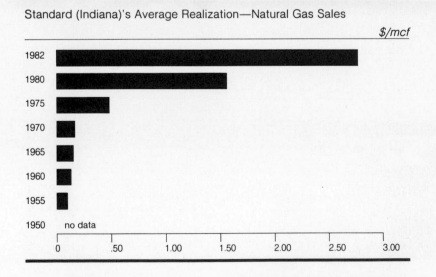

Standard (Indiana)'s Average Realization—Natural Gas Sales

$/mcf

Improved prices for natural gas made it possible to drill wells and utilize expensive hydrafracing which resulted in much higher producing rates from otherwise low productivity, tight gas sand reservoirs. The industry had known about such reservoirs but couldn't develop them at previous, below-cost prices. Special price incentives were granted under federal price regulations for these development areas which included some parts of eastern Texas, Colorado, Wyoming, and New Mexico. As an example, Galloway reported to the 1977 management conference that in the Wattenberg area of Colorado the company had drilled 376 wells and proved more than 500 billion cubic feet of gas which would have been uneconomic just 10 years earlier.

In 1979, the company was able to announce that it had increased its domestic natural gas production for the first time since 1973 and had increased its worldwide natural gas reserves for the first time in more than a decade. Swearingen and Richard M. Morrow, by then president of Standard, attributed this increase to the company's steadily increasing exploration and production expenditures. In 1979, these expenditures of $1.5 billion were nearly double the amount spent three years earlier and more than five times as much as was spent for these purposes in 1970.

27. The natural gas processing plant in southwestern Kansas for Hugoton field production was put on stream in 1949 when this photo was taken. It was one of many built in the 1940s and 1950s by Amoco Production Company, then Stanolind Oil and Gas Company. Demand for natural gas, which only a few years before was an oil field byproduct with little or no market, was increasing with the growth of its use for industrial fuel, home heating and cooking, and for petrochemical feedstock.

Standard led the industry in number of wells drilled in the U.S. in each of the five years in the 1977–81 period.

Standard's aggressive programs at home and abroad raised its net production of crude oil, condensate and natural gas liquids to more than one million barrels per day in 1977 and 1978. The company suffered a setback in 1979 when the revolution in Iran caused it to lose proprietary production amounting to 180,000 barrels daily. Price-induced conservation by consumers coupled with production declines in mature fields caused worldwide liquids production to average 766,000 barrels daily in 1982.

Standard (Indiana)'s Net Natural Gas Production

in millions of cubic feet daily

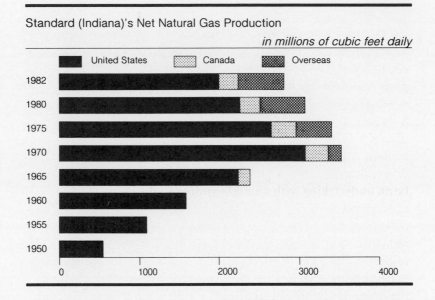

Worldwide natural gas net production averaged 2.8 billion cubic feet per day in 1982, falling below 3 billion cubic feet daily for the first time since 1968. Conservation efforts coupled with the economic recession of 1981–82 were largely responsible for the decline, as the company's 1982 U.S. production represented only about 70 per cent of its deliverable capacity.

Growth by Diversification/ Acquisition

19

In the 1960s and 1970s, diversification was a popular avenue of growth for many American corporations. Standard viewed diversification as a growth avenue if the opportunities fit long-range goals and were appropriate as to size and price.

"If we succeed in bringing off the plans discussed today," Swearingen told the 1973 Senior Management Conference, "our earnings in the early 1980s will be at the level of about $800 million. (Actually in 1979, they passed $1.5 billion.) For any diversification to be of genuine consequence to us, it will have to be an undertaking with annual earnings in the range of $50 to $75 million per year 10 years from now. To put this number in perspective, it should be noted that there are fewer than 70 industrial corporations in the United States which now make $75 million a year, and that a 10 per cent growth in earnings in our *existing* business will generate an annual increment of earnings in the order of $50 to $75 million."

It was Swearingen's view that diversification should not take the company too far from the skills it possessed. As he and his executive team examined the alternatives in terms of this framework, mining offered a logical extension of the company's capabilities. A report by the Stanford Research Institute, which Frank C. Osment presented to the board of directors in 1967, supported moving in this direction.

Mining was a business big enough to be of interest to Standard. It was a business that required geologists and engineers, the same kinds of disciplines employed in the oil and gas industry. Mineral resources were as widely dispersed around the world as oil and gas reserves. This meant that as the company sought new oil exploration rights in different countries, its mineral operations could be piggy-backed on top of the basic agreements for oil exploration. Finally, it was a business which required a large front-end investment, just as the exploration for oil. There was also a comparably long pay-out period.

Standard's board decided that the practical approach to the mining business was to form its own grass-roots organization. To investigate opportunities around the world and to consolidate the work that already had been done toward entering the field of mining, Standard brought in an experienced mining engineer-executive, Peter N. Pitcher, to be general manager of its mining operations, effective February 1, 1968.

Moving a step further, Standard in 1969 approved the organization of a new subsidiary, Amoco Minerals Company, to conduct mining operations in the United States, Canada, Australasia, Europe, and Africa. On April 1, 1970, Pitcher became Amoco Minerals' first president. In 1971, Standard reported stepped-up mineral exploration activities. It noted in its annual report for the year that exploratory core drilling indicated important reserves of high-grade copper-cobalt ore in the Republic of Zaire where Standard had acquired substantial interest in a 12,000-square-mile concession for a major project. The annual report also mentioned evaluation of copper, molybdenum, nickel, and other minerals prospects in three Canadian provinces and five states of the U.S.; drilling on a joint venture nickel prospect in western Australia; acquisition of licenses to prospect over some 490 square miles in Ireland; and the investigation of exploration opportunities in Mexico and in Saudi Arabia.

Soon, the search extended to Fiji, the Solomon Islands, Chile, and New Zealand. There were also feasibility studies on a northeastern Ontario gold discovery, and a joint venture to extract iodine from western Oklahoma brine discovered by Amoco Production Company. The copper-cobalt project in Zaire fell victim to rising capital costs and unsettled political conditions within the country.

Acquisition of proven reserves and management expertise seemed to offer another route into this new field of endeavor. A series of exploratory conversations with major mining companies followed: with Phelps-Dodge Corporation, Newmont Mining Corporation, Asarco, Inc., and with Amax, Inc.

In the case of Amax—the world's largest producer of molybdenum which also possessed significant holdings of coal as well as interests in silver, iron ore, nickel, aluminum, and petroleum—the initiative had come from Ian McGregor, chairman of Amax, who had inquired if Standard was interested in taking a position in the company with an accompanying commitment of capital. Swearingen told McGregor that Standard was not interested in passive investments but would be interested in acquiring control. Another series of negotiations followed, with the Standard board approving an offer in the range of $700 million for the Amax business.

But McGregor discovered when it came to selling or merging Amax that he was not in full control, although he was in fact chairman. The history of Amax began upon its incorporation in 1887 as American Metal Company, Ltd., and was for years prominently associated with the Hochschild family. The name was changed to American Metal Climax, Inc., in 1957 when it merged with Climax Molybdenum Company, a Guggenheim concern. The name Amax, Inc. was adopted in 1974. Walter Hochschild became president of American Metal in 1920 and was chairman and chief executive officer of Amax from 1960 to 1965. He became honorary chairman in 1966 and continued to be a director.

The Hochschild interests overruled McGregor's proposal to accept Standard's offer, and Standard did not press its case, continuing to pursue a policy of not becoming involved in an unfriendly takeover fight. It was Swearingen's philosophy that if a court fight were to be involved, the conditions of the original offer might be so substantially altered by the time the court fight was concluded that even if he were to win, the prize might no longer be worth the winning.

Pitcher retired as president of Amoco Minerals at age 65 in 1976, and was succeeded by R. W. Ballmer, who had been executive vice president. In 1977, Amoco Minerals undertook a pioneering project when it formed a consortium with three other major international companies to develop technology for recovering strategic metals from manganese nodules on the deep ocean floor. Amoco Minerals' 25 per cent interest in the consortium, Ocean Minerals Company, was later increased to 29 per cent. Nodules recovered in tests by the vessel Glomar Explorer were used in mini-pilot-plant studies to recover nickel, copper, and cobalt.

As Standard expanded its overseas operations in minerals with such projects as a three-stage program to develop a copper and gold mine in Papua New Guinea, it found a parallel between America's dependence on foreign oil and its dependence on foreign sources for strategic metals.

Writing in *SpaN* magazine in 1981, Swearingen cited the fact that the United States relied on unstable foreign sources for more than half of its supply of at least 22 strategic minerals. Among the examples he cited was cobalt, 90 per cent of which is imported and yet is essential to the manufacture of jet aircraft engines. Similarly, 89 per cent of the platinum so important as a catalyst in petroleum and chemical industries is imported, and 90 per cent of the chromium, an essential ingredient in high strength steels, comes from abroad.

The opportunity the company had been seeking to enter mining on a large scale in North America came in 1979 when Swearingen and James W. Cozad, an executive vice president of Standard, negotiated the purchase of Cyprus Mines Corporation.

Cyprus Mines was the sixth largest copper producer in the United States and held extensive interests in lead, zinc, silver, gold, molybdenum, and uranium including 51 per cent interest in a project to develop uranium reserves in Colorado. It also produced and marketed industrial minerals such as talc, kaolin, clay, calcium carbonate, barite, and diatomite. In Canada, near historic Whitehorse, Cyprus had 63 per cent interest in the Anvil lead-zinc-silver mine, the largest single mining development in the Yukon Territory since the Klondike gold rush of the 1890s. However, the Canadian Foreign Investment Review Agency refused to approve the transfer of this interest from Cyprus Mines to Standard. For this reason and because funds derived from the sale of the Cyprus Anvil interest would support additional acquisitions sought by Amoco Minerals, Standard in August of 1981 sold its interests in Cyprus Anvil to a subsidiary of Hudson's Bay Oil & Gas Company. The price was $212.6 million (Canadian).

Cyprus Mines became a wholly-owned subsidiary of Standard, and Kenneth J. Barr, formerly executive vice president of Amoco Production Company, was elected Cyprus president. Then, to conform to its organizational philosophy of streamlined functional operations, Standard integrated Cyprus Mines into Amoco Minerals Company on July 1, 1980, and named Barr president of that subsidiary. Standard's 50 per cent interest in the Standard-Gulf Oil Rio Blanco Oil Shale Company partnership was shifted to Amoco Minerals.

In 1980, Amoco Minerals aggressively pursued opportunities in mining. The board of directors authorized $300 million to develop the Thompson Creek molybdenum project in Idaho, which had been part of the Cyprus Mines acquisition. In February, Amoco Minerals purchased Empire Energy Corporation, with coal properties in Colorado, for approximately $64.5 million. In June of 1980, more coal properties were acquired when the company purchased the Emerald Mines Corporation, with properties in Pennsylvania, for approximately $118.9 million.

In August of 1981, Amoco Minerals acquired properties of the Harbert Corporation, a privately held Birmingham, Alabama, mining concern, in a stock transaction valued at $300 million.

The purchase included Harbert's coal mines in eastern Kentucky, a limestone quarry in Kentucky, other limestone operations in Louisiana, and barging operations on the Ohio and Mississippi rivers. The 7-million-ton-per-year capacity of the Harbert mines, together with the 2.1 million tons production of the Emerald Mine in western Pennsylvania and the Empire mine in Colorado, gave Standard a strong position in the coal business.

Prior to its interest in mining, Standard, in the 1960s, had eyed the possible acquisition of two petroleum companies, with operations restricted to the West Coast, which, if acquired, would fulfill the company's long-standing desire of becoming a nation-wide gasoline marketer. One of the companies was the Union Oil Company of California; the other was the Richfield Oil Corporation. Both were based in Los Angeles.

Negotiations were initiated first with Union, but the chairman, Reese H. Taylor, suddenly died. A former president and chief executive officer, Albert C. Rubel, was brought back from retirement to run the company and Swearingen started merger discussions with him, as well as members of the founding Lyman Stewart family, who still held a large block of stock.

At the same time, Gulf Oil Corporation was also making a bid for the company, with which it had been associated through loans it had extended to Union. Phillips Petroleum Company also coveted Union and in the process acquired 10 per cent of the stock, an act which promptly drew the attention of the Justice Department and a resounding threat of a veto of a proposed merger with any of the suitors. As a result, Phillips was forced to dispose of its stock, which it sold to Daniel K. Ludwig, the billionaire shipowner.

At about this time, investment bankers with a stake in the Chicago-based Pure Oil Company were deciding it was worth more dead than alive and sought a home for it in a merger with a healthier company. That company turned out to be Union, by that time headed by Fred L. Hartley. Because Pure was a Chicago-based company and shared the Midwest market with Standard, anti-trust implications ruled out any possible merger with the combined Union-Pure companies.

With one door closed, Standard turned its attention to the second possibility: a merger with Richfield Oil Corporation. Charles S. Jones, president of Richfield, met often over a period of a year with Swearingen, and provided the Standard negotiating team with complete data on the operating condition and profitability of the company.

Finally, Jones said he would be willing to recommend selling Richfield for a per-share price of $85; since there were about 10 million shares outstanding, this added up to about $850 million. Richfield was willing to take Standard stock in the deal, but Swearingen felt Standard's stock was undervalued at the time and preferred to make the acquisition a cash transaction. When the final figures were totaled up, Standard's board authorized Swearingen to make a cash offer of $750 million or $10 a share less than had been asked.

With this authority in his creel, Swearingen flew to Idaho where Charles Jones was on a fishing trip. For two days the two men fished and negotiated. Jones wanted the additional $10 a share and Swearingen wanted to give it to him. But search as he could among the assets and reserves of Richfield, Swearingen could not find the justification for the additional price and returned to Chicago.

About a month later, Swearingen picked up the paper to read that Robert O. Anderson, head of Atlantic Refining, had reached an agreement to merge Richfield with Atlantic at the asking price of $85 a share in stock. Anderson had entered the negotiations late; but his decision proved to be sound; the missing value of $10 per share turned out to be Richfield's interest in the Prudhoe Bay field in Alaska, then still undiscovered but later to be the largest oil field in North American history.

Not all attempts at acquisitions were met with a friendly reception. In the early 1970s Standard thought an acquisition opportunity might reside in Occidental Petroleum Corporation which in 1968 had acquired Island Creek Coal Company, the third largest coal company in the United States, and Hooker Chemical Corporation, at the time one of the ten largest chemical companies in the United States. Equally attractive to Standard were Occidental's crude oil properties in the North Sea. Each of these would fit nicely into Standard's operations. An oil strike in

Libya had been followed by an increase in the market price of Occidental stock to $55 per share, an all-time high. After the $55 per share high, the price per share of Occidental stock ranged downward into the 20s and teens. In 1974 through the first part of November, the high was $13¾ and the low was $7⅜.

A flurry of activity then developed in Occidental stock. On November 15, *The Wall Street Journal* noted that Occidental's stock "is back to making daily appearances on the most active list, and the price has climbed 27 per cent in about a week."

No one in the investment fraternity was able to figure out why. Although an advisory service and an investment banking firm had issued favorable comments on the company and some investors may have anticipated resumption of dividend payments, the *Journal* writer thought the stir of interest likely was due to rumors that Occidental was planning an acquisition, or itself was the object of a takeover attempt.

More than one million shares were traded in one week during the first part of November—637,500 on the biggest day. A persistent rumor had it that Arab interests were acquiring a position in Occidental. (Later in November, Occidental confirmed that Ghaith Pharaon, a Saudi Arabian businessman, had purchased about one million shares.)

Swearingen took the situation as an opportunity to open talks with Occidental, rationalizing that if a takeover was in process and Occidental wanted to head it off, Standard might be considered a better haven. Standard's board discussed the matter on November 13, and agreed that Swearingen should initiate discussions with Occidental. Swearingen met with Occidental's colorful chairman, Dr. Armand Hammer, in Los Angeles November 14.

Hammer thought that Swearingen was coming out to discuss experimental technology for oil shale recovery, in which both companies had an interest. In fact, Hammer brought his senior oil shale expert, Dr. Donald Garrett, to the meetings and Swearingen sat impatiently through a movie on Occidental's oil shale process before getting to the subject he had on his mind.

At the conclusion of the movie, Swearingen asked if Dr. Garrett could be excused as there was another matter he wished to discuss with Hammer that was extremely confidential. Hammer, noting that Swearingen was accompanied by Robert Greenhill, a representative of Morgan Stanley & Co., said he did not care to be outnumbered and Dr. Garrett, who, Hammer pointed out, was an executive vice president of Occidental, must stay.

255

As Hammer described it in his testimony at a subsequent senate subcommittee hearing, the following exchange took place:

"Mr. Swearingen then said, 'I would like to offer you some Standard of Indiana shares for all of Occidental Petroleum's shares'."

"I answered, 'I would like to offer you some of Occidental Petroleum's shares for all of Standard's shares'."

With this exchange, the battle was joined.

On November 15, Standard issued a news release in which it said it had explored with Occidental the possibility of combining the two companies, and that Hammer had indicated that he was unwilling to consider any such combination.

On November 21, Swearingen informed Standard's board of directors about his meeting with Hammer. In spite of Standard's policy against pursuing unfriendly takeovers, the stakes were high in this case and the board authorized investigation of whether an exchange offer should be made to Occidental's shareholders notwithstanding Hammer's objections.

But while Standard studied its case, Hammer mounted his defense in the flamboyant style for which he was noted. He filed suit in California Superior Court against Morgan Stanley & Company, Inc., charging breach of contract and alleging that while under contract to Occidental, Morgan Stanley had agreed to act as a dealer-manager for Standard's proposed tender offer. Occidental also filed suit in U.S. District Court, Los Angeles, seeking an injunction to prevent a takeover of Occidental by Standard.

The Federal Trade Commission began an investigation, and on December 3 hearings were held before the Special Subcommittee on Integrated Oil Operations of the Senate Committee on Interior and Insular Affairs to consider the proposed merger. Both Swearingen and Hammer testified.

In his testimony, Swearingen told the committee that an amalgamation with Occidental presented a unique opportunity for Standard to diversify in three major areas. He identified them as geographical diversification of petroleum operations into new foreign areas; new energy resources, especially coal; and diversification of chemical operations into new product lines. He also pointed to Standard's steadily increasing capital expenditures, production and exploration, while noting Occidental's decline in these areas during the preceding five years.

Over the next several weeks, Standard continued to explore the means by which a takeover might be accomplished. Faced with the determined opposition of Hammer and the uncertain value of much of Occidental's property, Standard's board on January 23, 1975, decided to make no offer to acquire Occidental. If the merger had gone through, Standard would have become at the time the sixth largest industrial concern in the United States.

Meanwhile, Standard undertook a series of studies to determine what new lines of business might be of a nature to have a meaningful impact on total profit performance. Standard was nearing the $30 billion mark in sales and was larger as a company than many total industries. As a result, the options for new businesses which would justify a commitment of management and resources were limited. Among those businesses which seemed to hold sufficient growth potential, electronics appeared to be promising. The industry's sales of integrated circuits had been growing at the rate of 50 per cent per year and the total field was expanding at an annual 15 per cent rate.

Corporate strategy called for Standard to invest in a company in which Standard's resources would have an impact through supporting a move of the smaller company into an expanded and strengthened market position.

In fulfillment of this strategy, Standard in 1977 purchased 15 per cent of the shares of Analog Devices, Inc., of Norwood, Massachusetts, which, under its chairman, Ray Stata, was a pioneer in designing and producing specialized precision electronic components. In 1980, Analog Devices formed a new division, Analog Devices Enterprises, to supply expansion capital furnished largely by Standard to young companies in businesses closely related to Analog Devices' long-term growth strategy.

The investment in Analog represented a break with past philosophy in a sense. However, the digital recorders of the kind manufactured by Analog Devices had been used by Standard to provide precise analyses of chemical products as well as to analyze computer-processed data from automated experiments. Standard always had been technologically oriented and its future largely depended on developing new technology. Analog offered an opportunity to participate in a field with growth potential.

The approach to research which recognized that new technology might be available through investment in innovative ventures as well as laboratory research also led, in 1979, to the purchase of a minority interest in the Solarex Corporation of Rockville, Maryland, the world's leading manufacturer of solar photovoltaic (solar electric) energy systems.

Two European corporations—Moteurs Leroy-Somer of Angouleme, France, and Holec n.v. of Utrecht, the Netherlands, had earlier taken minority positions in Solarex. Standard's purchase of about 20 per cent minority interest provided the final increments of investment capital to permit Solarex to construct an advanced production facility, one totally powered by solar energy. Standard also agreed to consider funding specific research and demonstration programs.

The first of these demonstration programs was the partial conversion to solar power of a service station in West Chicago, Illinois. In all, 72 panels containing 5,184 photovoltaic cells produced a peak output of 5,000 watts, more than half the amount required by a typical American household. The cells were made by Semix, Inc., a subsidiary of Solarex, which combined semicrystalline silicon material and a new proprietary cell-manufacturing technology to produce solar panels which were effective but cost considerably less than the conventional single-crystal silicon commonly used by the rest of the photovoltaic industry. It was proof of the assertion of Dr. Joseph Lindmayer, president of Solarex, that the Standard investment had permitted the company "to rapidly move our technology out of the research laboratory and into production."

Standard was also making other uses of solar technology. It had for a number of years used solar panels to apply a weak current to steel casings in pipelines and producing wells to halt or prevent corrosion. In remote oil and gas fields where utility power either was not available or excessively expensive, solar-powered telemetry systems were used to report well production data to district offices.

Kasch succinctly expressed the company's commitment to the use of solar energy. "Sunlight energy is enormous, providing 99.8 per cent of all the energy available on earth," he said. "It is also inexhaustible, clean, silent, and well-distributed: there's no solar OPEC . . . Semix's semicrystalline cell promises to break a major cost barrier to large-scale commercial application."

Opportunities to invest in companies with the possibility of expanding the field of microbiology into commercial applications were considerably more limited than those for investment in electronics. In 1977, however, Standard acquired 24.5 per cent interest in Cetus Corporation, a small California company doing research in the area of microbiology and recombinant DNA.

These acquisitions enabled Standard to stay on the leading edge of developing technology and to position itself for new directions of future growth.

Standard acquired the remaining outstanding shares of Solarex and Semix in 1983, and the two companies were merged into a subsidiary of Standard. Also in 1983, Standard formed a new subsidiary, Amoco Technology Company, as an umbrella organization for all of its wholly-owned and partially-owned high tech companies.

The Results of Change

20 ━━━━━━━━━━━━━━━━━━━━━━━━━━━━━━━━━

Through the years that Swearingen had been directing the affairs of Standard, he had consistently placed great emphasis on developing a self-reliant management—"giving the man the authority and letting him do the job," as he expressed it. To Swearingen, manpower planning was as important as financial planning. One of the main impediments to effective manpower planning had been overcome. The compartmentalized functions and independent fiefdoms that were working against achieving better utilization of human resources as well as improving rate of return when Swearingen became chief executive officer had disappeared as the one-company concept took hold.

Now, in 1978, Swearingen's mind turned to the time five years in the future when he would retire at age 65. George V. Myers had expressed a desire to take early retirement from the presidency in 1978 at the age of 62. Swearingen saw this as an opportunity to begin moving into place an executive structure which would provide continuity in company affairs after his own retirement. Meanwhile, there would be a five-year period for the new executives to be tested and to develop their own cohesion and dynamism.

When Myers retired on October 1, 1978, Swearingen began identifying key executives who would bear the responsibility for taking the company through most of the decade ahead. All came from within Standard. Together their average length of service with the company was 25 years; the average age of those taking new positions was 51.

As president of Standard effective October 1, 1978, the board of directors elected Richard M. Morrow, 52, who most recently had been president of Amoco Chemicals.

The office of vice chairman had been discontinued when Gunness retired in 1975. Parent company corporate responsibilities were assigned to four executive vice presidents: Frank C. Osment, 60, and Blaine J. Yarrington, 60, who had been elected in 1974; and Walter R. Peirson, 52, and James W. Cozad, 51, who were elected in 1978.

Leland C. Adams, 53, was elected president of Amoco International Oil Company in 1975. He became president of the combined Amoco Production Company on April 15, 1981. Reporting to Adams were John C. Meeker, 54, president, Amoco Production Company (USA), and Henry O. Boswell, 51, president, Amoco Production Company (International).

H. Laurance Fuller, 40, was elected president of Amoco Oil Company on October 1, 1978. In September of 1981, Fuller was elected an executive vice president and a director of Standard.

Lawrason D. Thomas, 44, was elected president of Amoco Oil Company on September 3, 1981.

Richard H. Leet, 51, was elected president of Amoco Chemicals Corporation on October 1, 1978.

Kenneth J. Barr, 52, was elected president of Amoco Minerals Company on July 1, 1980.

The new management team would direct an enterprise that had changed markedly during Swearingen's leadership.

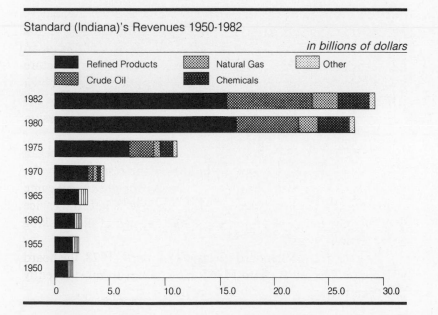

Standard (Indiana)'s Revenues 1950-1982

in billions of dollars

Refined Products Natural Gas Other
Crude Oil Chemicals

1982
1980
1975
1970
1965
1960
1955
1950

0   5.0   10.0   15.0   20.0   25.0   30.0

At the beginning of the 1980s, Swearingen and his associates were able to review with pride and satisfaction their progress toward achieving the goals which had been established by the planning task forces almost 20 years earlier. Specifically, Chairman Swearingen told a meeting of Boston Security Analysts, those goals called for:

The preservation of capital

A 10 per cent average annual earnings growth

Maintaining a 13 to 15 per cent return on equity

A 35 to 45 per cent dividend pay-out

A prudent financial structure

Comparing favorably with competitors in the industry

The degree to which these goals had been met and exceeded was indicated by financial reports. Standard's 1980 annual report to stockholders showed income of $1.9 billion on total revenues of $27.8 billion, compared with income of $145 million on revenues of $2 billion in the 1960 annual report. Even against a comparison of the value of the dollar in 1980 versus 1960, the growth revealed by the numbers was notable:

	1980	1960
Total Revenues		
as reported	$27,831,862,000	$2,038,208,000
1980 dollars		5,261,958,820
Net Income		
as reported	1,915,314,000	144,762,000
1980 dollars		373,726,177

The bite of inflation could not be ignored. In 1978, for example, Standard calculated that the replacement cost of its inventories had more than doubled to $2.4 billion compared with $1 billion on an historical cost basis.

At the end of 1980, Standard had total assets of $20.2 billion. It ranked ninth among U.S. industrial concerns and fifth among U.S. petroleum companies. Its total revenues of $27.8 billion were 38 per cent more than in 1979. Standard's net income in 1980 increased 27 per cent over the preceding year, to a record $1.9 billion. This ranked Standard sixth among the Standard and Poor's industrials and fifth among U.S.-based oil companies.

The market value of Standard's common stock at year-end 1980 was $23.4 billion, ranking it fourth behind IBM, AT&T, and Exxon, among companies listed on the New York Stock Exchange. Return on equity increased 2.2 percentage points from 1979 to 21.6 per cent, ranking Standard among the top 10 oil companies.

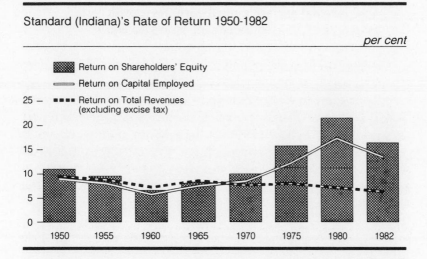

Standard (Indiana)'s Rate of Return 1950-1982

per cent

- Return on Shareholders' Equity
- Return on Capital Employed
- Return on Total Revenues (excluding excise tax)

Between year-end 1975 and year-end 1980, Standard's average total return to shareholders was 36 per cent per year based on the combined impact of both price appreciation and dividend yield, and assuming dividend reinvestment over the period. As a basis for comparison, the average total return to investors for 15 major oil companies was 27 per cent, while the Standard and Poor's 400 composite index showed a return of 14 per cent.

The evolution of Standard, as it adapted its organizational structure to changing opportunities and needs, was reflected in the proportion of capital employed in various subsidiaries.

George V. Myers noted in 1977 that the capital employed share of Standard's historic North American business, as represented by Amoco Production Company and Amoco Oil Company, had declined from 80 per cent of the total ten years before to slightly more than half. The reason could be found in the strategy adopted a little over 15 years before which called for an overall redirection of the company, a conscious effort to shift funds from the conventional North American oil and gas business to Amoco International Oil Company and Amoco Chemicals Corporation.

263

The share of the domestic Amoco Production subsidiary, which Frank C. Osment described as the major cornerstone of the company, had declined from an average of about 60 per cent in the early 1960s, to about 47 per cent toward the end of that decade, and to less than 40 per cent in 1975 and 1976. Allocations of capital spending to Amoco Oil also had been reduced over the years, and its outlook as the domestic manufacturing and marketing subsidiary was for relatively low growth.

By the end of the 1970s, Amoco International and Amoco Chemicals had grown to the point where their activities represented about 40 per cent of total capital employed. Amoco International activities for the next few years would be directed toward maximizing return from existing properties; new ventures in the overseas oil business would be undertaken on a selective basis. Chemicals, which Standard considered to be a high-growth business, would continue to be supported with cash infusions sufficient to sustain a growth rate materially greater than company and industry averages.

Standard now expected future corporate performance would be highly dependent on the ability of Amoco International and Amoco Chemicals to achieve earnings performance more nearly in line with their share of corporate capital employed. Amoco Production's reserves of both liquids and gas had been declining after peaking in 1968–69 and, following a period of sustained production levels, reserves were expected to decline further. This was a result of the limitations imposed on the reinvestment levels of Amoco Production and the cost and difficulty of finding oil in the U.S.

Standard's earnings topped the one billion dollar mark in 1977 and continued to climb through the end of the decade, providing a base for larger exploration and production expenditures. In 1979, Swearingen and president Richard M. Morrow told stockholders that in Standard's case there were signs of progress toward obtaining more reliable energy supplies from domestic sources.

"In response to price relief on natural gas production in recent years and the anticipation of federal relaxation of price controls on domestic crude, our company has steadily increased its exploration and production expenditures to nearly double the amount we spent just three years ago, and more than five times as much as we spent for this purpose in 1970," Swearingen and Morrow said. It was clearly the view of Swearingen and his management team that oil and gas would still be the company's primary business.

"We are optimistic about the future of the oil and gas business," Swearingen told the New York Society of Security Analysts in March of 1981. "We believe we have the know-how,

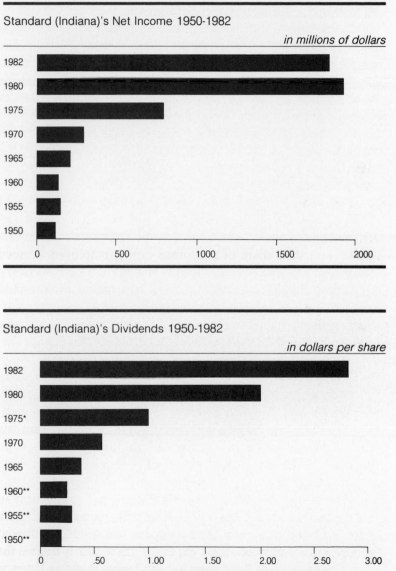

Standard (Indiana)'s Net Income 1950-1982

in millions of dollars

1982	
1980	
1975	
1970	
1965	
1960	
1955	
1950	

0   500   1000   1500   2000

Standard (Indiana)'s Dividends 1950-1982

in dollars per share

1982	
1980	
1975*	
1970	
1965	
1960**	
1955**	
1950**	

0   .50   1.00   1.50   2.00   2.50   3.00

*Restated for 100 Per cent Stock Dividend Paid on December 16, 1974
**Includes Market Value on Date of Distribution of Dividends in Capital Stock of Standard (New Jersey)

265

Standard Oil Company (Indiana)

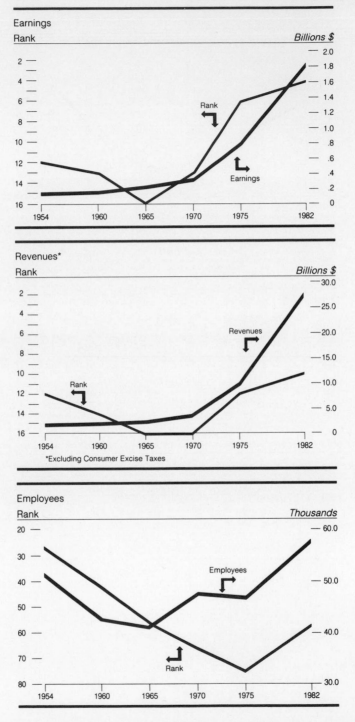

Earnings

Rank   Billions $

2 —   — 2.0
                                                         — 1.8
4 —   — 1.6
                                                         — 1.4
6 —   Rank   — 1.2
                                                         — 1.0
8 —   — 1.0
10 —   — .8
                                                         — .6
12 —   — .4
14 —   Earnings   — .2
16 —   — 0
   1954   1960   1965   1970   1975   1982

Revenues*

Rank   Billions $

2 —   —30.0
4 —   —25.0
6 —   Revenues   —20.0
8 —   —15.0
10 —   —10.0
12 —   Rank   — 5.0
14 —   — 5.0
16 —   — 0
   1954   1960   1965   1970   1975   1982
        *Excluding Consumer Excise Taxes

Employees

Rank   Thousands

20 —   — 60.0
30 —
40 —   Employees   — 50.0
50 —
60 —   — 40.0
70 —   Rank
80 —   — 30.0
   1954   1960   1965   1970   1975   1982

in the "Fortune 500"

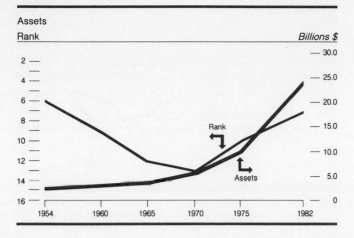

Assets
Rank

Billions $

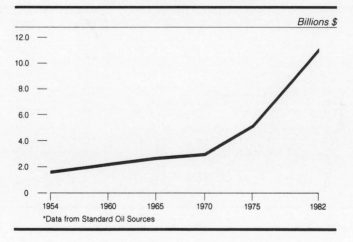

Year-end Book Value (Aggregate)*

Billions $

*Data from Standard Oil Sources

the people, and the capital to accept the physical, political, and economic risks to be successful. We believe there are large amounts of oil and gas yet to be discovered in the United States and that we can be in the forefront of their discovery. Moreover, we believe there will be a ready market for any oil and gas that we can produce here.

"We believe that there are large areas of the world outside the United States where oil can be discovered in paying quantities, where oil can be exported to markets that we now have, and where political risks are acceptable.

"We believe we should maintain our refining and marketing facilities in the U.S. and abroad in first-class shape so they will be as efficient as those of our competitors. We intend to continue our efforts to improve our position in areas of market strength and minimize our efforts elsewhere.

"We believe that the chemicals business and the mining business are logical extensions of our basic oil business and intend to broaden our activities in these directions."

In the summer of 1983, as Swearingen prepared for his retirement in early September, Standard's board of directors elected the new team of key officers who would guide the company's continuing growth and development. Each assumed his new position on September 7 upon Swearingen's retirement after 44 years as an employee, 31 years as a director, and 23 years as chief executive officer.

Becoming chairman and chief executive officer was Richard M. Morrow. James W. Cozad was elected vice chairman, and H. Laurance Fuller was named president. Walter R. Peirson, an executive vice president, was placed in charge of worldwide chemical operations as well as petroleum refining and marketing. Leland C. Adams was elected executive vice president responsible for worldwide petroleum exploration and production and for minerals exploration and development. Richard H. Leet was named executive vice president in charge of research, supply, marine transportation, corporate development, environmental affairs and safety, purchasing, and synthetic fuel development.

In the subsidiaries, Henry O. Boswell succeeded Adams as president of Amoco Production Company, and Robert D. Cadieux took Leet's place as president of Amoco Chemicals Corporation. Lawrason D. Thomas remained as president of Amoco Oil Company and Kenneth J. Barr as president of Amoco Minerals Company.

Richard M. Morrow, chairman of the board and chief executive officer, 1983-

James W. Cozad, vice chairman of the board, 1983-

H. Laurance Fuller, president, 1983-

Walter R. Peirson, executive vice
president, 1978-

Leland C. Adams, executive vice
president, 1983-

Richard H. Leet, executive vice
president, 1983-

Joe P. Hammond, vice president,
public and government affairs, 1975-

Edward A. Mason, vice president,
research, 1977-

L. Bates Lea, vice president and
general counsel, 1978-

Frederick S. Addy, vice president,
finance, 1983-

Robert K. Boknecht, vice president, employee relations, 1979-

Rady A. Johnson, vice president, government affairs, 1979-

Terence B. Redmond, vice president, planning and economics, 1979-

John J. Gobel, vice president and general tax counsel, 1981-

James E. Allard, controller, 1981-

Ronald E. Callahan, secretary, 1981-

William R. Hutchinson, treasurer, 1981-

William G. Lowrie, vice president, supply and marine transportation, 1983-

274

Arthur E. Rasmussen, director, 1971-

Robert H. Malott, director, 1973-

Richard D. Wood, director, 1973-

James C. Fletcher, director, 1977-

Karl D. Bays, director, 1978-

Richard J. Ferris, director, 1981-

Frederick G. Jaicks, director, 1981-

John H. Bryan, Jr., director, 1982-

Walter E. Massey, director, 1983-

Henry O. Boswell, president,
Amoco Production Company, 1983-

Kenneth J. Barr, president,
Amoco Minerals Company, 1980-

Robert D. Cadieux, president,
Amoco Chemicals Corporation, 1983-

Lawrason D. Thomas, president,
Amoco Oil Company, 1981-

Robert C. Gunness, vice chairman of
the board, retired March 1, 1975.

George V. Myers, president, retired
October 1, 1978.

Frank C. Osment, executive vice
president, retired September 1, 1982.

Blaine J. Yarrington, executive vice
president, retired March 18, 1983.

Herschel H. Cudd, senior vice
president, retired April 23, 1975.

F. Randolph Yost, senior vice
president, retired April 23, 1975.

L. Chester May, vice president,
finance, retired April 5, 1976.

Jack M. Tharpe, vice president,
employee relations, retired September
1, 1979.

George H. Galloway, president,
Amoco Production Company, retired
April 18, 1981.

Looking to the Future

21 ━━━━━━━━━━━━━━━━━━━━━━━━━━━━━━━━━━

Midway through his years as chief executive officer of Standard, Swearingen described his view of management's challenge as "not only to perform in the present, but to try to anticipate the future." As he neared the end of his tenure as chairman, he foresaw many changes for Standard in the years to come but believed it would still be very much in the oil and gas business well into the 21st Century.

He was optimistic about the future. "Throughout the world, the total hydrocarbon base is sufficient to carry us well through the next century," he told the International Oil Industry TBA Convention in Toronto, Canada, in 1980. "There are, for example, the great Free-World deposits of tar sands. In the United States, these in-place deposits represent the equivalent of about 30 billion barrels of oil. In Venezuela, the figure is at least 700 billion barrels. In Canada, it is estimated there are 900 billion barrels. But, as in the case of oil from shale and coal, we must be willing to pay the price for its development."

As he was throughout his career, Swearingen was scornful of the doomsayers about oil supplies. "This doomsday attitude is not a new one," he told the Young Presidents Club in Chicago in 1978. "About 30 years ago, Vice President Barkley told us that the United States would run out of oil by 1960. Yet the fact is we are using three times as much oil today as we were in Mr. Barkley's day, and at the same time our proved domestic reserves have grown from 25 billion to approximately 31 billion barrels."

Still, there were changes to be anticipated. Although oil would still be an important part of America's energy picture into the 21st Century, it would be less so as demand moderated through greater fuel efficiency and conservation. The trend was

281

already evident in 1980 when U.S. demand dropped more than 6 per cent for gasoline and 13 per cent for distillates such as fuel oil.

Entering the new decade, Standard's corporate strategy reflected its view that Americans would be using less gasoline. The best projections were that gasoline sales in the United States would decrease from a consumption rate of 7-8 million barrels a day in 1978-1979 to perhaps as low as 5 million barrels a day by 1990. As a result, Amoco Oil was expected to operate in a U.S. climate of relatively low growth. While the company was determined to maintain its posture as one of the three leading marketers of gasoline at retail in the United States, at the end of 1981 it moved toward ending the branded marketing of gasolines and heating oil in 11 states where results were unsatisfactory and where only 5 per cent of its refined products was sold. By the end of 1982, Amoco service stations were to disappear from Montana, Oklahoma, Arkansas, West Virginia, Maine, New Hampshire, Vermont, Washington, Oregon, and all of Texas but Houston and all of Kentucky but Louisville and Lexington.

Although possessing one of the healthiest balance sheets in American industry, Standard still found its subsidiaries growing at such a rate that all available funds were fully committed. This fact was reflected in the disciplined approach Standard took toward possible acquisitions. "A major diversification move, if any, will be accomplished in a manner which will not impair the availability of investment funds for existing operations," an internal policy statement declared.

Consistently, Swearingen emphasized financial performance as the end measure of the company's activities. The strategy for the eighties, he told a group of analysts, was to achieve a continuing high level of performance and rate of return. Although Standard's five-year spending plans did not include amounts for any commercial-scale synthetic fuel projects, Standard continued to support research in a number of synthetic fuels programs and others aimed at developing their potential to contribute significantly to America's energy needs in the future. These included tar sands, oil shale, coal-derived liquids, biomass, and solar energy.

The investment costs for development of these new areas were reflected in enormous numbers: $1 to $3 billion for shale oil development, $1 billion for tertiary recovery utilizing carbon dioxide and more for projects involving micellar fluid injection, and $1 billion for tar sands development.

282 Government policy continued to impact efforts to find new

energy sources, even as decontrol of oil and some natural gas prices went into effect. Industry leaders, such as Swearingen and Morrow, continued to press for the opening up of additional public lands for exploration. The potential of these federally controlled lands, which constituted one-third of the total land area of the United States, could be found in figures compiled by William H. Dresher, dean of the College of Mines and director of the Bureau of Geology and Mineral Technology at the University of Arizona. He estimated public lands contain 40 per cent of all U.S. coal; 70 per cent of all U.S. low-sulfur coal; 75 per cent of U.S. oil shale; 85 per cent of U.S. tar sands; 33 per cent of U.S. estimated oil resource base; and 43 per cent of the U.S. estimated gas resource base.

While government policy-makers debated the public lands issue and others affecting the nation's energy future, Swearingen told Standard executives at a planning meeting that "one of the things we must do is to maintain flexibility in our plans and programs. We must be able to move in other directions if the oil and gas business becomes physically or politically untenable."

One aspect of this pursuit of flexibility was the fostering of new grass roots entities or technologically pioneering ventures which had the potential for long-term contributions to corporate growth and earnings. It was Swearingen's concept that these innovative enterprises, in their early stages, required little funds, but over the long term might make significant contributions to future earnings and growth.

Environmental concerns and toxic waste treatment and disposal also moved to the fore as issues facing the corporation in the eighties. Corporate spending for environmental conservation from 1971 through 1982 totaled more than $2 billion, and review programs were established to ensure that facilities met all environmental and toxicological regulations. The testing of products to identify potential health hazards was assigned to an independent laboratory operated by the Illinois Institute of Technology; it became fully operational in 1980.

In all of its aspects, Standard seemed a corporation not so much finishing out the 20th Century as poised for new challenges and opportunities of the 21st Century. Significantly, it distributed to its shareholders and employees in 1981 a small booklet entitled "The Year 2000." While looking to the future, it reminded readers that there would be no panaceas.

The quality of leadership, as history has often recorded, is an intangible. But perhaps one of the elements which enabled John Swearingen to lead Standard so successfully over most of a quarter of a century was that he never lost his enthusiasm for the oil business or his conviction of its importance to America. Whether expressing himself philosophically or debating on television with critics of the industry during the national controversy over America's energy policy, he never wavered in his conviction that being in the oil business carried with it a very special sense of responsibility.

"I've seen people in many other businesses in my career," he told the author of this history, "and I've gotten to know something about a number of other businesses. But I think basically, that the oil business is the most fascinating business in existence, and it has people in it who, by and large, are superior in quality to any other line of business I know.

"That's not a popular thing to say about people in the oil business, but I can guarantee that there is more business done on a handshake in the oil business than is done on a handshake in any other ten lines of business in the United States. If you stick to your word, people will do business with you; if you don't, you're out.

"To me, this has been a very stimulating environment to work in. It is a business where it is necessary to have that kind of trust because time is always a valuable commodity in this business. Decisions can't wait until the lawyers and accountants draw up 50 to 100 pages of contracts to cover everything. Even when you draw up a contract there is something sure to occur that you have not anticipated, and you have to sit down and work it out again.

"There is another thing about the oil business that distinguishes it. In many lines of business you can't measure whether you really succeed or fail. In the oil business, if you have an idea there is a place that will produce oil, you put up the money and you drill the hole. Either oil or gas is there, or it isn't. It's as simple as that. You can measure whether you have accomplished something or not.

"Moreover, it is different from research activity, or teaching or banking, or manufacturing, because the gestation period between conception of an idea and its verification is relatively short. As you get an idea in the oil business, you go out and lease the land, you drill the well, and you know in two or three or maybe four years whether you were right or wrong. In other industries, you may go into a research laboratory and start research on a new

284

automobile or an advanced computer and it may be 20 or 25 years before you ever come to the end of the line and know you have or have not reached a successful conclusion.

"The exploration and production part of the business, of course, is where the romance lies. But there are opportunities in many other kinds of things, although perhaps to a lesser degree. The industry by-and-large has always been interested in developing new technology. For example, somebody may have a 10 per cent better way of finding oil than somebody else. This is an enormous advantage. People in all the history of the oil business have been looking for new ways of finding oil. But nobody has yet found or developed a direct tool for finding oil other than the drill. They have come pretty close, but they have never found a way other than drilling a hole. You can tell where a field *might* be, or where one *ought* to be, but whether it is there or not is the big question.

"So, I think it's a fascinating business and, as it's turned out over the last 50 to 75 years, it has been an absolutely essential business. We couldn't have automobiles or jet airplanes without having the ability to move these machines around with a simple, readily available, reasonably low priced fuel. And that's what oil provides."

There was no doubt that, as the major energy supplier in America, the petroleum industry touched the life of every citizen. But because of the scope, complexity and technical nature of its operations, it was an industry very difficult for an outsider to comprehend fully.

From the beginning it had been a uniquely American enterprise. It was pioneered in the United States, and American companies led in its development overseas. Through willingness to commit enormous sums of risk capital and through constant technological improvements, it had given Americans not only the lowest cost and most abundant supplies of fuel on the globe, but an impressive range of petrochemical and plastic products which conserved the country's resources, and lessened its reliance on natural materials of every variety.

Finally, it was appropriate for John Swearingen himself to sum up how the many people who served Standard through the years fit into this pattern of American life and what this record of accomplishment promised for the future.

"The record through the years has been one of challenge and response, of steady diversification and ever-widening scope; of the evolution of an enterprise with the strength and flexibility not only to withstand change but also to be itself a pioneer and a creator of change. Most of all, the record is one of service, and of progress toward a richer way of life.

"Increasingly, today's world also demands vision, flexibility, change, and growth as the price of survival, and we expect to measure up to these demands in the future as in the past. All of mankind stands today on explosive ground. Technological, political, and population problems confront us on a global scale. It is our belief that these problems can in time be surmounted and that our industry and our company can continue to play a role in their solution."

Standard (Indiana)'s Total Revenues 1911-1982

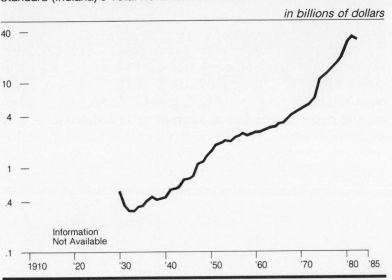

in billions of dollars

40 —

10 —

4 —

1 —

.4 —

Information
Not Available

.1

1910　'20　'30　'40　'50　'60　'70　'80　'85

Standard (Indiana)'s Net Income 1911-1982

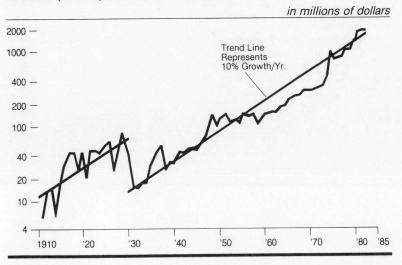

in millions of dollars

2000 —
1000 —

400 —

200 —
100 —

Trend Line
Represents
10% Growth/Yr.

40 —

20 —

10 —

4

1910　'20　'30　'40　'50　'60　'70　'80　'85

287

Biographical Notes

LELAND C. ADAMS

Leland C. Adams was elected a director of Standard Oil in 1976 and became president of Amoco Production Company on April 15, 1981, when domestic and worldwide exploration and production operations were consolidated.

Adams joined Standard in 1948 as a geophysicist for Amoco Production Company (then Stanolind Oil and Gas Company) following his graduation from the State University of Iowa at Iowa City with a degree in electrical engineering. Later he served as district and division exploration superintendent, then manager of exploration. In 1965, he was elected a vice president of Amoco Production and served as its Louisiana Gulf Coast division manager from 1965 to 1970. Adams became executive vice president of Amoco International in 1970 and president in 1975, serving in that position until the consolidation in 1981. Effective September 7, 1983, he was elected an executive vice president of Standard Oil, with worldwide responsibilities for minerals and for oil and gas exploration and production.

KENNETH J. BARR

Kenneth J. Barr moved from executive vice president of Amoco Production Company to president of Cyprus Mines Corporation in 1979 after its acquisition by Standard. He then was elected president of Amoco Minerals in 1980 when Amoco Minerals became the principal subsidiary responsible for all of Standard's worldwide mining activities.

Barr joined Amoco Production (then Stanolind) in 1948 as a junior petroleum engineer after graduation from Auburn University. He served in various capacities in Texas, Oklahoma, and New Mexico before being appointed chief engineer in 1963. He was placed in charge of Canadian oil and gas producing operations in 1965.

He subsequently served as vice president and division manager of

289

Amoco Production in New Orleans, general manager of supply and coordination for Standard in Chicago, executive vice president of Amoco International Oil Company, and executive vice president of Amoco Production.

ROBERT K. BOKNECHT

Robert K. Boknecht was elected vice president-employee relations of Standard on October 23, 1979.

Boknecht was named general manager-employee relations in 1977 and has been head of the employee relations department since September 1, 1979.

Boknecht joined Standard in 1955 as a consumer salesman. He has held a number of employee relations management positions in Chicago, Detroit, and Atlanta for both Standard and its wholly-owned subsidiary, Amoco Oil Company. He also served as manager of Amoco's Central Credit Card office.

A native of Decatur, Indiana, Boknecht received his B.A. degree from Valparaiso University, Valparaiso, Indiana.

HENRY O. BOSWELL

Henry O. Boswell was named president of Amoco Production Company (International) on April 15, 1981. Effective September 7, 1983, he became president of the consolidated Amoco Production Company.

Prior to the 1981 consolidation of worldwide exploration and production activities into a single subsidiary, Amoco Production Company, Boswell was executive vice president of Amoco International Oil Company in Houston.

Earlier he was Amoco International vice president managing exploration and production activities in Africa and the Middle East.

His career began in 1953 as a roustabout for Amoco Production (then Stanolind Oil and Gas Company). Boswell served in various engineering positions in Texas, Louisiana, and Oklahoma. In 1966, he was named division engineer at Amoco Production's Houston office.

In 1970, he became vice president-producing for Amoco Canada Petroleum Company Ltd., Calgary, and in 1973, he was appointed president of Amoco Canada.

A native of Texas, Boswell received his bachelor's degree in petroleum engineering from the University of Houston in 1954. He attended advanced management school at the University of Western Ontario in 1969.

ROBERT D. CADIEUX

Robert D. Cadieux became president of Amoco Chemicals Corporation on September 7, 1983. He had served as Amoco Chemicals' executive vice president since 1981.

Cadieux joined Amoco Chemicals in 1959 as an accountant. He was made manager-budgets and control reports for Standard Oil in 1971, manager of Amoco Oil Company's Kansas City administrative center in 1972, and was appointed Standard Oil's division controller for international petroleum operations in 1974.

Cadieux was named vice president of planning and administration for Amoco Chemicals in 1975 and vice president of plastics products and ventures management in 1977.

A native of Chicago, Cadieux holds a bachelor's degree in accounting and economics from the Illinois Institute of Technology and an MBA from the University of Chicago.

JAMES W. COZAD
James W. Cozad was elected vice president in charge of financial operations for Standard in 1971 after two years as financial vice president of Amoco Oil Company. He was elected vice president-finance, chief financial officer and a director in 1976, and an executive vice president of Standard in 1978.

After graduating from Indiana University in 1950, Cozad joined the accounting firm of Peat, Marwick, Mitchell & Company in Detroit. Prior to joining Amoco Oil in 1969, he had been treasurer and vice president-treasurer of HyGrade Food Products Corporation, and in 1967 had been named treasurer of Philip Morris, Inc. As an executive vice president of Standard he was in charge of all financial planning and operations. Effective September 7, 1983, he was elected vice chairman of Standard Oil.

HERSCHEL H. CUDD
See main text beginning at page 190.

JOHN W. ELIAS
John W. Elias became executive vice president responsible for domestic operations of Amoco Production Company, the worldwide oil and gas exploration-production subsidiary of Standard Oil Company (Indiana), on September 7, 1983.

Previously he was executive vice president for coordination of senior staff exploration, production, research, and gas sales activities. His new assignment was part of the functional restructuring of Amoco Production concurrent with the retirement of John E. Swearingen, chairman and chief executive officer of Standard.

A native of Texas, Elias received his Bachelor of Science degree in geology from the University of Oklahoma and joined the company in 1964 as a geologist. He served in various positions in Texas, Oklahoma, and Louisiana and was manager-exploration operations and vice president-exploration while Amoco Production's responsibilities were limited

291

to the U. S. and Canada. He served as Standard's general manager-planning and administration from 1977-1979.

RICHARD J. FARRELL

Richard J. Farrell, a director of Standard Oil for more than 15 years, elected to retire at age 62 on December 1, 1978, as vice president of law and public affairs, concluding a career with Standard of more than 36 years. He began his career in 1942 with a Standard subsidiary based in New York City following graduation from the University of Pennsylvania School of Law. By the late 1950s he was serving the parent company in Chicago as associate general counsel.

From 1961 to 1963, he was general counsel for Amoco (then American) Oil Company, then became vice president and general counsel and a director of Standard. He was elected vice president for law and public affairs in 1972 following the consolidation of all of the corporation's public and government affairs activities. When Standard decided to build a new international headquarters, Farrell was appointed the representative of senior management in charge of the project.

H. LAURANCE FULLER

H. Laurance Fuller was elected a director and an executive vice president of Standard Oil in 1981. From 1978 until 1981, he was president of Amoco Oil Company after serving as executive vice president of the subsidiary.

Fuller received a bachelor's degree in chemical engineering from Cornell University, Ithaca, New York, and a law degree from DePaul University, Chicago.

After joining Standard in 1961, he served as a chemical engineer, an attorney in the law department, assistant manager of budgets and control, manager of transportation development, manager of Amoco's refinery at Casper, Wyoming, manager of direct sales in the marketing department of Amoco Oil, and general manager of supply for Standard.

As an executive vice president of Standard, Fuller's responsibility included research and development, supply, environmental conservation and toxicology, corporate development, purchasing and marine transportation. Effective September 7, 1983, Fuller was elected president of Standard Oil.

GEORGE H. GALLOWAY

George H. Galloway, a member of the board of directors of Standard Oil Company (Indiana) for seven years and president of Amoco Production Company, then Standard's domestic exploration and production subsidiary, retired at age 65 on April 18, 1981, completing a 41-year career with the company. He also was chairman of Amoco Canada Petroleum Company Ltd.

292

A native of Nebraska, Galloway is a graduate of the University of Nebraska with a bachelor's degree in civil engineering and geology. He joined Amoco Production Company, then Stanolind Oil and Gas Company, in 1939 as a geologist and served in various Texas and Oklahoma field positions until 1951 when he was named assistant chief geologist in Tulsa.

He became vice president and manager of Amoco's Canadian division in 1952, vice president of exploration for Amoco Production in 1959, executive vice president in 1964, and president of Amoco Production in 1973.

ROBERT C. GUNNESS

Robert C. Gunness, vice chairman of the board of directors and former president of Standard Oil Company (Indiana), retired on February 28, 1975. He had more than 37 years of service with the company, 22 of them as a director.

Gunness was born at Fargo, North Dakota, in 1911, and grew up at Amherst, Massachusetts, where his father was head of the engineering department of the University of Massachusetts. Gunness received a B.S. degree in chemistry at the University, and a D.Sc. degree in chemical engineering at Massachusetts Institute of Technology where he remained as an assistant professor of chemical engineering for two years.

Gunness joined the staff of Standard's research department in 1938 as a group leader. He advanced to manager of research in 1947, became assistant general manager of manufacturing in 1952, and was elected a director in 1953 and general manager of supply and transportation in 1954. He was elected an executive vice president in 1956, president in 1965, and vice chairman in 1974.

JOHN E. KASCH

John E. Kasch, a vice president of Standard Oil Company (Indiana) from 1975 and a director from 1976, retired on September 2, 1981, after 39 years of service.

A native of Bloomington, Indiana, Kasch received B.S. and M.S. degrees and a doctorate in chemical engineering from the University of Texas. He joined the company in 1942 as a chemical engineer at Amoco Oil Company's refinery at Texas City, Texas, and transferred to Amoco Oil's New York office as assistant to the president in 1952. He was appointed manager of research and development of American Oil in 1956, was elected a director and vice president of administration in 1957, and general manager of supply and transportation in 1960.

Kasch was elected a vice president of Standard in 1965, then was named executive vice president of Amoco International Oil Company in 1966 and president in 1974. He returned to the parent company in 1975 when he was again elected a vice president of Standard.

293

LAWRENCE A. KIMPTON

Lawrence A. Kimpton, a director of Standard Oil Company (Indiana) from 1958, and an executive of the company from 1960, retired in 1971. He was a vice president from 1963 to 1968 when he became assistant to the chairman. During his career with the company his function first was planning, then he was concerned with corporate development, primarily with the company's broad program of diversification and new investment.

Born in Kansas City, Missouri, in 1910, Kimpton received bachelor and master of arts degrees from Stanford University and the doctor of philosophy degree from Cornell University in 1935. For the nine years prior to becoming an executive of Standard, he was chancellor and trustee of the University of Chicago. He first came to the University of Chicago in 1943 as chief administrative officer of the Manhattan District's Metallurgical Laboratory for the U. S. atomic bomb project, then became dean of students and professor of philosophy and education at the university in 1944 and vice president and dean of faculties two years later.

He served as dean of students and professor of philosophy at Stanford from 1947 until resuming his career at the University of Chicago as a professor and vice president in charge of development in 1950.

RICHARD H. LEET

Richard H. Leet was elected president of Amoco Chemicals Corporation in 1978 after serving as the subsidiary's executive vice president since 1977. Leet earned a doctorate in physical chemistry at Ohio State University after graduating from Northwest Missouri State University. He began his career with the company as a research chemist at Whiting in 1953. He became director of long-range and capital planning for Amoco Oil Company in 1964, and in 1966 transferred to the parent company's planning department.

Leet rejoined Amoco Oil in 1968 as manager of operations planning in the manufacturing and transportation department, and was appointed regional vice president of Amoco Oil's southern marketing region in Atlanta in 1970. In 1974, he was appointed vice president of planning and administration for Amoco Chemicals, and marketing vice president in 1975.

Effective September 7, 1983, Leet was elected an executive vice president of Standard Oil, with responsibilities for research, supply and marine transportation, corporate development, purchasing, environmental affairs and safety, and synthetic fuels development.

L. CHESTER MAY

L. Chester May joined Standard Oil Company (Indiana) as vice president, finance, and was elected a director in 1963. He retired on April 5, 1976.

A native of West Virginia, May is an alumnus of the University of West Virginia, and holds a law degree from Fordham University. He was admitted to the New York Bar in 1945.

Prior to joining Standard, May's business career covered a span of more than 30 years with American Telephone & Telegraph Company. From 1959 to 1963 he was treasurer of AT&T, and from 1958 to 1959, vice president and comptroller of Michigan Bell Telephone Company. Earlier he had served AT&T in financial capacities.

JOHN C. MEEKER

John C. Meeker became executive vice president responsible for international operations of Amoco Production Company, the worldwide oil and gas exploration-production subsidiary of Standard Oil Company (Indiana), on September 7, 1983.

Joining the company in 1948 as a geologist for Stanolind Oil and Gas Company, predecessor of Amoco Production, Meeker served in various positions in Texas, Louisiana, and in Canada. He was elected president of the newly-formed Amoco Canada Petroleum Company Ltd., in 1969, became vice president-exploration of Amoco Production in 1973, then served as executive vice president of Amoco International Oil Company.

After international and domestic exploration and production operations were consolidated in 1981, Meeker headed domestic operations until Amoco Production was functionally restructured concurrently with the retirement of John E. Swearingen, chairman and chief executive officer of Standard, on September 7, 1983.

A native of Titusville, Pennsylvania, Meeker received his bachelor's degree in geology from Princeton University. He also attended Williams College and the Northwestern University Institute for Management.

RICHARD M. MORROW

Richard M. Morrow became a director of Standard Oil in 1976 and was elected president on October 1, 1978. Morrow's entire business career has been with Standard.

After three and a half years of navy service, Morrow, a native of Ohio, decided to finish his education at Ohio State University, majoring in mining engineering with a petroleum option. Following graduation in 1948 he went to work as a junior engineer in Standard's large Hastings field in Texas.

After a variety of assignments in the Houston division, Morrow was named district engineer at New Orleans for Pan American Petroleum Corporation, the name which had replaced Stanolind for the exploration and production subsidiary. Succeeding promotions came in rapid succession: as engineering group supervisor in Tulsa, as assistant division engineer in Houston, and then back to New Orleans as district superintendent. In 1961 he became division engineer for the Oklahoma City division.

In 1962, he was named chief engineer for the production department in Tulsa. Next came a short tour of duty as assistant division production superintendent in Houston, followed by reassignment to Tulsa in 1964, this time as production superintendent for Alaska.

In June of 1965, he was named vice president and division manager of the Denver division. In the fall of 1966, Morrow was assigned to the international company as executive vice president for exploration and production.

Morrow became executive vice president of Amoco Chemicals Corporation in 1970. In 1974, he was elected president of Amoco Chemicals and served in that position until his election as president of Standard in 1978.

Effective September 7, 1983, Morrow was elected chairman of the board and chief executive officer of Standard Oil, succeeding John E. Swearingen upon the latter's retirement after 44 years as an employee, 31 years as a director, and 23 years as chief executive officer.

GEORGE V. MYERS

George V. Myers elected to retire at age 62 on October 1, 1978, after more than 25 years of distinguished service, 22 of them as a director. He had been president of Standard Oil Company (Indiana) since February, 1974.

Myers transferred from Standard's U.S. exploration and production subsidiary, now Amoco Production Company, to become general manager of production for Standard in 1956 and was elected to the board of directors later that year. He became vice president of production in 1958 and executive vice president in 1959. For a number of years he coordinated crude oil production, crude transportation, and crude purchasing operations of all subsidiaries, and foreign activities.

Myers joined Stanolind Oil and Gas Company in Tulsa in 1953 as manager of the financial departments and a director, and was elected financial vice president later in the year.

Myers previously had been controller of Westinghouse Air Brake Company at Pittsburgh, Pennsylvania, and a special agent for the Federal Bureau of Investigation.

A native of Townsend, Montana, Myers graduated from high school and junior college in Kansas City, Missouri. He holds a B.A. degree in business administration from the University of Chicago and also studied at the University of Pittsburgh.

FRANK C. OSMENT

Frank C. Osment was elected a director of Standard in 1968 and an executive vice president of Standard in 1974. He took early retirement at age 64 on September 1, 1982. He received a bachelor's degree in geology from Birmingham Southern College (Alabama) and a master's in geology from the University of Illinois, and started his career with Standard in 1945 as a geologist at the Stanolind Oil and Gas Company Shreveport, Louisiana, district office. During the next ten years, he advanced through increasingly responsible professional geology positions in Texas and Oklahoma. In the mid-1950s, as Stanolind's manager of exploration planning, Osment had a leading role in Stanolind's stepped-up Western Hemisphere activity outside the United States. In 1959 he became vice president, director, and manager of its Canadian division, then returned to Tulsa in 1964 as executive vice president of Pan American Petroleum Corporation (formerly Stanolind).

In 1965, Osment was elected a vice president of Standard with worldwide staff coordinating responsibilities in crude oil and natural gas exploration and production. He was elected president in 1967 of Amoco International Oil Company.

WALTER R. PEIRSON
Walter R. Peirson was elected a director of Standard Oil in 1976 and became an executive vice president in 1978. Effective September 7, 1983, he has worldwide responsibilities for chemicals manufacturing and marketing, and for manufacturing and marketing of petroleum products. Peirson's academic background includes degrees in mechanical engineering and law from the University of Illinois. He joined Standard's law department in Chicago in 1955, then served as executive vice president and president of General Gas Corporation at Baton Rouge, Louisiana, until it was merged in 1964 into Tuloma Gas Products Company.

He was president of Tuloma, then marketing vice president of Amoco Oil Company when it absorbed Tuloma in 1968. He became executive vice president of Amoco Oil in 1971, and president in 1974.

JOHN E. SWEARINGEN
See main text beginning at page 68.

LAWRASON D. THOMAS
Lawrason D. Thomas was elected president of Amoco Oil Company in 1981 after serving as executive vice president of the subsidiary. With a bachelor of science degree in chemical engineering and a master's in business administration from the University of Michigan, Thomas joined Standard in 1958 as a salesman with Amoco Chemicals Corporation. His early assignments included service as administrative manager of Amoco Oil's Southern marketing region, as a district manager in Chicago, director—marketing in Kansas City, and managing director of Amoco International's Australian operation.

BLAINE J. YARRINGTON

Blaine J. Yarrington was elected a director in 1970 and became an executive vice president of Standard in 1974. He retired on March 18, 1983, at age 65. Yarrington went to work as a $27-per-week truck driver for Railway Express Company in 1937 after completing two years of junior college at St. Joseph, Missouri. On his father's advice, he applied for work at Standard's marketing division office at St. Joseph. After waiting seven months, he was hired as a $15-per-week mail boy. He later described going from a $27 to a $15 a week job as "my first big risk decision."

Yarrington studied LaSalle Extension University correspondence courses in his off hours. His rise from his beginning mail boy job took him through a series of clerical and field auditing positions, including manager for marketing administration. A major career period was his service as regional manager for American Oil Company in New York City from 1961 to 1964.

In 1965, Yarrington was elected a Standard vice president with responsibilities for worldwide marketing and distribution. In 1967, Yarrington became executive vice president of American Oil Company, then served as president of that company (its name was changed to Amoco Oil on January 1, 1973) from 1970 to 1974.

F. RANDOLPH YOST

F. Randolph Yost, a member of the board of directors of Standard Oil Company (Indiana) and president of Amoco Production Company for 10 years, retired on April 23, 1975, as a senior vice president of Standard after 40 years of service as an employee.

A native of Beaumont, Texas, Yost attended the University of Texas where he studied business administration. He began his career in the oil industry with Yount-Lee Oil Company and came into Amoco Production, then Stanolind Oil and Gas Company, when Yount-Lee properties were acquired in 1935.

Yost became operating superintendent in 1947 and manager of the production department and a director of Amoco Production in 1949. After serving in field executive positions during the early 1950s, he became vice president, exploration, in 1956, executive vice president in 1958, and president in 1963. He also was chairman of Amoco Canada Petroleum Company Ltd. after it was formed in 1969.

Officers and Directors
Standard Oil Company (Indiana)
Circa 1950-1983

ABBOUD, A. ROBERT
Chairman of the Board, First
  Chicago Corporation and The
  First National Bank of Chicago
Director, 1976-1980
Resigned in 1980

ADAMS, LELAND C.
Director, 1976-
President, Amoco Production
  Company, 1981-1983
Executive vice president, 1983-

ADDY, FREDERICK S.
Treasurer, 1977-1980
Vice President and Treasurer,
  1980-1981
Vice President-Financial Opera-
  tions, 1981-1983
Vice President-Finance, 1983-

ALLARD, JAMES E.
Treasurer, April 1, 1981-
  September 21, 1981
Controller, 1981-

BAITY, R. F.
Director, 1947-1951
Vice President, 1949-1951
Died September 30, 1951

BAYS, KARL D.
Chairman of the Board,
  American Hospital Supply
  Corporation
Director, 1978-

BENTON, DWIGHT F.
Director, 1949-1965
Vice President-Sales, 1951-1960
Vice President, 1961-1963
Executive Vice President,
  1963-1965
Retired in 1965

BLAUSTEIN, JACOB
President, American Trading and
  Production Corporation
Director, 1954-August 17, 1955
Director, September 12, 1955-
  1970
Died November 15, 1970

BOKNECHT, ROBERT K.
Vice President, Employee Relations 1979-

BOSWELL, HENRY O.
Director, 1983-
President, Amoco Production
  Company, 1983-

299

BRISTOL, MERWIN
Director, 1959-1963
Retired in 1963

BROWN, BRUCE K.
Director, 1940-1942
        1944-1949
Vice President-Development,
    1945-1949
Resigned in 1949 to become presi-
    dent, Pan-Am Southern Corpo-
    ration
Retired in 1956

BROWN, VICTOR H.
Comptroller, August 1, 1971
Vice President and Controller,
    1976-1981
Resigned October 10, 1981

BRYAN, JOHN H., JR.
Chairman of the Board, Consoli-
    dated Foods Corporation
Director, 1982-

BUGAS, JOHN S.
Retired businessman, formerly
    Vice President, Ford Motor
    Company
Director, 1963-1979
Retired in 1979

BULLARD, EDGAR F.
Director, 1961-1963
President, Stanolind Oil and Gas
    Company (Amoco Production
    Company) 1945-1958
Chairman, Pan American
    Petroleum Corporation (Amoco
    Production Company) 1958-
    1963
Retired in 1963

BURNHAM, JOSEPH A.
President and Chief Executive Of-
    ficer, Marshall Field & Com-
    pany
Director, 1976-1977
Died October 10, 1977

CAIN, GEORGE R.
Chairman of the Board, Abbott
    Laboratories
Director, 1968-1972
Died July 2, 1972

CALLAHAN, RONALD E.
Secretary, 1981-

COZAD, JAMES W.
Director, 1976-
Vice President, 1971-1976
Vice President-Finance, 1976-
    1978
Executive Vice President, 1978-
    1983
Vice Chairman of the Board,
    1983-

CUDD, HERSCHEL H.
Director, 1963-1975
President, Amoco Chemicals
    Corporation, 1963-1973
Vice President, 1967-1969
Senior Vice President, 1974-1975
Retired in 1975

CULIN, WALTER A.
Treasurer, 1949-1960
Retired in 1963

DUCOMMUN, JESSE C.
Director, 1956-1960
Resigned in 1960 to become vice
    president and director,
    American Oil Company
Died July 7, 1966

FARRELL, RICHARD J.
Director, 1963-1978
Vice President and General
    Counsel, 1965-1972
Vice President-Law and Public
    Affairs, 1973-1978
Vice President, October 1, 1978-
    November 30, 1978
Retired in 1978

FERRIS, RICHARD J.
Chairman of the Board, UAL,
    Inc.
Director, 1981-

FLETCHER, JAMES C.
Professor, University of
    Pittsburgh
Director, 1977-

FULLER, H. LAURANCE
Director, 1981-
President, Amoco Oil Company,
    1978-1981
Executive Vice President, 1981-
    1983
President, 1983-

GALLOWAY, GEORGE H.
Director, 1974-1981
President, Amoco Production
    Company, 1973-1981
Retired in 1981

GLAIR, HARRY F.
Director, 1934-1953
Director of Purchases, 1951-1953
Retired in 1953

GOBEL, JOHN J.
Vice President and General Tax
    Counsel, 1981-

GRAHAM, DAVID
Director, 1952-1962
Financial Vice President, 1952-
    1962
Resigned in 1962

GUNNESS, ROBERT C.
Director, 1953-1975
Executive Vice President, 1956-
    1965
President, 1965-1974
Vice Chairman of the Board,
    1974-1975
Retired in 1975

HAMMOND, JOE P.
Vice President, Public and Gov-
    ernment Affairs, 1975-

HANSON, H. EDWARD
Director, 1944-1947
General Manager, Sales, 1945-
    1947
Retired in 1947

HARMON, LABAN E.
Secretary, 1945-1956
Retired in 1956

HUTCHINSON, WILLIAM R.
Treasurer, 1981-

JAICKS, FREDERICK G.
Chairman of the Board, Inland
    Steel Company
Director, 1981-

JOHNSON, RADY A.
Vice President, Government
    Affairs 1979-

JOHNSTON, LOGAN T.
Chairman, Armco Steel Corporation
Director, 1963-1971
Retired in 1971

KASCH, JOHN E.
Director, 1976-1981
President, Amoco International
Oil Company, 1974-1975
Vice President, 1965-1966
1975-1981
Retired in 1981

KIMPTON, LAWRENCE A.
Director, 1958-1971
Vice President, 1963-1968
Assistant to the Chairman of the
Board, 1968-1971
Retired in 1971

LEA, L. BATES
Vice President and General
Counsel, 1978-

LEET, RICHARD H.
Director, 1983-
President, Amoco Chemicals
Corporation, 1978-1983
Executive Vice President, 1983-

LINDQUIST, RUBERT J.
Director, 1946-1951
Financial Vice President, 1945-
1951
Died May 5, 1951

LIVINGSTON, HOMER J.
Former Chairman of the Board,
First National Bank of Chicago
Director, 1956-1970
Died May 9, 1970

LOWRIE, WILLIAM G.
Vice President, Supply and
Marine Transportation, 1983-

MALOTT, ROBERT H.
Chairman of the Board, FMC
Corporation
Director, 1973-

MASON, EDWARD A.
Vice President-Research, 1977-

MASSEY, WALTER E.
Vice President-Research,
University of Chicago
Director, 1983-

MAY, L. CHESTER
Director, 1963-1976
Vice President-Finance, 1963-
1976
Retired in 1976

McCLOUD, BENTLEY G.
Director, The First National Bank
of Chicago
Director, 1949-1956
Died May 10, 1956

McCONNELL, ROY F.
Director, 1938-1949
Vice President-Sales, 1944-1949
Retired in 1949

McGILL, WILLIAM J.
Director, 1953-1959
General Manager, Employee and
Public Relations, 1952-1959
Retired in 1959

McGOWEN, RICHARD M.
Comptroller, 1961-1971
Retired in 1971

302

McNULTY, MARTIN A.
Comptroller, 1945-1959
Retired in 1959

MILLER, WILLIAM H.
Director, 1959-1960
Resigned in 1960 to become Vice
    President and Director,
    American Oil Company
Retired in 1969

MONTGOMERY, SAMUEL A.
Director, 1951-1961
Vice President-Manufacturing,
    1956-1961
Died January 24, 1961

MOORE, L. WILLIAM
Director, 1961-1970
President, American Oil
    Company (Amoco Oil
    Company), 1957-1970
Retired in 1970

MORROW, RICHARD M.
Director, 1976-
President, Amoco Chemicals
    Corporation, 1974-1978
President, 1978-1983
Chairman of the Board and Chief
    Executive Officer, 1983-

MYERS, GEORGE V.
Director, 1956-1978
Vice President-Production, 1958-
    1959
Executive Vice President, 1959-
    1974
President, 1974-1978
Retired in 1978

OSMENT, FRANK C.
Director, 1968-1982
Vice President, 1965-1967
President, Amoco International
    Oil Company, 1967-1974
Executive Vice President, 1974-
    1982
Retired in 1982

PATTERSON, HERBERT P.
President, The Chase Manhattan
    Bank, N.A.
Director, 1970-1972
Resigned in 1972

PAULUS, MAX G.
Director, 1932-1956
Vice President, 1932-1956
Retired in 1956

PEAKE, ALONZO W.
Director, 1930-1955
Vice President-Production, 1930-
    1945
President, 1945-1955
Retired in 1955

PEIRSON, WALTER R.
Director, 1976-
President, Amoco Oil Company,
    1974-1978
Executive Vice President, 1978-

PRIOR, FRANK O.
Director, 1945-1960
President, Standard Oil and Gas
    Company, 1930-1945
Vice President-Production, 1945-
    1951
Executive Vice President, 1951-
    1955
President, 1955-1958
Chairman of the Board and Chief
    Executive Officer, 1958-1960
Retired in 1960

RASMUSSEN, ARTHUR E., JR.
Former Chairman of the Board,
  Household Finance
  Corporation
Director, 1971-

REDMOND, TERENCE B.
Vice President, Planning and
  Economics, 1979-

ROBERTS, JOSEPH K.
Director, 1947-1960
Vice President-Research and
  Development, 1956-1958
Vice President, 1958-1960
Retired in 1960

RUBASH, NORMAN J.
Vice President, 1979-1981
Resigned in 1981 to become
  President, Amoco Canada
  Petroleum Company Ltd.

RUSSELL, EARL W.
Secretary, 1956-1969
Retired in 1969

SAILSTAD, ALTON C.
Director, 1951-1959
General Manager, Sales, 1951-
  1959
Resigned in 1959

SEUBERT, EDWARD G.
Director, 1919-1946
Secretary and Treasurer, 1919-
  1927
Vice President, 1920-1927
President, 1927-1945
President and Chief Executive
  Officer, 1929-1945
Retired in 1945

SMITH, F. CUSHING
Director, 1958-1960
Resigned in 1960 to become Vice
  President and Director,
  American Oil Company
Vice President, 1967-1975
Retired in 1975

SNYDER, JOHN T., JR.
Treasurer, 1964-1973
Retired in 1977

STONE, JUDSON F.
Representative, McCormick
  Estates
Director, 1937-1958
Died February 20, 1958

SUNDERLAND, THOMAS E.
Director, 1949-1959
Vice President and General
  Counsel, 1956-1959
Resigned in 1959

SWEARINGEN, JOHN E.
Director, 1952-
Vice President-Production, 1954-
  1956
Executive Vice President, 1956-
  1958
President, 1958-1965
President and Chief Executive
  Officer, 1960-1965
Chairman of the Board and Chief
  Executive Officer, 1965-1983
Retired in 1983

TAYLOR, LOWELL B.
Treasurer, 1961-1964
Retired in 1968

THARPE, JACK M.
Vice President, Employee Rela-
  tions, 1969-1979
Retired in 1979

THOMPSON, ROBERT D.
Secretary, 1969-1981
Retired in 1981

TURNER, J. HOWELL
Director, 1959-1965
General Manager, Employee and
  Public Relations, 1959-1965
Resigned in 1965

UNDERWOOD, WILLIAM A.
Controller, 1959-1961
Retired in 1962

VREDENBURGH, JOHN C.
Treasurer, 1973-1977
Retired in 1977

WELCH, LEON C.
Director, 1944-1947
General Manager, Lubricating
  and Sales Technical Service,
  1945-1947
Retired in 1947

WILSON, ROBERT E.
Director, 1931-1934
          1945-1958
Vice President, 1932-1934
Chairman of the Board and Chief
  Executive Officer, 1945-1958
Retired in 1958

WOOD, RICHARD D.
Chairman of the Board, Eli Lilly
  and Company
Director, 1973-

WRIGHT, JOSEPH S.
Chairman of the Board, Zenith
  Radio Corporation
Director, 1966-1981
Retired in 1981

YARRINGTON, BLAINE J.
Director, 1970-1983
Vice President, 1965-1967
President, Amoco Oil Company,
  1970-1974
Executive Vice President, 1974-
  1983
Retired in 1983

YOST, F. RANDOLPH
Director, 1965-1975
President, Amoco Production
  Company, 1963-1973
Vice President, 1973-1974
Senior Vice President, 1974-1975
Retired in 1975

Evolution of Principal Subsidiaries of Standard Oil Company (Indiana)

AMOCO PRODUCTION COMPANY—
explores for, develops, and produces crude oil, natural gas, natural gas liquids, and sulfur worldwide.

Organized December 12, 1930, and began business January 1, 1931, as Stanolind Oil and Gas Company as a result of consolidation of properties of Dixie Oil Company, Mc-Man Oil and Gas Company, and Midwest Exploration Company. Took the name Pan American Petroleum Corporation on February 1, 1957, and changed name to Amoco Production Company on February 1, 1971. Organized a subsidiary, Pan American International Oil Company January 21, 1958, and changed its name to Pan American International Oil Corporation in June, 1959. It became a direct subsidiary of Standard Oil Company (Indiana) July 1, 1962, and its name was changed to American International Oil Company (AIOC). The name was changed to Amoco International Oil Company (AIOC) October 1, 1969. The names of the domestic and international arms were changed to Amoco Production Company (USA), and Amoco Production Company (International), respectively, on April 15, 1981, upon consolidation of foreign exploration and production activities into Amoco Production Company. The (USA) and (International) parts of the names were dropped September 7, 1983.

AMOCO MINERALS COMPANY—
explores for, develops, and produces minerals worldwide.

Organized September 2, 1969, as a grass-roots minerals exploration venture. Took Cyprus Mines Corporation as a subsidiary after Standard Oil Company (Indiana) acquired Cyprus on September 21, 1979. Acquired Empire Energy Corporation on February 29, 1980, Emerald Mines Corporation (Emway) on June 30, 1980, and coal and other properties of Harbert Corporation in September, 1981.

AMOCO CHEMICALS CORPORATION—
manufactures and markets chemical products worldwide.

Organized on September 12, 1945, as a sales unit for chemicals manufactured at refineries. The name of Hidalgo Chemical Company, a subsidiary of Stanolind Oil and Gas Company, was changed to Amoco Chemicals Corporation on June 25, 1956. Gillock Chemical Company, a subsidiary of American Oil Company, was acquired, and Indoil Chemical Company, a subsidiary of Standard (Indiana), and Pan American Chemicals Corporation, a subsidiary of American Oil Company, were merged into Amoco Chemicals Corporation under the reorganization and simplification of corporate structure on February 1, 1957.

AMOCO OIL COMPANY—
refines, transports, and markets petroleum products worldwide.

Organized in 1922 by Louis Blaustein and his son, Jacob, and named The American Oil Company. It formalized a Blaustein retail kerosene and gasoline jobbership begun in 1910. On August 17, 1954, The American Oil Company became a wholly-owned subsidiary of Standard (Indiana). On December 31, 1960, Utah Oil Refining Company, a wholly-owned Standard subsidiary, was merged into American Oil, and refining and marketing operating assets of Standard were transferred to American Oil, increasing its territory to 45 states plus limited marketing in three others. Name changed to Amoco Oil Company on January 1, 1973. Became a worldwide operation upon the consolidation of foreign and domestic refining and marketing assets on April 15, 1981.

Status of Standard Oil Companies Separated by the 1911 Decree

Note: Of 37 subsidiaries and affiliates of Standard Oil Company (New Jersey) charged in the U.S. Government's suit in St. Louis in 1906, by 1911 The Manhattan Oil Company had been liquidated, liquidation of Standard Oil Company (Iowa) was nearing completion, and the Navarro (formerly Corsicana) Refining Company and Security Oil Company had been severed from Jersey Standard by a Texas court decision in 1909. Consequently, the four companies did not appear in the final 1911 list of companies to be separated from Jersey Standard.

Names in 1911	Names in 1982
Cumberland Pipe Line Company, Inc. Southern Pipe Line Company	Ashland Oil Company
The Atlantic Refining Company The Prairie Oil & Gas Company	Atlantic Richfield Company
Borne, Scrymser Company	Borne Chemical Company
Indiana Pipe Line Company The Buckeye Pipe Line Company Northern Pipe Line Company New York Transit Company	Buckeye Pipe Line Company (subsidiary of Penn Central Corp.)
Chesebrough Manufacturing Company Consolidated	Chesebrough-Pond's Inc.
Continental Oil Company	Conoco, Inc. (subsidiary of DuPont Company)
Anglo-American Oil Company, Ltd. Standard Oil Company (New Jersey)	Exxon Corporation

Names in 1911	Names in 1982
The Ohio Oil Company	Marathon Oil Company (acquired by U.S. Steel Corp. 1982)
Standard Oil Company of New York Vacuum Oil Company	Mobil Corporation
South-West Pennsylvania Pipe Lines National Transit Company South Penn Oil Company The Eureka Pipe Line Company	Pennzoil Company
Standard Oil Company (California) Standard Oil Company (Kentucky)	Standard Oil Company of California
Standard Oil Company (Indiana) The Standard Oil Company (Kansas) Standard Oil Company (Nebraska)	Standard Oil Company (Indiana)
The Standard Oil Company The Solar Refining Company	The Standard Oil Company (Ohio) (NOTE: The company adds "(Ohio)" when necessary to differentiate from other companies.)
Union Tank Car Company	Union Tank Car Company (A division of Trans Union Corp.)
Washington Oil Company	Dissolved 1977
The Crescent Pipe Line Company Galena-Signal Oil Company	Liquidated in late 1920s.
Colonial Oil Company	Liquidated (date unknown)
Waters-Pierce Oil Company	Dissolved in 1940
Swan & Finch Company	Liquidated in 1965

Index

All page numbers in italic typeface refer to illustrations.

Amoco International Oil Company, 233–34, 261–62, 264; *see also* American International Oil Company *and* Pan American International Oil Company
Amoco Iran Oil Company, 229
Amoco Marine Transportation Company, 234
Amoco Minerals Company, 202, 235, 250–53, 261, 266, 306
Amoco Oil Company, 89, 133, 160–62, 234–35, 261, 263–64, 266, 286, 307; *see also* American Oil Company
Amoco Production Company, 65, 201, 232, 236, 240, 252, 261, 263–64, 266, 306; and domestic exploration, 238–42, 244–45, 250; and foreign exploration, 202, 210; and research, 162, 172, 175, 178; foreign operations of, 232–35; *see also* Stanolind Oil and Gas Company *and* Pan American Petroleum Corporation
Amoco Super Premium, 122, 123
Amoco Technology Company, 259
Amoco Trading Corporation, 89, 203, 206
Amoco (U.K.), 213; *see also* British Gas Council-Amoco (U.K.) Group
Analog Devices Enterprises, 257
Analog Devices, Inc., 114, 257
Anderson, Robert O., 254
Andrus, Cecil, 145
Anglo-Iranian Oil Company, Limited, 47
Anniversary, 75th, 1964, 93
"Anti-discrimination" laws, 8
Antigua, 212
Antitrust suits, 9, 10, 15, 54, 242
"A Penny and a Half is Not Enough," 1957 address by R. C. Gunness, 66
Arab oil embargo, 108, 136, 143, 145, 148–50, 154–55, 172, 196–97, 234, 238
Arabian peninsula, Eastern, 231–32
Arabian Seaoil Corporation, 234
Archbold, John D., 6
Arctic Islands, exploration of, 237
Ardeshir field, 216
Argentina, 206, 211–12, 225, 227
Arthur D. Little Company, 160
Asarco, Inc., 250
Athabasca oil sands, 171
Atlantic Monthly, 9

Atlantic Ocean, 1981 offshore lease sale in, 240
Atlantic Refining Company, 254
Australia, 207, 212, 225, 233–34, 250
Automation, 129, 177–79
Automotive parts, use of polypropylene in, 192
Avisun Corporation, 161, 190–91; purchase of, 192–93
Bacton, England, natural gas terminal at, 214
Bailey, Daniel G. F., 211, 213
Bailey, Jennings, 32
Baity, R. F., 299
Balke, W. H. (Herbert), 181
Ballmer, R. W., 251
Baltimore Canyon, 1976 lease sale in, 239, 240
Baltimore, Maryland, refinery, 134
Barnett, Roy J., 32
Barr, Kenneth J., 202, 252, 261, 266, *277,* 289
Battle of the Atlantic, 49
Bays, Karl D., *276,* 299
Benzene, 181
Benzol, 61
Benton, Dwight F., 299
Bertoia, Harry, 118
Biddle-Murray truck, 17
Big Bertha, 165, 166
"Big Step," 80
Biomass, 282
Bitumen, *in situ,* 171–2
Blackmer, Henry M., 26, 27, 29, 32
Blast furnace, Chester, Pennsylvania, 74, 75
Blaustein family, 59, 60–62
Blaustein, Jacob, 57, 61, 63, 79, 98, 119, 122, 208, 299
Blaustein, Louis, 60–62, 119
Board of Patent Interferences, 186
Boknecht, Robert K., *273,* 290, 299
Boston Security Analysts, 262
Boswell, Henry O., 202, 216, 233, 261, 266, *277,* 290, 299
Botsford, Samuel K., 53, 55
Bottles, from polyester resin, 195
Bottom draw-off concept, 47
Brandeis, Louis D., 15
Bransky, O. E., 12, 16
Brassert, steel-maker for Andrew Carnegie, 75
Bravo Dome, carbon dioxide deposits at, 175
Bristol, Merwin, 300

British Gas Council-Amoco (U.K.)
  Group, 213–14, 225
British Institute of Petroleum, Lord
  Cadman Memorial Medal of, 54
British West Indies, Antigua, 212
Brown & Root Company, 74
Brown, Bruce K., 50, 300
Brown, George, 74
Brown, Victor H., 300
Bryan, John H., Jr., *276,* 300
Bugas, John H., 300
Bulk plants, 49, 66, 67
Bullard, Edgar F., 37, 39–40, 43–44,
  52, 57–58, 77, 201, 203–07, 213,
  237, 300
Burnham, Joseph A., 300
Burton-Clark still, 14
Burton-Humphreys cracking process,
  12–16, 23, 45, 47, 72, 120
Burton, William M., 7, 12–16, 18, 19,
  35, 55, 71, 120
Butadiene, 48, 181
Butane, 183, 187
Cabinet Task Force on Oil Import
  Controls, 138–40
Cadieux, Robert D., 266, *277,* 290
Cadlao field, 233
Cain, George R., 300
Callahan, Ronald E., *274,* 300
California Company, The, 243
Calumet Nitrogen Products
  Company, 187
Canada, 59, 104, 201–02, 225–26; *see
  also* Stanolind Oil and Gas
  Company *and* Amoco Canada
  Petroleum Company Ltd.
Canadian Foreign Investment Review
  Agency, 252
Candles, 16, 17
Capital employed, American Oil, 126
Carbon dioxide, use of, in tertiary
  recovery, 175
Carmody, Donald R., 185
Carpet backing, 192, 193
Carrollton, Missouri, 24
Carter, President James C., 146, 154
Casper, Wyoming, refinery, 134
Cassia field, 212
Castro, Fidel, 203
Catalytic converter, 122–24
Catalytic cracking process, fluid,
  47–48, 70, 73, 120, 180–81
Catalytic Research Associates, 47
Celanese, 196
Cetus Corp., 258

Champlin Petroleum Company, 244
Chapman, Steven, 146
Charter, change of original, 16, 18
Chase Manhattan Bank, 96, 99
Chemical Industry Medal, 54
Chemical Warfare Service,
  World War I, 49, 54
Chemicals business, beginnings of, 59
Chemicals, manufacturing and sales
  strategy, 191
Chemicals manufacturing plants, 184,
  187, 189–90, 192–95, 197–98
Chemicals, marketing, 191
Chemicals, petroleum based; in 1920s,
  180; in World War I, 180; in World
  War II, 181–83
Chemicals, production, 191–99
Chemicals, research, 161–63, 175–76,
  180–91, 195
Chemists in oil industry 1900–10, 12
Chicago Tribune, 21, 34
Chicago, University of, training needs
  study, 127
Chief Executive Officers, 1889–1918,
  18, 19
Chili, 250
China, People's Republic of, 232–33
Chocolate Bayou, chemicals
  manufacturing complex at, 194
Civil engineering fabrics, 197
Civil rights movement, 111, 112
Clark, Edgar M., 13
Clark, John D., 30
Clarke, George W., 45, 76, 78
Clean Air Act, 173
Cleveland, Grover, 8
Climax Molybdenum Company, 251
Coal, 286–87
Coal conversion, 170
Coca-Cola, 195
Cody, Cardinal John Patrick, 117
Columbia, 202, 206, 212
Columbia University, 54
Columbian West Coast Oil
  Company, 202
Communication and motivation, 3
Compartmentalized specialties, 3, 79
Competition among former Standard
  Oil Trust companies, 22
Competitive oil cracking processes, 14
Competitive pricing, 124, 125
Composition of matter; and
  interference proceedings, 186–87;
  patent on, 185–86; *see also*
  polypropylene *and* Zletz, Alex

313

Geophysics, early development
of, 164–67
Germany, 25
Giddens, Paul H., ix, 53
Glair, Harry F., 301
Glomar Explorer, 251
Goal, fundamental, 91–92
Gobel, John J., *273*, 301
Gold, discovery of, 250–51
Governmental controls, 105–07,
133, 136–40, 143–44, 146–57,
238, 247, 283
Graham, David, 95, 96, 301
Grand Banks, exploration of, 237
Greenhill, Robert, 255
Gregoire Lake, Amoco's lease area
at, 172
Greybull, Wyoming, refinery, 135
Grimm, Paul, 228
Growth and profits, no conflict
between, 4–5
Gulf of Mexico, productive oil and
natural gas area of, 237
Gulf Oil Corporation, 25, 136, 172, 253
Gunness, Robert C., 47–48, 65–68, 90,
92, 102, 110, 113, 118, 161, 189,
230, 261, *278*, 293, 301
Hammer, Dr. Armand, 255–57
Hammond, Joe P., ix, *272*, 301
Hammond Research Center, 71
Hanson, H. Edward, 301
Harbert Corporation, 253
Harmon, Laban E., 301
Hartley, Fred L., 253
Hastings oil field, 44–45, *46*, 62
Hay Associates, 95
Heating oil, 1972 shortage of, 148
Heavy oil, 171
Hidalgo Chemical Company, 64
Hill, V. G. (Vic), 76
"History of Geophysical Prospecting,
The," 164
Hitler, Adolph, 183
Hochschild family, 251
Hochschild, Walter, 251
Hod field, 227
Holec n.v., 258
Holmes-Manley process, 15
Honolulu Oil Corporation, 242
Hooker Chemical Company, 254
Houdry, Eugene P., 45, 46
Houdry process, 45–47, 70, 180
Houdry Process Corporation, 46
House Committee on Interior and
Insular Affairs, 138, 140

Household appliances, use of
polypropylene in, 192
Houston, as Amoco Production
Company operations
headquarters, 233
Hudson's Bay Oil and
Gas Company, 252
Hugoton field, natural gas processing
plant for, 183
Humboldt, Kansas, 24
Humphrey, William E., 204, 211, 213
Humphreys, Albert E., 26–27, 29
Humphreys, Robert E., 12–15, 55, 71
Hutchinson, William R., *274*, 301
Hydrafracing, 246; *see also* Tulsa
Research Center *and* Patents,
licensing
Hydrafrac, 167–68
Hydrocarbon Research, Inc., 184
Hydrocarbon Synthesis
Corporation, 182
Hydroforming process, 48, 113, 181
I. G. Farbenindustrie, 47, 183
Import controls, 41–43, 137, 139,
149, 206
Imports, Eastern Hemisphere,
estimates of, 230
Imports, refinery bias, 137, 138
Indefatigable field, 214
Indiana Oil Purchasing Company, 64
Indoil Chemical Company, 64
Indonesia, exploration in, 206, 212
Industrial Relations Counselors,
Inc., 89
Insulin, 176
Internal cyclones, 47
Internal Revenue Service, 149, 156
International Energy Agency, 153
International Minerals and Chemicals
Corporation, 191
International oil arena,
reentry into, 59
International Oil Industry TBA
Convention, 281
Interstate Commerce Commission, 38
Investment policies, service
stations, 127
Iodine, extraction of, 250
Iran, 104, 204, 212, 216, 248;
nullification of agreement with, 229;
revolution in, 228–30
Island Creek Coal Company, 254
Isomerization technology, 181
Isooctane, 181
Italy, 205, 207, 212, 234

316

Jackson, Allan, 17
Jaicks, Frederick G., *276*, 301
Jamaica, 202–03
James, Thomas S., 216
Japan, seismic surveys and wildcat
   drilling, offshore of, 225
Job descriptions, 2
Jobbers, Amoco Oil, 153
Jobo field, 225
Johnson, President Lyndon B., 104, 138
Johnson, Rady A., *273*, 301
Johnston, Logan T., 302
Joliet, Illinois, chemicals
   manufacturing facility at, 189
Jones, Charles S., 254
Kappel, Frederick R., 95, 96
Kasch, John E., 102, 169, 176, 258,
   293, 302
Keating, M. J., 157
Keleher, Francis J., 57, 58
Kendrick, Senator John B., 28
Kennedy, President John F., 111, 138
Kennedy, Judge T. Blake, 30
Kennel, William E., 188, 192, 195
Kerogens, 239–40
Kerosene, 7, 8, 17, 61
Kerr-McGee Petroleum
   Company, 237
Khomeini, Ayatollah Ruhollah, 228
Kimpton, Lawrence A., 93, 109,
   160, 294, 302
King, Martin Luther, Jr., 111
Kozary, Myron T., 213
Lake Maracaibo, Venezuela,
   production in, 225
Lambertsen, John G., 192
Laramie, Wyoming, refinery, 135
Law and Government Affairs,
   department of, established, 106
Lea, L. Bates, *272*, 302
Lead, tetraethyl, 119–23, 133
Leduc, discovery of, 201
Leet, Richard H., 261, 266, *271*,
   294, 302
Leman field, 214
Liberty Bonds, U.S., 29, 31
Libya, 205
License-fee system, imports, 149–50
Licensing oil cracking technology, 14
Lima, Ohio, oil found near, 7
Lima, Ohio, refineries, 7
Lindmayer, Dr. Joseph, 258
Lindquist, Rubert J., 302
Litton Industries, 164
Livingston, Homer J., 98, 302

Lloyd, Henry Demarest, 9
Lockhart Crossing field, 242
Lord Baltimore Service Stations, Inc.,
   26, 61, 62
Lowrie, William G., *274*, 302
Ludwig, Daniel K., 253
MacDonald, Walter, 213
Magnetometer, 164
Mallet, Robert, 164
Malott, Robert H., *275*, 302
Mammoth Oil Company, 28–30
Mandan, North Dakota, refinery, 134
Manpower planning, 109, 235
Mapping, subsurface, 166–67
Marketing territory, 16, 65, 80
Mark, Herman Francis, 188
Martindale, Charles, 54
Mason, Edward A., 169–70, 176,
   272, 302
Massachusetts Institute of
   Technology, 54
Massey, Walter E., *277*, 302
May, L. Chester, 96, *280*, 294, 302
McCabe, Warren, 69, 70
McCloud, Bentley G., 302
McConnell, Roy F., 302
McClure's, 9
McGill, William J., 302
McGowen, Richard M., 302
McGregor, Ian, 250–51
McKee, Ralph H., 54
Mc-Man Oil and Gas Company,
   38, 40
McNulty, Martin A., 303
Mechanical thumper, 164, 166
Meeker, John C., 202, 261, 295
Mellon, Andrew W., family of, 25
Mexia oil deal, 26, 27, 29, 30, 32, 33
Mexico, 25, 43
Micellar recovery, 168
Michell, John, 164
Microbiology, 175–76
Mid-Century Corporation, 189
Midgley, Thomas, Jr., 119
Midwest Exploration Company, 40
Midwest Oil Company, 23, 65
Midwest Oil Corporation, 64, 65
Midwest Refining Company, 23, 24,
   26, 29, 33, 38, 39, 40, 242
Milford Haven, South Wales, oil
   refinery at, 225
Military leaves, number of,
   World War II, 50
Miller, William H., 303
Milne, John, 164, 166

317

319

Pomerene, Atlee, 28–31
Pond, Peter, 170
Port Hudson field, 242
Poui field, 212
Power centers, operating, 51
Powerplant and Industrial Fuel Use
    Act of 1978, 148
Prairie Oil and Gas Company, 22, 24,
    26, 27, 29, 30, 32
Prairie Pipe Line Company, 24
President's Materials Policy
    Commission, 148
Price and allocation regulations,
    litigation, 156, 157
Price Waterhouse and Company, 95
Prices; crude oil, 41; gasoline, 124;
    government controlled new natural
    gas vs. imported Algeria LNG, 146
Prior, Frank O., 1, 39–40, 43–44, 52,
    55, 57–59, *60*, 68, 73–74, 77–79, 89,
    98–99, 159, 190, 201,
    203–07, 237, 303
Process Management Company, 182
Producing fields, early famous
    name, 237, 238
Production; fluctuations in,
    1977–1982, 248; host government
    control of, 226; vs. reserves, 107–08
Production research, 162, 236
Production Training Center, 114, 115
Profitability and growth, no conflict
    between, 4, 5
Propane, 183, 187
ProPex Geotextiles, 197
Proxy fight, 34
Prudhoe Bay field, 254
Purchasing from minority
    suppliers, 113, 114
Pure Culture Products, Inc., 176
Pure Oil Company, 27, 253–54
Purified terephthalic acid;
    see Terephthalic acid
Rangely field, 243
Ras al Khaimah, 232
Rasmussen, Arthur E., Jr., *275*, 304
Rate of return, American Oil, 126
Raw Materials Division, Natural Gas
    and Petroleum Section, 49
Reagan, President Ronald, 157
Recombinant DNA, techniques of;
    see DNA
Recruiting goals, 109–10
Red Crown Lodge, 56, 168–70
Redmond, Terence B., *273,* 304

Reentry into foreign operations,
    200–01
Refineries; location of, 67, 134; names
    and closings of, 134–35, 207,
    212, 225
Refinery; per cent capacity utilized,
    133; runs, 44, 108
Refinery, Whiting, explosion and fire
    at, 132
Refining; economic analysis of, 70–73;
    foreign crude, 132–33; products of,
    130–31; processes, 129–30
Refining research, 12–14, 45–47,
    129–35, 162
Regan, T. L. (Pat), 76
Regulatory changes, retroactive, 156
Reorganization, 1967, 102
Republican National Committee,
    32, 33
Research, 7, 12–14, 45–47, 74, 129,
    131, 159–77, 180–91, 195, 239;
    exploration, 236; four precepts for,
    168–69; *see also* Chemicals research,
    Production research, *and* Refining
    research
Research centers, 48, 71, 159
Reserves, 1973–1979 increase in, 247
Reserves, U.S. oil, negative forecasts
    on, 238
"Resources for Freedom," 142
Responsibilities, parent company,
    defined, 80
Restraint of trade, charges of, 9, 10
Restructuring, functional, 79, 80;
    see also Compartmentalized
    specialties, barriers of
Rhea, Walter, 132
Richfield Oil Corporation, 253–54
Rio Blanco Oil Shale Project,
    172–74, 252
Ritts, L. Chase, 206, 213–14
Roberts, George, Jr., 183
Roberts, Joseph K., 71, 73, 189, 206,
    207, 304
Roberts, Owen J., 28–31
Rockefeller, Frank, 7
Rockefeller, John D., 6–9
Rockefeller, John D., Jr., 14, 18,
    30, 33–35
Rocky Mountain Oil and Gas
    Producers Association, 28
Roebuck, Allan K., 185
Rogers, F. M., 12
Roosevelt, President Franklin D., 49
Roosevelt, President Theodore, 8, 20

Rouse, John E., 36, 54, 73, 74, 75, 183
Royal Dutch-Shell Company, 47
Royal Dutch/Shell Group, 43
Royalty rates, Canadian, 225
Rubash, Norman J., 202, 304
Rubber, synthetic, 48, 181, 190
Rubel, Albert C., 253
Ruhrchemie, A. G., 182
Russell, Earl W., 304
Sailstad, Alton, C., 304
St. Mary's church, site of, 117
Sajaa field, 232
Salt Creek oil field, 23, *25,* 39, 65
Salt dome, 165
Salt Lake City refinery, 134
Salvatori, Henry, 163–64
Samaan field, 212
Santa Marta Oil Company, 202
Savannah, Georgia, refinery, 134
Scheineman, F. W. (Fred), 47
Schlesinger, James, 146, 148
Schock, Charles F., 201
Schultz, Paul R., 73, 183
Schwartz, Bernard, 193
Science Press, 164
Scientific Design Company, 188–89
Sea carpet, 197
Secondary recovery, 168
Secrecy, early philosophy of, 21–23
Segregated restrooms, 111–12
Seismograph, 44, 164–66
Seismology, 164
Semix, Inc., 258–59
Senate Antitrust and Monopoly
    Subcommittee, 145
Senate Committee on Interior and
    Insular Affairs, 256
Senate Committee on Public Lands
    and Surveys, 28, 31, 33
Senior Management Conference, 1964,
    1–5, 93, 94
Senior Management Conference, 1968,
    103–05
Senior Management Conference, 1970,
    105
Senior Management Conference, 1973,
    106–08, 230, 249
Senior Management Conference, 1977,
    143
Service Pipe Line Company, 38, 64; *see
    also* Stanolind Pipe Line Company
Service stations, 17, 18, 112, 119, 121,
    123–28, 136, 282; closing of, 128;
    full service, 127–28; long lines at,
    136

Seubert Edward G., 35–38, 41–44, 47,
    48, 50, 51, 95, 200, 304
Seymour beverage bottle plant, 195
Shah of Iran, the, 153, 205, 228
Shale oil; *see* Oil shale
Sharjah, United Arab Emirate
    of, 232
Shell Offshore, Inc., 240
Shell Oil Company, 183
Sherman Anti-trust Act of 1890, 8–10
Shortages, gasoline, distillates, 153
Shultz, George P., 138–39
Sinclair Consolidated Oil
    Company, 24
Sinclair Crude Oil Purchasing
    Company, 24, 26, 27, 29, 30, 33, 38;
    see also Stanolind Crude Oil
    Purchasing Company
Sinclair, Harry F., 24, 27–33
Sinclair Pipe Line Company, 24, 29,
    37; *see also* Stanolind Pipe Line
    Company
Sinclair Refining Company, 187
Singapore, refinery at, 225
Six-Day War, Arab-Israeli, 140, 149;
    evacuation during, 208–11
Small refiner bias, 151
Smith, F. Cushing, 103, 304
Smith, L. L. (Larry), 192
Smith, William T., 243–45
Snyder, John T., Jr., 304
Social climate, 107, 110–12
Societe Civile Amoco, 206–07
Socony-Vacuum Oil Company,
    45, 46
Solar energy, 257, 282
Solarex Corporation, 257–59
Solliday, Albert L., 39, 203, 205
Solomon Islands, 250
Sound ranging, 164–65
"Sour crude," 7
South Carolina Institute of Archeology
    and Anthropology, 194
Southeast Asia, 225
Southern Crude Oil Purchasing
    Company, 40
South Marsh Island Block 48 field,
    investigation of, 145
SpaN, 146, 170, 252
Special Subcommittee on Integrated
    Oil Operations, 256
Standard-Gulf Oil Rio Blanco Oil
    Shale Company, 172–74, 252
Standard Oil Band of Whiting, 22, 41
Standard Oil Building, *81,* 116–18

dependence on foreign oil, 149; on diversification, 249–50; on domestic operations, 241, 247, 264–65; on foreign operations, 201, 203–04, 232, 235; on "Fundamental Challenge," 1–5; on future of oil business, 1, 4–5, 281–86; on governmental controls, 137–39, 142, 146, 150, 152; on job descriptions, 2; on management, 2–5, 90–99, 260–62; on national energy policy, 142–43; on profits and growth, 4; on research, 159–60, 162, 168–70, 183, 189–90; promotions of, 75–78; retirement of, 266

Sweet, George Elliott, 164

Switzerland, 207

Synthetics research, 161, 171

Taiwan, seismic surveys, wildcat drilling, off, 225

Tankers, number of, 234

Tank truck, first, 17

Tarbell, Ida M., 9

Tariffs, 41–43; see also Import controls

Tar sands, 170–72, 282–83

Task forces, internal, 3, 90, 91, 100–02, 123, 126, 262

Taylor, Lowell B., 304

Taylor, Reese H., 253

Teak field, 212

Teapot Dome investigation, 28–33

Temple, Mickey, 229

Temple, V. W. (Vern), 228–29

Ten-Year Plan, 3, 91–93, 101, 103

Terephthalic acid, 188–89, 191–95

Tertiary recovery, 168, 174–75, 282

Tetraethyl lead, 119–21, 133

Texaco, Inc., 15, 18, 47, 136–37, 182–84

Texas City refinery, 48, 132–34, 181

Texas Company, the; see Texaco Inc.

Texas Liquor Control Board, 191

Thailand, exploration rights off of, 225

Tharpe, Jack M., 97, 98, 110, *280*, 304

"The Fundamental Challenge," 2

Thermal recovery, 168

Thermoplastics, 190

"The Story of a Great Monopoly," 9

"The Year 2000," 283

Thiele, Ernest M., 55, 70

Thomas, Lawrason D., 261, 266, *278*, 297

Thompson Creek, molybdenum project at, 252

Thompson, David, 75

Thompson, Robert D., 305

Thumper, mechanical, 164, 166

Tight gas sands, 246–47

Tilford, W. H., 18

Titusville, Pennsylvania, 6

TNT, 16, 181

Toluene, 16, 48, 49, 181, 188

Torch and Oval, 80

Torfelt area, discoveries in, 214

Tor field, 227

Torsion balance, 44, 164–65

Trademark, protection of, 80, 89

Tradition, scientist to executive, 71

Trans-Cuba Oil Company, 203

Transportation, rail, water, pipeline, truck, 17, 67, 71

Traylor, Melvin A., 35

Trinidad, 206, 211–13, 225; field discoveries, 212

Trinidad and Tobago Electricity Commission, 212

Trinidad and Tobago, Government of, 211–12

Trinidadian National Gas Company, 212

Trudeau, Prime Minister Pierre, 225, 226

Truman, President Harry S., 141

"Trust-busting," 8

Tube still, 13, 14

Tuloma Gas Products Company, 64, 187

Tulsa Data Center, 178

Tulsa Research Center, 159, 163–65, 167–68, 171, 177–78, 183, 239, 240

Turner Construction Company, 117

Turner, J. Howell, 97, 98, 305

Tuscaloosa Trend, 241–246; production estimates of, 242

"Twenty-Five Ways to Save Fuel Oil," 49

Underwood, William A., 305

Unfair price discrimination, charges of (the "Detroit Case"), 124–25

Union Carbide, 196

Union Oil Company of California, 253–54

Union Pacific Railroad Company, 243–45

United Arab Republic, 208

United Kingdom, 104, 207, 211, 234

U.S. Circuit Court of Appeals, Eighth District, 30

323